CLAUDE LÉVI-STRAUSS SOCIAL PSYCHOTHERAPY & THE COLLECTIVE UNCONSCIOUS

Thomas Shalvey

The University of Massachusetts Press
Amherst, 1979

Grateful acknowledgment is made to the following for permission to reprint copyrighted material: The University of Chicago Press, for material from Claude Lévi-Strauss, *The Savage Mind,* copyright © 1966 by The University of Chicago Press. Basic Books, Inc., for figures from *Structural Anthropology,* by Claude Lévi-Strauss, translated from the French by Claire Jacobson and Brooke Grundfest Schoepf, pp. 128, 145, and 146, copyright © 1963 by Basic Books Inc., Publishers, New York.

Library of Congress Cataloging in Publication Data
Shalvey, Thomas, 1937–
Claude Lévi-Strauss: social psychotherapy and the
collective unconscious.
Bibliography: p.
Includes index.
1. Lévi-Strauss, Claude. 2. Subconsciousness.
[DNLM: 1. Anthropology, Cultural—Biography.
2. Philosophy—Biography.   3. Psychology, Social—
Biography. WZ100 L664S]
GN21.L4S5   301.2′092′4   78-19695
ISBN 0-87023-260-6

Contents

To my parents

Acknowledgments

I acknowledge my very deep debt of gratitude to two people who guided the progress of this volume during the course of its creation and thus helped to bring it into existence: Professor Wilfrid Desan of Georgetown University, Washington, D.C., who first suggested the book's theme and who piloted it along with his cogent insights and experiences; and Leone Stein, Director of the University of Massachusetts Press, whose encouragement and persistence were both supportive and heartening. I also express thanks to Professor John Manfredi of the University of Massachusetts, Department of Sociology, who lent his time and experience to the reading of the manuscript and to strengthening my perseverance. Finally, but not least, my thanks to Richard Martin, Editor of the University of Massachusetts Press, who read the manuscript and helped to transform it into publishable shape; to the entire staff of the Press for cooperation and encouragement at all times; and to Anne Granger, who tirelessly gave of herself and her time in the process of ordering, editing, and typing the final copy. In the area of motivation, a special recognition is due Jeffrey Ponnel, A.C.S.W., Long Island-Jewish Medical Center, Hillside Division, for our numerous discussions involving social psychotherapy as both an analytic yet concerned unraveling of the structures of the human spirit.

Thomas Shalvey
New Haven, Connecticut

List of Abbreviations and Translations

Abbreviations for and Translations of the Works of Lévi-Strauss

L-S, *SEP*   *Les structures élémentaires de la parenté*. Paris: Presses universitaires de France, 1949. Rev. and corr. ed. The Hague and Paris: Mouton and Co., 1967. With one (noted) exception, my citations are from the latter edition. In English, *The Elementary Structures of Kinship*. Translated by James Bell, John von Sturmer, and Rodney Needham. Boston: Beacon Press, 1969.

L-S, *RH*   *Race et histoire*. Paris: UNESCO, 1952. In English, *Race and History*. Paris: UNESCO, 1968.

L-S, *TT*   *Tristes tropiques*. Paris: Libraire Plon, 1955. In English, *Tristes Tropiques*. Translated by John Russell. New York: Atheneum, 1967. Chapters 14, 15, 16, and 39 of the French edition are omitted. Because this is a partial translation of the original, it has a different pagination.
Tristes Tropiques. Translated by John and Doreen Weightman. New York: Atheneum, 1974.

L-S, *AS*   *Anthropologie structurale*. Paris: Librairie Plon, 1958. In English, *Structural Anthropology*. Translated by Claire Jacobson and Brooks Grundfest Schoepf. Garden City, N.Y.: Doubleday, 1967.

L-S, *T*   *Le totémisme aujourd'hui*. Paris: Presses universitaires de France, 1962. In English, *Totemism*. Translated by Rodney Needham. Boston: Beacon Press, 1963.

L-S, *PS*   *La pensée sauvage*. Paris: Librairie Plon, 1962. In English, *The Savage Mind*. No translator named. Chicago: University of Chicago Press, 1966.

L-S, *CC*   *Mythologiques: Le cru et le cuit.* Paris: Librairie Plon, 1964. In English, *Introduction to a Science of Mythology.* Vol. 1, *The Raw and the Cooked.* Translated by John and Doreen Weightman. New York: Harper and Row, 1969.

L-S, *MC*   *Mythologiques: Du miel aux cendres.* Paris: Librairie Plon, 1967. In English, *Introduction to a Science of Mythology.* Vol. 2, *From Honey to Ashes.* Translated by John and Doreen Weightman. New York: Harper and Row, 1973.

L-S, *OM*   *Mythologiques: L'Origine des manières de table.* Paris, Librairie Plon, 1968.

L-S, *HN*   *L'homme nu.* Paris: Librairie Plon, 1971.

In Collaboration

L-S, *E*   Charbonnier, Georges. *Entretiens avec Claude Lévi-Strauss.* Paris: Plon-Juillard, 1961. In English, Georges Charbonnier. *Conversations with Claude Lévi-Strauss.* Translated by John and Doreen Weightman. London: Jonathan Cape, 1969.

In Volume of Another Author

L-S, *IMM*   *Introduction à l'oeuvre de Marcel Mauss.* In Marcel Mauss, *Sociologie et Anthropologie.* Paris: Presses universitaires de France, 1968.

In Private Circulation

L-S, *LI*   *Leçon inaugurale,* Chaire d'anthropologie sociale. Paris: College de France. 5 January 1960. In English, *The Scope of Anthropology.* Translated by Sherry Ortner Paul and Robert A. Paul. London: Jonathan Cape, 1967.

Introduction

Claude Lévi-Strauss is not a philosopher, but a social anthropologist. Although prepared academically for a philosophical vocation, he has committed himself to anthropology. His view toward philosophy, subsequently, is somewhat ambiguous. In describing one of his most philosophically oriented books (*The Savage Mind*), he states that, despite the possibility of formulating in it an indigenous philosophy, he was determined not to set out upon this route. He seems quite convinced in his determination not to enter philosophical realms; yet, since Lévi-Straussian structuralism, at its core, is an epistemology and has already produced an ethic,[1] it is doubtful that he can be considered to have successfully extricated himself from this philosophical perspective.[2]

One overall problem forms the core of this observation. In Lévi-Strauss, the basic opposition out of which all primitive logic is structured is that between nature and culture. The bridge that logic forms between these binary terms is the priority of the collective over the individual.[3] The question that Lévi-Strauss constantly sets before himself is how the collective is ontologically prior to the individual.

This problem has a long history. Its *locus classicus* is the debate that takes place between Glaucon and Socrates in the second book of the *Republic*.[4] The general question of the dialogue is "What is justice?" Glaucon had maintained that the words *justice* and *injustice* have no meaning, since individuality is ontologically prior to the collective. If the "just" man and the "unjust" man were both provided with a talisman that would render them invisible (the ring of Gyges), they would both take and do whatever their (*individual*) natures urged upon them. Hence, for Glaucon, individuals are intrinsically unrelated one to another, and *justice* is, then, simply a conventional term, not a natural one.[5] The intrinsic nature of each particular man is to seize the advantage and to take what he can without being punished. "Justice" applies to those conventions that the weak have imposed upon the strong, to save themselves from annihilation.

Socrates formulates his reply to Glaucon's empiricism by eliciting agreement from Glaucon that individuality within the state best appears in the *division of labor* in each society. He intends Glaucon to admit that intersubjectivity is as primary an ingredient of man's (individual) being as is Glaucon's idea of an isolated ego. Socrates tries to show that we speak of an individual and his "rights" only because we understand him in the broader context of responsibilities. Hence, *individuality* in Socrates' notion is founded upon the division of labor, itself resting upon intersubjective exchanges. The collective, here, is ontologically prior to the individual:

> A state . . . arises, as I conceive, out of the needs of mankind; no one is self-sufficing, but all of us have many wants. Can any other origin of a state be imagined?
>
> There can be no other.
>
> Then, as we have many wants, and many persons are needed to supply them, one takes a helper for one purpose and another for another; and when these partners and helpers are gathered together in one habituation the body of inhabitants is termed a State.
>
> True, he said.
>
> And they exchange with one another, and one gives, and another receives, under the idea that the exchange will be for their good.
>
> Very true.[6]

Lévi-Strauss's position is similar to Plato's: in placing the collective over the particular, he breaks with the tradition of individualism in French philosophy running from Descartes to Sartre. The significance and character of this break calls not only for a description of Lévi-Strauss's accomplishment but also for critical interpretation.

1 ✿ The Intellectual Context

Robert Burns, the Scottish poet, once asked in a poem for an almost impossible grace: "the gift to gae us, to see ourselves as others see us." In such a state of existence, the other would be internalized in the self and the self in the other; yet such a state represents a radical denial of an important modern philosophical notion: that of the autonomy and self-sufficiency of the Cartesian *cogito*. A similar expression of this denial stems from the application of the insights, primarily from the Freudian idea of the unconscious but also from Marx's notion of praxis, to a theory of mind called structuralism. Its chief proponent is the social anthropologist Claude Lévi-Strauss.[1]

The Freudian notion of the unconscious permits structuralism to reject the correspondence, coming from Descartes, between experience and consciousness. Structuralism disclaims the agreement of expression with understanding,[2] or, as we may say, with Lévi-Strauss, structuralism abrogates the continuity, postulated by phenomenology, between experience and reality. The very character of the Cartesian *cogito* is thus challenged. This aspect of structuralism has been termed "the displacement of the source of language." With insights derived from Marx's notion of praxis, structuralism rejects the autonomy of the Cartesian *cogito*. This repudiation is what I will call the naturalization of the *cogito*, or the unity of mind with matter. It is this naturalization of the *cogito* in structuralism (or the discovery, *in the world*, of the roots of the *cogito*) of which Merleau-Ponty writes here:

This notion of structure . . . establishes a whole system of thought. For the philosopher the presence of structure outside us in natural and social systems and within us as symbolic function points to a way beyond the subject-object correlation which has dominated phil-

osophy from Descartes to Hegel. By showing us that man is eccentric
to himself and that the social finds its center only in man, structure
particularly enables us to understand how we are in a sort of circuit
with the socio-historical world.

In Lévi-Strauss, this radical turning-to-the-world to find the structures
of mind lies in what, generally, he has called his "everyday materialism."
Central to this position is that reinterpretation of the Freudian notion
of the unconscious which is both chronologically prior to Lévi-Strauss's
empirical quest for the structures of mind and of central importance in
understanding his later deliberations on the nature of society and history.[3]

The Original Encounter with the Unconscious

In his deeply personal chapter in *Tristes Tropiques* entitled "The Making of an Anthropologist," Lévi-Strauss records that, as a young Sorbonne
student preparing for his major examinations in philosophy, he realized
an intense distaste for the abstract philosophy of academe and especially
for the then-in-vogue mechanical application of the Hegelian triadic
method. On the other hand, he had been attracted to another, more concrete, study since early childhood, that of geology. This science he calls
a form of "the very image of knowledge" (*la connaisance*) by which we
search, for example, "along the flank of a limestone plateau in Languedoc
to determine the line of contact between the geological strata." When
we have embarked upon a geological expedition, what first confronts us
is an immense *disorder* in the landscape; and it may be ordered in any
direction we please. Eventually the marvelous discovery is made: we
realize that the rock formation contains two ammonites and that one of
the now extinct mollusks has shell involutions more complex than the
other. The inspiration dawns that here we have before us two entities
that transcend the gap of time—they come from two eras many thousands of years apart. Geology transports us into a realm in which the
hands on the clock are frozen, in which time and space become suddenly
intermingled.[4]

Lévi-Strauss has consistently maintained these early insights. He observes that the theories of Freud are quite like the application to individual human beings of a method of which geology has established the
canon. For, as the geologist, with a massive expenditure of effort, chips

away at the stone and uncovers the underlying layers of fossil that have contributed to creating our present world as it now appears—as the geologist discovers, blow by blow, the centuries that lie beneath the now-revealed present—so too the psychoanalyst, with great effort, reveals the underlying layers of the unconscious that form consciousness and, through a constant effort to find the key that would make the landscape intelligible, discloses "seemingly impenetrable phenomena. . . . The order which is thus introduced into a seemingly incoherent mass is neither contingent nor arbitrary. Unlike the history of the historians, that of the geologist is similar to the history of the psychoanalyst in that it tries to project in time . . . certain eternal truths . . . which in other fields are referred to specifically as laws. In all these instances, the arousing of aesthetic curiosity leads directly to an acquisition of knowledge." [5]

Lévi-Strauss records an intuitive moment in his own career when, one Sunday during the period known as "the phony war" in the last few months of 1939, while he was acting as a liaison officer between the French and British armies, the force of the structuralistic archeological method clarified in his own thoughts under the impetus of his perception of a simple daffodil. To perceive a single daffodil, to see it, we must first see the other plants and contrast it with them. The daffodil becomes intelligible, not in itself, but in a process of "much more" ("beaucoup plus"), that is, through relations of likeness and of difference that allow us to isolate it. The daffodil is perceived only in a "bundle of relations" ("paquet de relations"), much as notes are perceived in a musical score, in which one has no meaning in itself, apart from its relationship with the others. [6] To comprehend this somewhat surrealistic contemplation of the daffodil, it helps to recall that Lévi-Strauss's father and uncle were both painters. This sort of contemplation is like that of the archeologist, in that the objects of both comprise a "paquet de relations"—relations that are nontemporal and, in fact, are somewhat perpendicular to the horizontal temporal axis.

In a very perceptive fashion, this brief anecdote about the daffodil illustrates what Lévi-Strauss is directly about. His is the attitude of the aesthetician who is enamored by the totality of the self-enclosed system. For him, beauty is its own excuse for being. Art exists for the sake of art. The structure exists for the sake of the structure. The work of Lévi-Strauss, claims Paul Ricoeur, represents the triumph of syntax and system over meaning. [7] "Structure," in the view of Lévi-Strauss, always signifies elements that are defined by purely internal relationships, and it may be defined as "a syntax of transformations which cause the passage from one variant to another while revealing that the number of such passages is limited." In the last analysis, Lévi-Strauss, like the painter of internal landscapes the elements of which represent nothing beyond the canvas itself, represents the triumph of aestheticism.[8]

And Lévi-Strauss is willing to accept the role of *aesthete* (Sartre's term, incidentally, for anyone who intends to study men as if they were ants), if to be an aesthete is to be a scientist who, like the geologist and the psychoanalyst, is intent upon reintegrating culture into nature and life into the totality of its physicochemical conditions.[9] The geological spirit of this science is well expressed in the quotation from E. B. Taylor's 1871 *Primitive Culture* that Lévi-Strauss offers as part of the epigraph of *The Elementary Structures of Kinship*: "The tendency of modern inquiry is more and more towards the conclusion that if law is anywhere, it is everywhere." [10]

Lévi-Strauss's goal is to uncover the laws of systems, the particular styles that shape peoples' customs and cultures. These systems are not unlimited, so that "human societies, like individuals, never create absolutely, but merely choose certain combinations from an ideal repertoire that it should be possible to define." With an inventory of dreams, customs, mythology, and psychopathological behavior, Lévi-Strauss would hope to construct, for societies, something like the periodic table of chemical elements. In short, he puts societies upon the couch of psychoanalysis and explores the structures of the intersubjective unconscious of each. The notion of an intersubjective unconscious is not self-evident and we must explore both its character and its sources in French ethnology. There, according to Lévi-Strauss, we encounter the linguistic idea of rigorous mental structures.[11]

The Totalizations of French Sociology: Durkheim and Mauss

The foundation of the turning to the world in Lévi-Strauss is built upon a mode of anthropological investigation that he inherited from the school of French sociology dominated by Emile Durkheim and his successor, Marcel Mauss. The orientation of this school is toward viewing social phenomena in their totality. Each social phenomenon is to be seen in its relationships with all the spheres in which society operates: the economic, the religious, the juridical, the moral, and so on—in short, that "circuit (of man) with the socio-historical world" of which Merleau-Ponty speaks. "We are concerned with 'wholes,' with systems in their entirety," writes Mauss.[12]

Durkheim comments upon "the collective consciousness." This consciousness can be described as the totality of beliefs or feelings generated among any number of individuals who belong to the same group or society. It is distinct, however, from the individual members who compose it, insofar as, though they pass on, it remains. It thus does not change with successive generations but, rather, connects generations one with another. It differs, then, from particular consciousnesses, and, although its own reality is dependent upon them, the collective consciousness and the individual consciousnesses are not mutually interdependent.[13]

Adopting this notion of a social phenomenon as part of a totality, Mauss adds to it the important conception of the role of exchanges—economic, matrimonial, and religious—in forming the collective unconscious. This is the content of his major work, *The Gift.* For Mauss, every social institution reveals the same psychological, intersubjective pattern. Food, children, women, land, services, rank—all are viewed by the natives as grist for their intersubjective mill, as objects to be given away and received back again in a constant round af barter.[14]

Although Mauss conceived of his own work as simply an extension of the Durkheimian enterprise, he essentially changed the notion of the "total social fact." In Durkheim's *Rules of Sociological Method,* law, language, logic, art, and religion are all considered as aspects of the social. But too often (according to Lévi-Strauss), the "social" is then treated by Durkheim as if it were a new quasi-metaphysical entity and not simply the interrelations of various specific functions or codes. Mauss frees the notion of totality from "some metaphysical phantoms" and protects it "from the icy winds of dialectic, the thunder of syllogisms, and the lightning flashes of antinomies." [15] Most importantly for Lévi-Strauss, Mauss does not first postulate the social as underlying cause (in the mode of substance), but conceives of it as "foliated" and composed of many distinct and yet interconnected levels. It thus becomes, not a postulate, but an empirical reality open to empirical observation.[16]

There are, for Mauss, three obligations that each member of a primitive society takes upon himself as a member of society: giving, receiving, and repaying. Ultimately, the "basic theme" of Mauss's classic work, as Evans-Pritchard expresses it, is that "one belongs to others and not to oneself." Mauss carries the notion of *prestation,* or exchange of gifts, one step further and conceives of it not only as exchanges exercised among individuals but as conversions between groups as groups. This he calls "total prestation," or one that functions between clan and clan, in which individuals and groups trade everything. This entire theory of prestations is called the principle of reciprocity.[17]

Lévi-Strauss signifies that the reading of Mauss (which was for him "like Malebranche hearing Descartes lecture") inspired him toward the study of unconscious as well as conscious universal social phenomena. Social facts cannot be reduced to "scattered fragments": such was the message of Mauss; and it taught Lévi-Strauss that the preliminary socio-logical analysis must always be "carried as far as the unconscious cate-gories." It is, then, within the context of the Durkheim-Mauss ethno-logical tradition that Lévi-Strauss offers his crucial reinterpretation of Freud.[18]

2 ✿ The Logic of the Unconscious

Structure and Unconscious Exchanges: Freud

The collective consciousness of Durkheim and the totality through which social exchanges operate in Mauss are those strange entities, those "some-things" that are neither material things nor constructs of an order of reason alone (*entia rationis*) but partake of both formal and material aspects. They are, as we have seen above, considered to be revealed by material exchanges (of goods, services, women, and so on), and yet they do not pass out of existence with the destruction of these individual material entities. Lévi-Strauss attempts to express this intermediate character (between "thing" and "idea") of a society based upon exchanges by calling the ways in which exchanges are performed "structures." A structure is simply "the way in which exchange is organized in a sector of society or in society as a whole. . . ." Thus, as Merleau-Ponty finds it important to observe, although structures are psychical entities, they are not ideas (in the sense of either conscious percepts or concepts). Just as a speaker does not have to perform a conscious linguistic analysis of his language's grammar in order to speak, so the subject living in the midst of society does not necessarily know the principles of exchange that govern that society. Rather than the subjects of society possessing the structure, it possesses them.[1]

Thus, the structures that unconsciously govern the transactions within the subject's society are kindred to the unconscious linguistic structures that govern the message of the speaker.[2] Preoccupation with the uncon-scious linguistic code has also given rise in France to that school of psy-choanalysts, led by Jacques Lacan, who interpret Freud linguistically, and Lévi-Strauss's reinterpretation of Freud is of major moment in his work. To understand properly the Lévi-Straussian enterprise, we will reexamine Freud as a structuralist might.

For the structuralist, Freud's descent into the unconscious reveals the hidden logic that first appeared in his interpretation of dreams. Freud, like most people, found dreams absurd and illogical until each detail of each dream and, then, each dream in its relationship with preceding or successive ones was interpreted systematically. All at once, the dream revealed itself as a rebus, and the task of the analyst was to find the key unlocking the order of its logic.[3] The psychoanalyst, in this conception, is really a language cryptologist; he is adept at code-breaking. The analyst should, therefore, no longer rely upon fixed criteria for interpretation of images recurring in dreams and fantasy (for example, taking all long objects as symbols of the male genitals and all round or square ones as symbols of the female). On the contrary, no set criteria can be admitted other than the relative position of the image in the dream or association of ideas.[4]

How is this logic of the unconscious formed? The answer is that it is molded through a linguistic device—censorship, or, as it is more commonly called, repression. The unconscious is that part of the subject's history which is expressing itself without being understood. The barriers and taboos of society suppress the more instinctual drives.[5]

The Unconscious as the Realm of the Other

Let us analyze in some detail the role played by this logic of the unconscious, insofar as it constitutes the foundation of Lévi-Strauss's enterprise. In order to understand the roots of Lévi-Strauss's transformation of Freudian repression into linguistic censorship, we must begin with Freud's postulate of the "pleasure principle." Our source will be the explanation given in *Civilisation and Its Discontents*: after having rejected the question of the meaning of life as an unanswerable one, Freud explicitly states, in response to the question of the purpose of individuals' lives, that, since all behavior begins in painful excitation, the individual's goal becomes the pursuit of the pleasurable and the reduction of the pain. In conformity with this aim, "the purpose of life is simply the programme of the pleasure principle," which, in its turn, "dominates the mental apparatus from the start."[6]

Yet even from the earliest day of infantile experience, the program of the pleasure principle is doomed to frustration. The realities of existence in the world soon rush in, and no pleasures can be maintained forever. We are "threatened" by suffering from three quarters: *our bodies,* which decay; the *external world,* which may "rage" against us; and "our relations to other men." These will become the source of the power of "the reality principle." [7]

To achieve pleasure and avoid reality, the organism will seek ways of escaping from the body, which situates it in the external world and relates it to other men. Freud then enumerates six of these ways. The first four are (1) intoxication ("crudest" but "most effective" method); (2) mastery of the sources of our instinctual passions (through, for example, yoga, Platonic asceticism, and so on); (3) sublimation (or displacement), the shifting of the instinctual aims to satisfactions that are "finer and higher," so that such "instinctual aims cannot come up against frustration from the external world" (through, for example, artistic and creative work); and (4) the development of the life of fantasy ("of the imagination"), in which "the connection with reality is still further loosened." Of the realm of the imagination, Freud writes: "At the time when the development of the sense of reality took place, this region was expressly exempted from the demands of reality-testing and was set apart for the purpose of fulfilling wishes which were difficult to carry out." The last two methods by which the pleasure principle seeks to subordinate reality to itself are (5) madness, which is a total withdrawal from reality, and (6) love. Like sublimation, love makes use of the "displaceability" of the libidinous drives of the pleasure principle, insofar as it "locates satisfaction in internal mental processes." [8]

In all of these ways, the organism under the command of its desire for pleasure seeks withdrawal from reality into the area of a life of unconscious fantasy, where the pleasure principle, not the reality principle, remains supreme. What we should notice is that through the pleasure principle the world of intersubjective experience is interiorized. The other is made part of the self, for the other is precisely the area where, in the *conscious* state of the ego, the individual's drive for personal pleasure is thwarted by the reality principle. This frustrated intersubjectivity leaves the realm of consciousness and, as it were, goes underground, so that the *natural* object of libido is replaced by an ideational libidinous object. [9] Thus, we can at least partially understand why Jacques

Lacan can speak of the unconscious as "the language of the *Other*," although we have not yet analyzed what is the meaning of the *language* of the Other.[10]

All these modes of escape from suffering (the reality principle) to pleasure (the pleasure principle) utilize "displacement" of libido.[11] Since libido energy motivates the pleasure principle, this energy is transferred to another area, that of "internal mental processes" (the unconscious), when blocked by reality. In this area the pleasure principle holds absolute sway. Displacement is the chief meaning of a number of Freud's expressions: *dislozieren* ("dislodge"), *transponierent* ("transpose"); *Übertragung* ("transference," "translation"), all of which refer to the power of the pleasure principle to channel instinctual, biological energy away from its primary object and convert it to a secondary object of desire. More accurately, Freud elsewhere refers to this bifurcation of the ego into two realms—that of its external functioning, governed by the reality principle, and that of its internal (mental) functioning, governed by the pleasure principle—as a "splitting of the ego in the mechanism of defence." [12]

In addition to the role played by displacement in the working of the pleasure principle, there is a further element of this splitting (*Spaltung, dédoublement*) of the ego, an element that Freud calls condensation. In this function of the unconscious, the individual's creativity, or his ability to form a new symbol out of preexisting unconsciously maintained elements, comes to the forefront. Condensation is especially evident in dreams. Freud writes, in explanation:

> In my *Interpretation of Dreams* . . . I have demonstrated the part played by the work of *condensation* in forming what is called the manifest dream-content out of the latent dream-thoughts. A similarity of any sort between two elements of the unconscious material —a similarity between the things themselves, or between their verbal presentations—is taken as an opportunity for creating a third, which is a composite or compromise idea. . . . The formation of substitutions and contamination which occurs in slips of the tongue is accordingly a beginning of the work of condensation which we find taking a most vigorous share in the construction of dreams.[13]

An interesting illustration of the process of condensation appears, according to Freud, in Alexander the Great's "satyr" dream on the night before he captured Tyre. This is an especially good example, for, instead of applying a *fixed* symbolic interpretation of the elements of the dream as sexual symbols, Freud interprets the dream as an unfixed concatenation of unconscious elements. That is, the symbol of the satyr manifests itself in the unconscious discourse of Alexander as simply a condensation of the two Greek words *où Túpos*: "Tyre is yours." We will later see that, for Lévi Strauss, the *collective dream* becomes the area in which the unconscious manifests itself in the mythology, the art, and even the village structure of primitive peoples.[14] For him, the "symbolic function" in society is dependent upon the law that founds society, the law of all intersubjectivity, the incest-prohibition, in the same way that Lacan, building upon the Oedipus complex in Freud, maintains that the symbolic order depends upon the law of the Father.[15]

The work of Jacques Lacan follows the formulation of a structural model of the psychic operations, introduced by Freud in 1923 in *The Ego and the Id*. The tripartite divisions of the id, the ego, and the superego are all parts of the psychic functions, but in differing modalities. The id is dominated by primary process. In primary process, psychical, instinctual energy flows freely under the domination of the pleasure principle. Here what are important are wish fulfillment and a capacity for regression under tension. For Lacan, as for Freud, the dream content provides a manifest example of the functioning of primary process. For Lacan finds that the formula

$$\frac{\text{signifier}}{\text{signified}}$$

becomes the basis for condensation and displacement in primary process functioning. The *signifier* means the sound, and *signified* means the concept. Both, together, make up the sign. In primary process, it is the signifiers themselves and the relations, or arrangements of differences, between them that create their meaning. "No meaning is sustained by anything other than reference to other meaning." In primary process there is a constant sliding of the signified under the signifier. Language is like a dictionary, each word having a ratio of equivalency to the other words; it is an endless tautological system. The distortion recognized by Freud as so manifest in dreams displays this constant sliding. Displacement is the way in which the original emphasis of an idea will veer off and pass onto other ideas. Condensation explains the brevity and seemingly paltry content of dreams as compared to the elaborateness of dream thoughts. For Lacan, metonymy, which substitutes one word for another, is the language instrument by which displacement functions. Metaphor, which retains a covert signifier, when one signifier stands in another's stead, is the instrument of condensation.[16]

But what of secondary process (waking thought, reasoning, judgment, and so on)? Surely this constant sliding of the signified under the signifier must have some (temporary, at least) halt. Lacan introduces here what he calls *points de capiton* ("spaced upholstery buttons"), at each of which the meaning of a word is nailed down at the point of its last term in the signifying chain or system. The *points de capiton* belong, retrospectively, to the diachronic order (the order of time and events). Lacan attempts an explanation of the all-important question of the construction of the subject in relation to meaning.[17]

Having dealt with the id of Freud linguistically, Lacan turns to the construction of the area of the ego. This construction occurs when speech "evokes a third term as witness to its meaning, and thereby [can] complete the signifying chain." Lacan frequently refers to this area as that of "Thirdness," the locus of neither one's own speech nor that of one's interlocutor. He claims that "the unconscious is the discourse of the Other (with a capital O)"—the Other "that even my lie invokes as a guarantor of the truth in which it subsists." This is the "third locus" of "signifying convention" of the kind illustrated in the adversary's complaint to his opponent: "Why did you tell me you are going to Cracow so I'll believe you are going to Lvov, when you really are going to Cracow?" When Lacan invokes "Thirdness" or "the Other" (*l'Autre*), he intends "the symbolic order [that] is a third order, which means that it is organized between the subject and the real world and that it is possible to make use of it without any direct empirical references." Lemaire offers five uses of *l'Autre* in Lacan: "The Other is: (i) language, the site of the signifier, the symbolic. . . . (ii) the site of the intersubjectivity of patient and analyst, and hence the analytic dialogue. . . . (iii) the unconscious in that it is constituted by signifying elements and that it is the subject's other . . . (iv) the third party witness invoked in analysis as soon as it is a question of formulating a truth. . . . (v) it is the Father or the Mother." [18]

We begin to reach the heart of the Freudian antecedents of Lévi-Strauss's interpretation of the unconscious as a hidden language when we examine Freud's treatment in *Beyond the Pleasure Principle* of the *Fort-Da*: the compulsion to repeat. Freud recounts the story of the game invented by the little boy of one and a half. The child was, on the whole, quite well behaved, and, as would naturally be true of any child that young, quite attached to his mother. He had, however, one small but somewhat disturbing habit. He would take any small objects, like his toys, on which he had laid his hands and would throw them off into the corners, under the bed, and so on. While doing this he would utter a prolonged "Oooo," and his face would manifest great satisfaction. Both Freud and the mother were agreed that the *Oooo* sound represented the German word *fort* ("gone"). One day Freud noticed that the child elaborated upon this primitive game by taking a string with a reel attached to it, holding it by the string and throwing the reel into the hidden recesses of his curtained crib, while saying "Oooo," then pulling it back into sight while exclaiming "da" ("there"). The total game, then, was that of "disappearance and return." [19] One usually only witnessed the first part of the game, but unquestionably, the greater satisfaction was derived from the second part of the act. The game was *repeated* by the child ad infinitum. Here is Freud's exegesis of this *absence-presence* syndrome: "The interpretation of the game then became obvious. It was related to the child's great cultural achievement—the instinctual renunciation (that is, the renunciation of instinctual satisfaction), which he had made in allowing his mother to go away without protesting. He compensated himself for this, as it were, by himself staging the disappearance and return of the objects within his reach." [20]

The game was an active repetition of an experience the child had passively received many times over: his abandonment (at least temporarily) by the mother. The mother's disappearances were the major occurrences in this young child's life of those experiences to which we have referred above: the frustrations wrought by the reality principle upon the individual's desires for intersubjectivity. These desires, as illustrated, turn underground: the child's unconscious is literally formed through a repetition of this recurrent experience of presence and absence of the other. The formation of an unconscious is, at this age, expressed by the formation of language in the conscious life of the child, which language expresses the dialectic of presence and absence in which all dialogue consists.[21]

For a very young child, the disappearance of the other literally means "out of sight, out of mind." When the mother disappears, she has, for the child, for all intents and purposes, completely vanished. Thus, the very young child is always surprised when the "absent" person reveals herself in the game of peekaboo; and, invariably, the child will be content to repeat this game endlessly. Gradually, however, he gains control of the game insofar as he has learned to interiorize the Other. This process of interiorization is fostered as the child develops the area in which the Other resides in the self.[22] Whereas he cannot *in reality* control the presence of the Other (the mother), he can do so in the area of the pleasure principle. "At the outset he was in a *passive* situation—he was overpowered by the experience; but, by repeating it, unpleasurable though it was, as a game, he took on an active part.[23]

Freud offers one other example from the life of this young child that helps explain the genesis of the collective unconscious. One day after the child's mother had been away for several hours, she was met upon her return with the words "baby-oooo" (baby-gone). What made the seemingly enigmatic statement comprehensible was the child's discovery, during the mother's absence, of his own reflection in a long mirror. Since this mirror didn't quite reach the floor, the child found that by crouching down he could make his image in the mirror disappear, and by standing up, he could bring it back into view (presence).[24]

Both stories well illustrate the *dédoublement* (split representation) of the ego that Freud had cited as the outcome of the ego's attempt to defend itself against the encroachments and frustrations of reality. The absence-presence polarity of the *Fort-Da* symbolizes the fundamental binary opposition upon which the logic of the unconscious is formed. For Lévi-Strauss, this logic, based upon binary opposition, consists of the relationships between the opposite poles, just as articulated language basically consists of the formal relations existing between the sonorous features of oppositions, such as vocalic/nonvocalic, compact/diffuse, tense/lax, strident/mellow, and so on. The sonorous oppositions *Fort* and *Da* are at play in Freud's example.[25] According to Wilden,

> When Freud introduced the concept of the "splitting of the Ego" in his later works, he laid emphasis upon the message of the dream, which, . . . is a message from the level at which "reality" is recognized as the co-existing level at which it is disavowed, the two attitudes existing in simultaneous contradiction.
>
> . . . This view of the dream returns us to Lacan's use of the Symbolic. If no man's actions are symbolic in themselves, as Lévi-Strauss asserts, then their symbolic nature is dependent upon the Other (upon the unconscious and the other).

For Lévi-Strauss, as for Lacan, the formal relations of language are the area of "Otherness" ("Thirdness"), which, by totalizing the contact between self and other, enables the self and the other to establish a relationship through communication! [26]

Metonymy

The role of structural psychoanalysis in Lévi-Strauss's thought is indicated, not only in his reliance upon the Freudian conception of the logic of the unconscious, but also in extensions and refinements of that conception. Lacan, Lagache, Leclaire, and even Piaget view the very young infant as an "absolute subject"; that is, an infant views the world as simply an extension of himself and not as differentiated from himself— as ob-jective. But, for ob-jectivity to occur, the object must, at some time, be absent, as it is made absent through the game of *Fort-Da*. By making the object absent (and, subsequently, interiorizing it), the child discovers "difference," or objectivity.[27] Thus, as Lacan never ceases to point out, the mediating power of the unconscious Other is that which enables the individual to possess an objective and an intersubjective world.[28]

The unconscious Other, governed by the pleasure principle, opens the world of intersubjectivity to the individual, since *desire* for the other is a "movement toward identification"; "identification is itself dependent upon the discovery of difference, itself a kind of absence." [29] This "lack of object" (Lacan's term), which gives rise to anaclytic (as opposed to narcissistic) development, is derived, then, from this absence, the pole of differentiation.[30] Lacan views speech as "a movement toward something, an attempt to fill the gaps." Speech, in this view (as in the *Fort-Da* articulation of Freud's grandson) becomes "as dependent upon the notion of *lack* as is the theory of desire." [31] Nor is thought something different from speech. The transposition of meaning from word to word in metonymy is the manifestation, at the level of signifiers, of the underlying dialectic of desire of the basic intersubjectivity of the individual.[32] It is at this point in the logic of the unconscious that the introduction of linguistic theories becomes significant.

Metaphor: Jakobson

The establishment of metaphor as the area of the functioning of the unconscious owes a major debt to the work of the linguist Roman Jakobson.[33] In a commanding article, published in 1956 under the title "Two

Aspects of Language and Two Types of Aphasic Disturbances," he attempted to establish the relationship between the unconscious level of experience ("the dream") and the linguistic devices of metonymy and metaphor: "A competition between both devices, metonymic and metaphoric, is manifest in any symbolic process, either intrapersonal or social. Thus in an inquiry into the structure of dreams, the decisive question is whether the symbols or temporal sequences used are based on contiguity (Freud's metonymic 'displacement' and synecdochic 'condensation') or on similarity (Freud's 'identification and symbolism')." [34]

The "contiguity disorder" that Jakobson discovers as one type of aphasia is really an inability "to combine linguistic entities into more complex units." The first words that disappear in the language of such aphasiacs are those whose function is entirely grammatical, for example, conjunctions, prepositions, pronouns, and articles. The patient thus develops the "telegraph style" of speaking. *Contexture* (metonymy) in his speech disintegrates, and his speech deals solely with similarities, or metaphoric phrases. He will substitute, for example, *spyglass* for *microscope,* or *fire* for *gaslight.* In more advanced cases of this aspect of the disease, every utterance will be reduced to a "single one-word sentence." [35]

The other type of aphasia Jakobson calls "similarity disorder." Here the patient possesses the ability of metonymic utterances but loses that of metaphoric propositions. Contexture is retained, so that the patient will constantly transpose one word for another on the same level of language (without recourse, that is, to the level of metalanguage). For example, a particular patient of Kurt Goldstein's would never say the word *knife* alone, but, depending upon the context in which the word appeared, would transpose it to *pencil sharpener, apple-parer, bread knife,* or *knife and fork,* "so that the word knife is changed from a free form, capable of occurring alone, into a bound form." Utterances in this type of aphasia are never single words; grammatical expressions are the last to be lost. The patient, quite frequently, readily completes scraps of words or sentences, but his speech is almost completely reactive: he can carry on a conversation but cannot initiate one. Finally, his utterances are dependent almost entirely on the context: "It is particularly hard for him to perform or even to understand such a closed discourse as the monologue." [36] Whereas the last things retained are grammatical relationships, the first thing to be omitted is "the main subordinating agent of the sentence, mainly the subject." [37]

Against this Freudian background, it is easy to understand why the patient who lacks a metalanguage (an unconscious code, guided by the pleasure principle) has difficulty in initiating a dialogue or even understanding a monologue. The monologue, especially, depends on the Other within the self, whose language appears as the area of metaphor within the self—a monologue being, after all, a conversation with oneself. The aphasiac type called the similarity disorder is, as Jakobson states, a "defect in the capacity of naming," or, "properly, a loss of metalanguage." The aphasiac with such a loss of the code underlying our object language, through which alone can one "speak about any object language," can employ only metonymy based on contiguity. Thus, he will widely substitute *fork* for *knife*, *table* for *lamp*, *smoke* for *pipe*, *eat* for *toaster*, and so on. The patient suffering from contiguity disorder, on the other hand, could speak only in metaphors, substituting *spyglass* for *microscope*, *fire* for *gaslight*, and so on. In short, "metaphor is alien to the similarity disorder, and metonymy to the contiguity disorder." [38]

In Sum: The Unconscious and Language

Metonymy is conceived as displacement, or the process by which thought slips from one term to another because of resemblance. To offer an example, in a celebrated analysis of the unconscious text of a dream, Jean Laplanche and Serge Leclaire show that the image of a unicorn (*licorne* in French) is related to its composite phonemes *lit* and *corne* (bed and horn) and represents "the metonymy of the desire" of the man for a woman.[39]

But, without metaphor, unconscious thought would simply slip along indefinitely from word to word without ever approaching any meaning. Meaning is built upon *mots-carrefours* ("crossroads words"), which condense in themselves a plurality of significations.[40]

An analytic session, in an urban set-up or in anthropological fieldwork, is always a discourse between two parties—the patient who is talking and the analyst who is listening. The words of the patient must be studied for their intrinsic structure, as Jakobson has shown a connection between this structure and various forms of mental disturbance.[41] The unconscious is a hidden language to be deciphered. The anthropologist, the analyst of primitive mentality, will become a cryptologist.

Accordingly, real self is never directly revelatory to itself but appears only in a transference of its hidden desires toward the person of the analyst, in combination with the analyst's counter-transference of his latent feelings toward the patient. What emerges is the analysis itself: a mutual convertibility of feelings, a crossroads word. In such a world, the conscious self is regarded as a phantasm, a dream, even as only a symptom of an underlying linguistic structure that alone is real. The very works that Lacan calls "canonical" for the theory of the unconscious— Freud's *The Interpretation of Dreams, The Psychopathology of Everyday Life,* and *Jokes and their Relation to the Unconscious*—are nothing other than "a web of examples" in "the formulas of connexion and substitution" applied to the signifier in "its *transference*-function." *Übertragung* ("transference"), first introduced in *The Interpretation of Dreams,* would later give "its name to the mainspring of the intersubjective link between analyst and analysand." The unconscious is a *text* (to be interpreted by the psychoanalyst or the social anthropologist) consisting of an interweaving of allusions through which one thing is known in another thing.[42]

In the case of Freud's *Fort-Da* example, recounted above, the child, who previously was (using Piaget's terminology) a total subject through the binary opposition of the phonemes *o-a,* divides the entire universe into an opposition of presence and absence. Thus, the *o-a* are the signifying terms standing for the signified, the presence and absence of the mother. One is known in the other, but not univocally; rather, what is known is an analogy: the *o* is related to the sound *a* as the maternal presence is related to the maternal absence. Metaphor does not compare two things identically the same, but rather two things *partially* the same and *partially* different. The comparison in Freud's example is bound up in the word *as:* the way that maternal presence *is related* to maternal absence *is similar to* (*as*) the way that *o* is related to *a* in the spoken language of the boy. Expressed otherwise, the analogies that the structuralists find to constitute mental life are composed of relations of relations[43] that in turn can be related. The reference to Plato by Laplanche and Leclaire is not unintentional in this regard.[44] And, again, the mutual convertibility of the natives' transference to the social anthropologist's counter-transference, explained above, is but another example of the structural use of analogy. For in the (psycho)analytic situation, the patient relates (now) to the analyst as the patient related (then) to his or her parent. And this transference-relation of two relations, in its turn, can be compared (related) to the anthropologist's counter-transference, which, in its structure, is the mirror image (reverse) of the natives'.[45]

Lacan's contribution to the notion of a structuralistic reinterpretation of Freud is furthered by his explanations of the mirror stage and the castration complex. The mirror stage (between the sixth and fifteenth months) describes the infant's fascination with its own "spatialization" as it appears when the infant sees itself in a mirror. Its groping but unified sense of self is set into motion at this moment. The subject undergoes a separation, or splitting, in which the mirror image of self becomes the prototype for the world of objects. The infant situates its identity in separation. The domination of the continual flow of instinctual drives, which have previously prevailed, becomes situated in a specular image and through it unified into an ego. Within and by means of the mirror phase, the "imaginary" is constructed. The imaginary counterpart exists only because originally the *I* (ego) is another.[46]

The mirror phase begins the detachment of the subject from dependency on the mother as the source of satisfaction of its needs. For it now captures its own spatiality, albeit in an essentially narcissistic way. As this is accomplished in a specular fashion, the unconscious is the phase of the Other. This mirror image helps the infant unify and integrate its somatic experiences into an *I*. This reflected self means that the *I* continues, throughout its life, its integration through the affirmation given it by the Other, the symbolic order itself.

The castration complex puts the subject squarely in the midst of sociality. The Freudian thesis of the primacy of the Oedipus complex in the production of sexuality enters our consideration here. The fear of castration by the parent of the same sex, as punishment for the desire for the parent of the opposite sex, forces the infant out of the mold of narcissism into the development of intersubjective sociality. The reproduction of the species through kinship systems is based upon the threat of a privation; and only with the child's domination of the anxiety of castration can his place in the social order (the human's place in truth) be assured. According to Lacan, the work of Lévi-Strauss on the function of totemism and on kinship systems clearly confirms, anthropologically, the Freudian hypothesis of the primal murder of the father explained in the Oedipus myth. Lévi-Strauss's work has shown the function of the two taboos that bear the transmission of all culture: (1) the taboo against the destruction of the totemic figure that represents the dead father, and (2) the taboo against incest (the reverse side of the laws decreeing exogamy). This Lacan calls the "symbolic" order. Because the child is threatened by the anxiety of castration, the prohibition against incest is created as the law that founds the human (symbolic) order.[47] The work of Freud's *Totem and Taboo* (1912–13) and *Beyond the Pleasure Principle* (1920) confirms the existence of the castration complex and the mirror stage.

The later *Civilisation and Its Discontents* (1930) confirms the primacy of the aggressive instinct turned inward as the foundation of guilt in Freud's newly adopted structural *superego (ego* and *id).* For years, Freud had sought to avoid the existence of an aggressive instinct, lest it be confused with Adler's theory. But, finally, acknowledging that Adler's was more "in the nature of an instinct of self-assertiveness," he adopted (in *Beyond the Pleasure Principle*) an aggressive instinct that he preferred to call the "destructive" or "death instinct" (thanatos). It is this principle, Freud maintained in the last decade of his life, that carries forward the banner of civilization. In a revealing letter, written to Princess Marie Bonaparte on 27 May 1937, Freud unveiled the following view of the process of civilizing: "The turning inwards of the aggressive instinct is of course the counterpart to the turning outwards of the libido when it passes over from the ego to objects. We should have a neat schematic picture if we supposed that originally, at the beginning of life, all libido was directed to the inside and all aggressiveness to the outside, and that in the course of life this gradually altered. But perhaps this may not be correct.[48]

These multifarious streams flowing from sociology (Durkheim and Mauss), linguistics (Jakobson), and psychoanalysis (Lacan), passing through the reservoir of Freud, emerge in the synthesis of Lévi-Strauss's social psychoanalysis. Lacan, as mentioned above, acknowledged Lévi-Strauss's contribution.[49] And we may now ask ourselves what further transformations of all that we have seen this social anthropologist provides.

3 ☼ The Lévi-Straussian Reinterpretation of the Unconscious

Child Thought

Lévi-Strauss maintains that, if we are ever to discover whether or not any mental structures do exist in human thought,[1] we must turn to "la pensée infantile," or infant thought, for, since it is the least affected by the variable customs of different cultures, it is the most universal area of human experience. When we look at infant thought, we find that there are certain "mecanismes" that correspond to the most basic needs of the child.[2] They are most apparent in infant thinking simply because the infant's experience is least influenced by the particular culture to which it belongs, but not because its mind represents any "early" state of intellectual development.[3]

The child manifests, to a great degree, a basic identification with the entire surrounding universe, exhibited in the wish, common to all children, to have exclusive possession or the biggest share of whatever is the center of interest at the moment. Included in this attitude are not only material objects but also immaterial rights, such as the hearing or singing of a song. For example, learning to take turns is one of the most difficult lessons for the pre–five year old to learn.[4] All of this is to say that the child does not regard the world as anything but a simple extension of himself; his thought is marked, according to Piaget, by "syncretism," and, according to Lévi-Strauss, by "polymorphism." The child, in the language of Freud's *Pleasure Principle*, wishes the world to conform to his own pleasure-pursuit. But, as we have seen, he soon finds that the reality principle conflicts with his primitive egotism. In place of the world's conforming with his idea of it (*autism*), his idea must conform to the world. Learning to take turns is part of that learning to conform. The child learns the principle of reciprocity: if I receive, I must equally give.

The unconscious thus formed always expresses an equalization of two opposing inequalities. Clearly, the desire to possess is not an instinct, and it is not founded upon an objective relation between subject and object. Rather, the object receives its value by relationship to the other.[5] The child immediately desires the object in which someone else has expressed an interest, or which someone else possesses. The object, specifically, possesses value (or meaning) for one person insofar as it is valuable (meaningful) for another.[6]

We have referred to this mediatory function of the unconscious as "Thirdness" and, in the Lacanian phrase, as "the language of the Other." In Lévi-Strauss, it simply means that the individual cannot symbolize (give meaning) alone; symbolization (value making) is a collective enterprise, and language itself is the mediator in the formation of objects, the denominator par excellence. The attitudes of two individuals in communication, then, acquire a meaning of which they would otherwise be devoid. The unconscious is the mediatory term between oneself and others. Thus, not only is symbolization a collective enterprise, it is also the mark of mental normality for the self to be alienated through a relationship of self to others.[7]

For Lévi-Strauss, all the elements of social life are present in the child, from the very beginning of infant life, in innate (nonacquired) mental structures. The child's thinking, to be sure, lacks the experience of the adult's, but this experience introduces nothing that in any way could be conceived as something essentially (qualitatively) new.[8]

From its earliest years, the child shows itself implicitly cultural. For illustration, Lévi-Strauss elicits the difficulties that Brainard experienced in attempting to repeat on his little daughter Köhler's experiments with monkeys. One experiment consisted in placing candy outside a window and seeing whether the child could discover a method of reaching it. But instead of trying to reach the candy, the child says, "Hi! Daddy, get it." The difference between Brainard's daughter and Köhler's monkeys is that the child has a highly developed social sense, exhibited in her use of *language* in place of direct action, so that all of Köhler's *experiments* became simply *discussions* ("I can't," "Yes you *can*," and so on) between father and child. In no way, then, asserts Lévi-Strauss, can even the youngest child's action be equated with animal activity.[9]

We return here to the problem with which we began: is the social an empirically acquired characteristic of man, or is it innate and native to man's very structure? Do men form the social (Glaucon), or does the social form men (Socrates)? [10] Lévi-Strauss answers unequivocally: "Infantile thought represents a sort of common denominator for all thoughts and all cultures. This is what Piaget has frequently expressed in speaking of the 'syncretism' of child thought. . . . The further we penetrate towards the deeper levels of mental life, the more we are presented with structures diminishing in number but increasing in strictness and simplicity." There is, of course, a difference *in extension* between the thought of children and that of adults, and it is basically found in the fact that every newborn child carries with him, at birth, the sum total of possibilities in an embryonic form. But each culture and each period in history will keep and develop only a very few of these. Although every newborn child is equipped, through its mental structures, with all the means that mankind possesses in defining its relations to the world, those structures are exclusive. Consequently, every type of social organization represents a choice, imposed and perpetuated by the particular group into which the child is born. [11]

Adult Thought

The learning of a language is similar to the infant's entrance into social life. And it is here, especially, that the analogy between social anthropology and phonological linguistics, as explained by Troubetzkoy and Jakobson in the thirties, takes hold. Lévi-Strauss is taking from phonological linguistics the idea of the relationship between an infrastructure of binary phonemic oppositions and the superstructure of morphemes to serve as a model of the relationship existing between "reality" (the immanent structure) and appearances (the social data). [12] It is important to understand from the outset that he does not intend that phonological linguistics be literally applied to social anthropology—as if the ethnologist were to attempt an analysis of kinship terminology (for example, *father*) into its components (sex, relative age, generation, and so on). One could never achieve a science out of such a procedure, for if structural linguistics teaches us anything, it is precisely the idea that there are no necessary relationships at the level of vocabulary. Troubetzkoy, the founder of structural linguistics, reduced the structural method to four operations. First, structural linguistics shifts from the study of conscious linguistic phenomena to the study of their unconscious infrastructure. Secondly, terms are not treated as independent entities, but the relations between them are analyzed. Thirdly, the concept of system is introduced. Fourthly, structural linguistics aims at discovering general laws.[13] Lévi-Strauss proposes to introduce this methodology into the study of kinship systems and mythology—because kinship and mythology systems, like phonemes, are elements of meaning and, like phonemes, acquire meaning only when they are integrated into systems; like phonemic systems, they are constructed by the mind on the level of unconscious thought.[14]

The analysis of structural linguistics proceeds, then, by a reduction from an object language to a metalanguage and, ultimately, to a series of binary oppositions, much as all languages, known or unknown, can be reduced to the fundamental binary opposition of the consonant and the vowel. The further distinctions among the consonants and among the vowels come from the contrasts between "compact et diffus, ouvert et fermé, aigu et grave." In all the languages of the world, the complex systems of oppositions among the phonemes serve no other purpose than to elaborate in many directions a system that is simpler and is common to all languages—the contrast between consonant and vowel, which, through the play of a double opposition between compact and diffuse, sharp and heavy ("grave"), creates what can be called the "triangle vocalique":

$$a \qquad\qquad\qquad k$$
$$u \quad i \text{ and the "triangle consonantique": } p \quad t.^{15}$$

This linguistic scheme is all referred to Jakobson.[16] For Lévi-Strauss, these oppositions are those that begin to appear "first in the speech of an infant"; they are those that existed between the *a* and the *o* in the *Fort-Da* illustration in Freud. At the moment of articulation of these oppositions, the child entered a particular culture (in that case, German) whose collective symbols (whose metaphors, or codes) were limited to a particular aspect or aspects of the universal structures.[17]

The different sounds that the human speech organs are capable of articulating are almost unlimited. But each language retains only a very small number of all possible sounds. During the period of infantile babbling, before articulated language, the child produces the entire range of human sounds; later (after entering into an articulated language), he will find great difficulty in reproducing them and will never be able to reproduce them satisfactorily when he learns languages different from his own. On the other side of the coin, infantile babble is meaningless, whereas language allows communication among individuals; thus, utterance is inversely proportional to significance. All signification, then, comes through the selection of the particular communications system or systems presided over by the child's particular culture. The particular language into which the child is incorporated selects or produces a certain set of metaphors. Selection is, according to Jakobson, one of the two ways in which linguistic signs can be arranged (the other being "combination," or metonymy, the absence of which indicates the contiguity disorder).

> A selection between alternatives implies the possibility of substitut-ing one for the other, equivalent to the former in one respect and different from it in another. Actually selection and substitution are two faces of the same operation. . . . Selection [according to de Saussure] "connects terms *in absentia* as members of a virtual mne-monic series." That is to say, selection (and, correspondingly, substi-tution) deals with entities conjoined in the code but not in the given message. . . . in a substitution set signs are linked by various degrees of similarity which fluctuate between the equivalence of synonyms and the common core of antonyms.[18]

According to Lévi-Strauss, the child, in entering a particular language code, encounters a realm of particularized metaphors, which, as we have seen, disappear in that form of aphasia Jakobson called similarity dis-order. All this says that, as we have seen in the *Fort-Da* of Freud, there is a displacement of libidinous energy from consciousness into the un-conscious at the moment when the child comes to "objectivize" (that is, name things). This displacement of the area of the pleasure principle occurs through the symbolic function, so that naming means a destruc-tion of the child as a total subject and his incorporation in the realm of reciprocities into the collective, so that, according to Lévi-Strauss, the social, like language, is an autonomous reality, symbols always being more real than the things they symbolize.[19]

Participatory Mentality

There is, however, a very important distinction to be made here. Lévi-Strauss most emphatically disagrees with Piaget's notion of the child as total subject (Piaget's syncretism of child thought), if by this Piaget means a stage of development unstructured in itself, out of which the child will mature. Piaget, Lévi-Strauss feels, fails to recognize that there is no sudden, mysterious appearance of the child's social instincts at the age of seven or eight years. On the contrary, these instincts exist from the very earliest moment of life, anterior to the individuality of the *I*. If, by child syncretism, Piaget means a state of confusion and primitive undifferentiation between himself and another, between people and objects, between objects themselves, then Piaget is mistaken, for this state is not so much an absence of differentiation as it is a system of differentiation different from ours, or, more accurately, the result of several systems coexisting, with a constant transition from one to another. In place of the "total subjectivity" or "syncretism" of the child's thought, Lévi-Strauss, borrowing terminology from Freud, suggests that we speak of the "polymorphous" state of the child's mental structures. When the psychoanalyst describes the child as a "polymorphous pervert," he means that the child presents in a rudimentary and coexisting form all the types of eroticism that the adult will specialize (through a selective process) into normal or pathological eroticism. In his own way, Lévi-Strauss is rethinking the Freudian notion of repression and applying it to the mental state of the child. Just as the child manifests all erotic forms, the adult, through a process of displacement and substitution, narrows the scope of his eroticism through repression into an unconscious of all forms other than genital. In an analogous way, the forms (systems/codes) of the unconscious are formed through displacement and selection of some systems and exclusion of others, so that, for Lévi-Strauss, culture becomes the area of permitted relations (law), whereas nature is that of unacceptable relations —permitted or not permitted in the conscious life of the group (Freud's reality principle). Thus, the child should be called a "polymorphous socialite." [20]

The Freudian Model Transformed

There is one area in which the Freudian model is not uncritically accepted by Lévi-Strauss, and this area marks Lévi-Strauss's creative transformation of the Freudian model. It has been a quite common theme in anthropology, psychology, and sociology to compare infantile thought with the type of thinking found among primitive peoples, so that the children of our own culture are compared with the adults of another. [21] This theme is expressed in the famous dictum that "ontogenesis reproduces phylogenesis," meaning that the development of an individual reproduces the history of the species. Primitive society then corresponds to man's infantile state.

Freud argued differently. In the monumental *Totem and Taboo,* he traces the origins of social life after the genetic origin of the Oedipus complex in each individual. According to the Freudian story, the prim-eval horde, a band of male siblings, rose against their father and defeated him. They then married his wives, their mothers. The universal prohi-bition against murder (expressed in the protection of the totem) is de-rived from their guilt and desire to become reconciled with their father. The universal taboo against incest restrained their fraternal sexual rivalry and forced them to seek wives elsewhere, outside the group, thus giving rise to society. This theory, expressed by Freud to account for the tempo-ral origins of society, holds, therefore, that "phylogenesis reproduces onto-genesis." An Oedipus conflict is, according to Freud, reproduced in the life of each individual member of the race: the individual's ontogenesis mirrors the early primal horde murder of the father, and so on.[22]

Let us understand Lévi-Strauss's creative transformation of the Freudian theory by examining the theory. The Oedipus complex (an ambivalent love-hate relationship to the father and desire for the mother) is linked to Freud's concept of infantile sexuality. The child (who has not yet resolved the Oedipal conflict into heterosexual genitality) exists at an early stage of sexuality; he is called a "polymorphous pervert." [23] The resolution of the conflict comes about through a splitting of the ego into an unconscious, where incest is desired, and a conscious, where it is for-bidden.[24] The incest taboo, as explained in *Totem and Taboo,* represents a resolution of the Oedipus conflict on the level of the group; that is, it represents security for the group, insofar as it establishes an exogamous society.

Lévi-Strauss's utilization of Freud differs from this pattern primarily in that, to Lévi-Strauss, the resolution of Oedipal conflict functions on the synchronic level,[25] rather than on the diachronic level as it does in Freud. We have already seen that for Lévi-Strauss the child is both poly-morphously perverse in his eroticism and also polymorphously social or polymorphously metaphorical. Lévi-Strauss approvingly cites Rousseau's statement that the first language must have been figurative (metaphorical) and emotional, and it is this stage of "total identification" that precedes the consciousness of oppositions expressed in articulated (and meaning-ful) language. Rousseau's text is cited here, both for its beauty and for its capital importance:

It seems, then, that need dictated the first gestures, while the passions stimulated the first words. . . . The language of the first men is represented to us as the tongues of geometers, but we see that they were the tongues of poets.

And so it had to be. One does not begin by reasoning, but by feeling. . . . The natural effect of the first needs was to separate men, and not to reunite them. It must have been that way, because the species spread out and the earth was promptly populated.

As in Freud, through the stage of polymorphous eroticism, the child is relationally united through his sexuality to all erogenous zones, in Lévi-Strauss the original babbling of the child, expressing his intersubjectivity, is equally polymorphous.[26]

The splitting of the ego into two indigenous halves is mirrored in the dual organization of primitive societies into two unequal moieties and the reunification of the two in the group life of the native tribe, and so on.[27] Consequently, in no way can primitive thought be compared to child thought, for the splitting of the ego is a normal function, manifested in both primitive peoples and modern adult peoples. As we have seen, it is the way in which one enters a collective. The child's thought, not yet conforming to the specialized symbols (metaphors, myths, structures) of a particular group, is, as it were, floating and unstable, like that of the mentally ill person. Yet there is a synthetic structure to the child's thought, insofar as the child's thought represents "a sort of universal substratum the crystallizations of which have not yet occurred, and in which communication is still possible between incompletely solidified forms." Since the reason for the precariousness of the child's thought differs from that of the instability of the pathological (the child is autistic and egocentric because he represents the total possibilities or structures of all mankind; whereas the mentally ill adult represents only his own individual synthesis), the child thus differs from the pathological. Whereas the child is *in via* to adulthood, the mentally ill person is *ex via*. Lévi-Strauss rejects the notion that primitive thought is in any way less systematic—less linguistic—than that of the modern adult. Ontogenesis might reproduce phylogenesis in embryology, but not in sociology.[28]

Phylogeny, on the other hand, does not reproduce ontogeny. Claiming that it does was the error committed by Freud in *Totem and Taboo*. To the extent that it is the goal of *Totem and Taboo* to represent a resolution of Oedipal conflict by ensuring the security of the group, Freud's enterprise is accepted by Lévi-Strauss. But Freud should have recognized, according to Lévi-Strauss, that phenomena involving the most fundamental structure of the human mind could not have appeared once and for all. On the contrary, they are repeated in their entirety in each consciousness, and in each consciousness they transcend historical successions. In other words, the beginning of the species is constantly repeated in each individual consciousness and is repeated only in this atemporal (synchronic) way. *Totem and Taboo* explains, for Lévi-Strauss, not why incest is consciously condemned but how it is unconsciously desired. The story of the primal male horde is itself a myth expressing an ancient and lasting dream, whose magic seductiveness arises precisely from the fact that the acts it portrays have never been committed, because culture has always and everywhere opposed them. Such symbolic gratifications as this "myth" represent a permanent desire for disorder or counter-order, not because things were once thus chaotic, but because human life has never been, and never can be, that way.[29]

Here, then, in Lévi-Strauss, the Freudian model, the linguistic model (from Rousseau), and the phonological (Jakobsonian) model intersect: the incest-prohibtion (that is, Oedipal conflict) is universal—like a language.[30] But like the "passions" that constitute the beginning of language for Rousseau, the universality of the prohibition exists only insofar as there exists a positive side to the negative prohibition. The positive side consists of the rules of exogamy that constitute society and ensure, like language, the exchange of the matrimonial counterpart of words—women. The prohibition of incest is like exogamy, a rule of reciprocity, because one surrenders one's daughter or sister only on condition that one's neighbor does the same.[31] Thus, the transition from nature to culture is determined by man's linguistic ability to think of biological relationships as systems of oppositions: oppositions between the owners (men) and the owned (women), between wives acquired and wives (sisters and daughters) given, between bonds of alliance and bonds of kinship; opposition in the lineages between the consecutive series (same sex) and the alternate series (sex changes in passing from one to another); and so on.[32]

The elementary kinship structures are, for Lévi-Strauss, built upon a very basic opposition between two types of relationship in which a man may stand with a woman. She may be either a sister or a daughter, that is, a woman given (a kinswoman), or a wife, that is, a woman received (a relative by marriage). Upon this opposition is built a structure of reciprocity, through which one group must give but may also receive and the other must give but may also demand. The exchange is, in Mauss, a "total prestation." The distinction between cross cousins and parallel cousins delineates marriages that are universally allowed (sometimes even mandatory) and those that are forbidden (because parallel cousins are classified as brothers and sisters). The daughter of my paternal uncle is my parallel cousin; but the daughter of the sister of my father is my patrilinear cross cousin, the daughter of the brother of my mother is my matrilinear cross cousin, and so on. I can therefore marry the daughter of my paternal aunt or the daughter of my maternal uncle. Sometimes another patrilineal or matrilineal determination also enters the picture, and eventually the combinations become quite complicated.[33] Whatever the group, parallel cousins come from families in the same formal position, which is a position of static equilibrium, whereas cross cousins come from families in conflicting formal positions. Cross cousins are in a dynamic disequilibrium in relation to one another.[34] This disequilibrium is the inheritance of kinship, and alliance alone can solve it. Goods that, considered in isolation, would be identical (that is, women) cease to be identical when assigned to a proper place in the structure of reciprocity.[35]

Structures of Communication and of Subordination

Lévi- Strauss's analysis seeks to explore the level of language below that which he terms "the system of terminology." To prepare for this level, he acknowledges his debt to the work of modern phonologists, such as Jakobson, Halle, and others. He acknowledges that the function of language is to communicate; this we always knew. But the forms in which language was structured, the ways communication occurred, were known only with the dawn of modern phonology. The opposite was true of kinship systems; that is, the ways in which they functioned (their systems) were known but not their purpose (meaning). Lévi-Strauss seeks to bring out both the order and the signification of kinship systems.[36]

One begins to reach the deeper, nonvocabulary level of kinship structures when one explores what Lévi-Strauss terms "another system . . . the system of attitudes." All kinship systems are composed of two quite different orders of reality. There are, first, the terms through which different familial relationshps are expressed (father, brother, daughter, and so on).

But kinship goes beyond terminology. It incorporates feelings, rights, obligations, respect, hostility—in short, the system of attitudes. These, of course, go far beyond mere terminology. In *The Elementary Structures of Kinship*, Lévi-Strauss writes:

> The prohibition of incest is less a rule prohibiting marriage with the mother, sister or daughter, than a rule obliging the mother, sister or daughter to be given to others. It is the supreme rule of the gift. . . . Motherhood is not only a mother's relationship to her children, but her relationship to other members of the group, not as a mother, but as a sister, wife, cousin or simply a stranger as far as kinship is concerned. It is the same for all family relationships. . . .[37]

The system of attitudes thus insures the relationships of the individual to the group. The function of all kinship systems consists in assuring both the integration of the collective and the equal balance of all its parts. This exchange in marriage between two families revolves about "the unit of kinship" ("l'élément de parenté"), or the simplest possible kinship structure. It rests upon four terms (brother, sister, father, son), "which are linked by two pairs of correlative oppositions in such a way that in each of the two generations there is always a positive relationship and a negative one." Immediately, one can note the teleological character of such an outlook. Kinship systems function in order to enable exchange to ensue, and exchange functions in order to maintain the equilibrium of the group. On the grounds of the nonteleological explanations of natural science, Lévi-Strauss has been criticized for reintroducing final causality into scientific investigations. He has replied in his *Huxley Memorial Lectures*: "The objection that a teleological outlook is distasteful to modern sciences need not alarm us, for it is obviously false. The ghost of teleology was exorcised over twenty years ago by A. Rosenbluth, N. Wiener, and J. Bigelow who have explained teleology as a special case of determinism to be found in mechanisms capable of feed-back operations." Such observations provide some insight into the deterministic way in which Lévi-Strauss conceives the algebraic functioning of the collective unconscious.[38]

One should also note that, since we are dealing with an interchange between different generations (for example, in the simple example of exchange given above, the son of a union of a male from family *A* with a female from family *B* could not marry another female from family *B*, lest the collective become asymmetrical in its structures), we are dealing

also with two types of kinship structures: what Lévi-Strauss calls "structures de communication," which are static, and "structures de subordination," which are dynamic and nonreversible.[39] We have seen that kinship
systems, rules of marriage, and descent groups are all regarded by Lévi-
Strauss as a coordinated whole, whose function is to insure the perma-
nency of the social group through blood relations and affinal links.
Women are the unit of exchange. These mechanisms would continue
working indefinitely and the social structure would remain static if no
external factor were to affect the mechanism. However, diachronic
changes do affect the structure, and therefore there are changes in the
structure, producing relations of dominance or dependence. Structural
anthropology is conceived as dealing with both types of structure.

There are three levels of structures of communication: those that function through the communication of women (kinship structures), those
that function through the communication of goods and services (economic
structures), and those that function through the communication of
messages (language). All three function on the level of "grammar and
syntax, witnesses of unconscious structures." Economics forms the centerpiece of this triptych. Economic exchanges are the intermediaries between the two extremes, for, whereas kinship systems are involved with
the communication of persons and language systems with the communication of signs, economics concerns itself with the exchange neither of
persons nor of signs but of values. Therefore, whereas kinship systems as
a whole are structures of communication, within each set of kinship systems are the structures of subordination, and these provide the foundation for the constant flow from disequilibrium back to equilibrium within
the system. One should note that, within the structures of subordination,
the collective is dominant over the individual. One should also note that
these structures are atemporal (Lévi-Strauss's term is "synchronic"), insofar as they cut across chronological generations. Lévi-Strauss is, obviously,
most concerned with the synchronic. The distinction has its roots in
Saussure's attempt to separate an evolutionary linguistics from a static
linguistics. The former would study the derivation of a modern English
word from Old English, for example; the latter would study relational
identities amid morphological changes. For example, in an earlier state
of English, the second person singular was morphologically *thou,* and
the plural was *you.* Through diachronic development the *thou* became
morphologically identical with *you,* so that second person singular and
plural are now both spelled *you,* yet one still can note a relational dis-

tinction between them: one is singular, the other plural. In Lévi-Strauss, such syntactical structures will provide the meaning underlying the empirical morphology. To use an illustration given in *Tristes Tropiques,* if one were to reduce cannibalism (among non-Europeans) to its meaning, we would find that it celebrates the fact that man is spirit (not just matter), in that the cannibal wishes to incorporate, by his act, the "spirit" of the alien into himself. But we also condemn cannibalism on the same grounds, that man is more than matter. Therefore, the meaning of both acts (the practice of and the condemnation of cannibalism) is the same.[40]

The notion that signs function as elements of a system, precisely because the line between the *significans* and the signified is arbitrary (the "diacritical function" of signs), is also a Saussurian contribution. The illustration Saussure gives is particularly interesting because it will reappear in Lévi-Strauss's analysis of Caduveo face painting. It consists in an analogy between the diacritical function of the sign and the conception of individuality that appears in a game theory. Saussure claims that, in a chess game, the value of each piece depends upon its position in relation to every other piece on the chessboard. Or, if we were to cut transversely into the stem of a palm branch, instead of viewing the fibers all running together in the same direction (diachronic development), we would observe a pattern made between the longitudinal fibers. These designs or patterns are similar to synchronic structures.

Primitive societies, which, for Lévi-Strauss, are analogous to "machines mecaniques" ("mechanical machines"), produce (unlike thermodynamic machines) very little "entropy," or "the minimum of that disorder." They tend "to remain indefinitely in their initial state, and this explains why they appear to us as static societies with no history." In place of the disorder and inequalities that go hand in hand with (western) historical "progress," primitive societies seek to retain perfect symmetry amongst their members; the formation of kinship structures is one means thereby employed.[41]

Whenever a contradiction appears within a primitive society, caused by the asymmetrical grouping of families on the basis of intermarriage, the collective unconscious seeks to overcome all such inequalities through the establishment of symmetrical rules (laws) of logic. This attempt is made on the basis of a syntactical linguistic model: "The kind of correlation . . . which exists between the *system of terminology* and the *system of attitudes*. . . . is of a dialectical nature. The modalities of behavior between relatives express . . . the terminological classification

. . . a means of overcoming difficulties and contradictions. . . ." In brief, for Lévi-Strauss, all culture at the human level is linguistic in essence. The sign of the appearance of men is not toolmaking—for animals, too, can use instruments—but language. All art, religion, and law, and even the rules of cooking and etiquette, are languages. Culture, for Lévi-Strauss, is always regarded as a mediation between two contradictions. Culture functions like a linguistic code on behalf of exchanges (the "total pretestations" of Mauss), which operate on behalf of the eradication of inequalities among parts. Culture constitutes the collective in act; it is a system of total interchanges. The collective among primitive peoples is regarded as a veritable mechanical machine.[42] Finally, the unconscious modes of exchange that allow the collective in act to appear are translatable into conscious social systems, because such social systems reveal their underlying code. Our thanks for the opening of this structural method into social anthropology are due, Lévi-Strauss claims, to our having learned "from Freud that the grammatical can be achieved entirely within the individual.[43]

Mana and the Mind as Object

Lévi-Strauss has marvelously, then, combined Freudian Oedipal theory with structural linguistics and Mauss's notion of reciprocity to achieve— and this is perhaps his unique contribution—a totally mechanized notion of mental structures. There is always more in the exchange than the things exchanged. It is the essence of this "something more," which in the form of the exchange-relationships precedes the very things exchanged, to which we now must turn our attention. If, as we have already seen, metaphor joins (through a process of selection and substitution) entities conjoined in the code but not in the given message, then it follows that the mind always has more meanings available than there are objects to which to relate these meanings. This is the intellectual condition of man, that there is always more signified than there are signifiers. The disproportion between the two gives rise to the symbolic function that always seeks to integrate them. Magic among primitive peoples, mythology, kinship systems—all attest to this fact by providing new systems of reference within which thus far contradictory elements can be integrated.[44]

Furthermore, Lévi-Strauss quite frequently, while denying, as we have seen, any metaphysical existence to the structures of the unconscious, writes in philosophical fashion about the unconscious: "The universe signified before anyone began to know what it signified." "We don't attempt to demonstrate how men think through myths, but how myths think themselves through men." The myths "think themselves out" in men; there is "more" in exchange than the things exchanged; and this "more" signified even before men knew what it signified. This use of language seems very metaphysical. Lévi-Strauss acknowledges the complementarity of his ethnographic enterprise with that of Kant, and, like Kant, he definitely intends no metaphysical presuppositions. His approach, he claims, has never changed from *The Elementary Structures of Kinship,* even up through the four volumes of the *Mythologiques.* Its goal has been to show that apparently arbitrary data can always be reduced to order, that necessity reveals itself as immanent "in the illusions of freedom." His prime reason for studying mythology has been the idea that, in mythology, the mind seems to be at its most capricious and seems to be freed from mental restraints. Moreover, if the human mind can be shown to be determined even in its myths, then it must be *a fortiori* determined in all its manifestations. Unlike Kant, Lévi-Strauss takes as the starting point not the hypothesis of universal judgment but the empirical observation of collective judgments. Lévi-Strauss accepts the cognomen attached to his work by Paul Ricoeur: a "Kantianism without a transcendental subject." The transcendental subject is rejected by Lévi-Strauss as extraneous, insofar as the mind is not subject but object.[45]

The key to the entire nonmetaphysical, nonsubjective notion of mind lies in the idea of transformations. Transformation signifies, in a broad sense, the passage from one level of a system to another.[46] The entire structural methodology consists in establishing analogies. The methodology pursues conditions in which systems of truth become mutually convertible and, therefore, simultaneously admissible for several subjects. The entire ensemble of these conditions takes on the character of an object endowed with a reality proper to itself and independent of any particular subject. Thus, Lévi-Strauss says that the purpose of the first of his four volumes of *Mythologiques* is to have no subject; elsewhere, he says that the book about myths is itself a myth. His meaning is that not only do the myths think themselves out in men, but the myths even think themselves out among themselves. Whereas codes of the first order are those of language, and the myths themselves are codes of the second order, his own book would be a code of the third order, or one that would assure the reciprocal translatability of several myths. Since myths are simply codes showing the signification of that which is expressed at the vocabulary level, these books are the myth of mythology. Because what is being established is a code—which would demonstrate that myths of very diverse origin (in both time and space) objectively form a group—historical progression or geographical proximity is not a major consideration of structural analysis.

Thus, the mind, freed for conversation with itself and from the obligation of dealing directly with objects, finds itself reduced to imitating itself as object. The laws of its operations are in no way fundamentally different from those it manifests in its other functions, and it then affirms itself as a thing among things.[47] We return here to the theme that we have called Lévi-Strauss's turning-to-the-world: his "everyday materialism" (*materialisme vulgaire*). Unlike phenomenology and its offspring, existentialism, structuralism destroys, through its progressive analysis of the subject into its underlying codes, all hint of subjectivity.[48] In this way, we may say that in structuralism (unlike phenomenology and neo-Kantianism), I do not constitute the world, the world constitutes me.[49]

The structuralist methodology consists, then, in a doubly reflexive movement of two thoughts working upon one another;[50] that is, the reflections of the ethnologist's thoughts in those of the natives he studies, and vice versa. This is the psychoanalytic method of transference and counter-transference (see Chapter 2 above). Through this process the human mind (*l'esprit humain*), without any concern for the identity of its occasional carriers, manifests a structure that through a constant series of transformations reveals progressively greater intelligibility. Since all "objects" are universally coded, it should be possible to reduce all—even the most qualitative and emphemeral—to such scientific intelligibility: "We can thus hope to reach a plane where logical properties, as attributes of things, will be manifested as directly as flavors or perfumes; perfumes . . . result from combinations of elements which, if subjected to a different selection and organization, would have created awareness of a different perfume. Our task, then, is to use the concept of the sign in such a way as to introduce these secondary qualities into the operations of truth." [51] The entire method consists in elucidating schemes of reciprocal intelligibility or of transformations that will bring out the "global coherence" of the individual terms (myths and so on).[52] Lévi-Strauss expresses this doubly reflexive movement in a number of illustrations, the best of which is that of two mirrors placed on opposite walls, yet obliquely set upon the walls (that is, with slight variations in each mirror). The number of mirror images would not be infinite (as they would be if placed directly opposite one another), and four or five such images would probably give us at least enough coverage to make us feel sure that no large piece of furniture in the room would be missing in our description of it. In this way the ensemble of social relations can be disclosed even though new versions of the myth might later be revealed.[53]

The "more" that is uncovered in metaphor, the something extra in the exchange that is beyond the things exchanged, is therefore the systems of codes underlying the exchanges of men. Yet, we must answer the question of the nature of these codes, and whether there is any principle of unification to them.

We know that in Lévi-Strauss's view, in the manner of Mauss's "total prestation" and Jakobson's universal codes, society itself is a constant round of reciprocities. The power (*une vertu*) behind exchanges is not something physical, since we do not always exchange physical things (sometimes they are dignities, honors, privileges, and such). And yet we have already seen that it is not totally subjective.[54] It cannot be identical with the exchanges themselves, for then we would be explaining the exchanges by the exchanges. It is something more real in its unity than in its parts (for outside of being systematic, it does not exist). It is that which plays the role of copula in the proposition. Among primitive peoples, it is called "mana."

Mana, which always signifies force or power, among primitives signifies an impersonal supernatural force to which good fortune is attributed.[55] It is the foundation, for the primitive, of synthetic, *a priori* judgments, which provide the cement for the primitives' cognitional universe. Mana glues together the overabundance of signifier in the universe with the relative dearth of objects in the universe to be signified. In short, it is that area of thirdness (the unconscious) which surmounts and surpasses the inequalities and individualities of the self and the other. It is a "floating signifier" (*signifiant flottant*), or a "universal resource which is infinitely more rich than that of each particular culture." Mana, according to Lévi-Strauss, is to be interpreted in strictly scientific terms, as an algebraic symbol representing "an indetermined value of meaning," a "simple form," or, to be more exact, a symbol in its pure state capable of being transformed into any content whatsoever. Because it is nothing in itself it can become all things. It is a symbol that has a symbolic value of zero, much as zero-phoneme, in linguistics, is one whose entire function is to be opposed to all other phonemes without possessing in itself any constant phonetic value or differential character. Briefly, mana is a pure variable. It serves the same function a concept of proportionality would serve, allowing one to understand variability in the midst of invariability, discontinuity in the midst of continuity. It plays the same role played by the concept of alienation (mediation) in Hegel: again returning to the linguistic unconscious, it proclaims that to be an individual it is necessary to be in relation to an other. As the cement (the unconscious) between one thing and another, it metaphorically connects them. It is the absence spoken of, in the Freudian dialectic of presence and absence, explained in the *Fort-Da*. As Barthes perfectly expresses the case: "The zero degree is not, properly speaking, a nothing . . . it is an absence which signifies." [56]

Since mana is for the primitives the cement between the intelligible world and the actual world, it is analogous to, but not as perfectly symbolic as, the one science (and it must in this context be a science) that, for Lévi-Strauss, forms the apotheosis of all structuralist methodology. This discipline is neither psychoanalysis nor archeology, neither mathematics nor anthropology, but music: "a constant of my own personal history . . . my reverence . . . for 'that God, Richard Wagner.' If Wagner is . . . the undeniable originator of the structural analysis of myths and even of folk tales (as in *Die Meistersinger*) . . . the analysis was made, in the first instance, *in music*." [57] The structure of myths is comparable to a great musical score. For although both music and myth need a temporal dimension (unlike painting) in order to become manifest, both are, in effect, mechanisms intended to do away with time. Music is bound up with the physiological rhythms and time of the listener; thus it is diachronic and irreversible. But it operates on a synchronic level because it has a score, and, therefore, like a cloth blowing and billowing in the wind, music has caught up and enfolded time into itself. Listening to it, we achieve a sort of immortality.

Mythology, too, works on both a diachronic and synchronic axis. It is diachronic in that it utilizes historical occurrences and operates on the psychophysiological periodicity of the inner time of the listener (cerebral waves, organic rhythms, the capacity of memory, the power of attention); and it is also synchronic (as we shall presently see), linking together certain significations in a factual way. Again, the notion of the linguistic unconscious operates through both music and mythology. The composer's design takes on the aspects of reality, as does myth, through the listener and by him. But, inversely, we discover ourselves as signified in the message of the sender, in the area of unconscious Thirdness. "The intention of the composer, ambiguous while still in the score . . . becomes actual, like that of myth, through and by the listener . . . music has its being in me, and I listen to myself through it. Thus the myth and the musical work are like conductors of the orchestra, whose audience becomes the silent performers." In this analogy of mythology with music, Lévi-Strauss is stressing the very same notion emphasized in this statement from *The Elementary Structures of Kinship*: "Women are not primarily a sign of social value, but a natural stimulant." Social structures are both tangible and intellectual in that they are symbolic. It is the amazing property of mana and of the collective unconscious it composes to transcend the dichotomy between the actual and the intelligible, so that the social is neither purely intellectual nor purely material; it is symbolic or structural.[58]

The Transformational Method: A New Analogy of Being?

We have seen, then, that for Lévi-Strauss the notion of mana (the extraordinary symbolic function) embodies the concept of the variable: a capacity to recognize discontinuity in the midst of continuity, and vice versa. By attributing such advanced power to the primitive mentality, Lévi-Strauss is saying that the primitive mind achieves a degree of intellectuality as scientifically rigorous and as systematically socialized as the most advanced technological thought of the West.[59]

In order to comprehend a bit more clearly what exactly is involved in the mental use of variability (or, as phrased by the structural linguist, the use of "metaphor"), let us look at some examples gleaned from the experiments performed by Piaget and Jerome Bruner on young children. Recall that Lévi-Strauss, though accepting these and similar experiments as proof that the power of thinking analogically is a highly intricate and scientific mode of cognition, is quite wary of the theory of maturation that accompanies those specimens in Piaget and Bruner and others. As an innatist, he is uneasy because such theories are sometimes used to imply that mental structure can mysteriously appear on the scene out of that which was not structured at the very inception of mental life.[60]

The key concept in understanding the role played by mana among primitives is that of transformations. Each set of relationships compared to another set is itself transformed by the very comparison into another pole of a new binary opposition, which is the new comparison or new relationship established. Transformation, or systems of transformations, in the more usual phrase, can be understood in two senses. In a broad sense, it means the passage from one level of a system to another; in a narrower sense it means a change in time, which is accomplished according to a set of rules.[61]

The ability to transpose (that is, transformation in the broad sense) is a mental skill that represents a very advanced degree of abstraction. The experiments of Piaget and Bruner point to the character of this skill. The ability to recognize proportion is the power of using the variable [62] (that is, to think analogously, or in the structuralists' terminology, "metaphorically") and is one that is not developed fully even by the age of five. A simple experiment conducted upon five year olds confronted with two equal beakers, each filled to the same level with water, betrays their inability to think analogously. The child will typically say that both beakers are equal. But if the experimenter pours the contents of one of the beakers into another one that is taller and thinner and then asks the child whether there is the same amount of water in both, the child will deny the equivalence, saying that the water is higher in one beaker than in the other. Bruner concludes, "This incapacity to recognize invariance of magnitude across transformations in the appearance of things is one of the most striking aspects of this stage." [63]

The power of thinking according to structural transformations is the ability to recognize invariance in the midst of variations.[64] In another interesting but somewhat more complex experiment conducted along the same lines, children between the ages of four and eleven were presented with two half-filled glasses of unequal volume. The larger glass was identified as *A,* the smaller as *B.* When asked, many of the children said that *A* was fuller than *B* but also that *A* was emptier than *B.* Or some would say that both were equally full, but *A* was emptier. To the experimenter, these replies seemed like patent logical contradictions.

Even more astounding was that the proportion of contradictory answers increased with age; more seven year olds answered "illogically" than five year olds, and so on. However, when the experimenter examined the way in which the children went about making their judgments of "fullness" and "emptiness," he found that logic or illogic was not the issue at all. Rather, children from ages four to eleven *all* judge "fullness" in the same way: by using a direct method of observation, rather than by computing proportion. Hence, greater apparent volume of water —with equal levels, the width of the glass; and when water level and width are equal, the height of the glass—is the factor equated with "fullness." But when asked which glass was emptier, the older children displayed a movement toward knowledge of proportion, though not a complete grasp of it. For "emptier," they displayed "an appreciation of the complementary relation of filled and empty space"—although an incorrect one. Whereas the younger children equated emptiness with liquid "littleness" (never even approaching knowledge through proportion), the older children equated "emptiest" with the largest volume of unfilled space (just as "fullest" meant to them the largest volume of filled space). Superficially, the answers of the older children seemed logically contradictory, because they had begun to dissociate two variables, empty space and full space. However, they were still limited to "ostensive definitions," those based upon pointing; hence, they could not yet handle the two variables by the use of proportion: "What is intriguing about proportion is that it cannot be pointed at since it is a relation of two variables." [65] What the experiment calls for is the ability to employ transformational structures, to identify invariability in the midst of variability; in short, to relate the relations of empty space to filled space in one glass with the relation of empty space to filled space in another. This ability is, indeed, an advanced mental achievement.

For Lévi-Strauss, the mind of the primitive, so often thought by modern man to be illustrative of early, nonadvanced mental development, is marked in its metaphorical abilities (that is, the power of using proportion) by the touchstone of advanced mental capacities. According to Bruner: "Intellectual development is markedly increasing capacity to deal with several alternatives simultaneously, to tend to several sequences during the same period of time, and to allocate time and attention in a manner appropriate to these multiple demands." [66]

Another aspect of language is its reversibility. That is, having encoded language, we can recode it, transform it, change the direction of the temporal overt action it symbolizes, and so on. Mental growth from infancy to adulthood consists in the internalization of action, its transformation into symbols, and the employment of reversibility. Lévi-Strauss calls this atemporal aspect of mental structures "synchrony." Such atemporal cuttings into the temporal flow form, according to Lévi-Strauss, "a mechanical and reversible time," the opposite of "a statistical and irreversible time." And if the mind is a symbol-producing mechanism, social anthropology is (like structural linguistics and structural psychoanalysis) one of the semiological sciences. It is the property of signs and symbols to function only insofar as they are part of systems, ruled by their internal laws of implication and of exclusion.[67] In other words, it is proper to a system of signs to be transformable or translatable into the language of another system with the aid of permutations. Lévi-Strauss's method (the structuralistic method) would be "a transformational rather than a fluxionist" one. The "very close relationship between the concept of transformation and the concept of structure" that plays so important a role in social anthropology means that two conditions are necessary in order for any arrangement of social "facts" to be structured: first, that it be a system, governed by an internal coherency; second, that this coherency, which is not open to observation in an isolated system, be revealed in the study of transformations, through which the properties in systems that appear to be different are revealed as similar.[68] It is, as we have seen, the role of mana to provide the logical cement.[69]

Transformational Systems in the Study of Mythology

In Chapter 11 of *Structural Anthropology,* entitled "La structure des mythes," Lévi-Strauss offers the ground plan that he will follow throughout his later four-volume *Mythologiques*[70] and, more importantly, for our purposes, a concrete example of the way in which metaphor and analogous thinking are discovered in the syntactic structures of human thought. The example he offers is a structuralist analysis of the Oedipus myth. His preliminary remarks about myths indicate that they present an ambiguous character, in that they are both universal (many myths throughout the world are quite similar) and also contingent (in that there appears to be no logic, no continuity—anything may happen in a myth).

The same problem was encountered by early linguistic philosophers: in different languages the same sounds appear as universal elements but convey different meanings. In linguistics, the contradiction was resolved through the Saussurian principle of the arbitrary character of linguistic signs, whose conclusion must be that not the sounds themselves but the combinations of sounds provide the meaning of a word. A second Saussurian distinction helps us to understand the position of myth in society and Lévi-Strauss's explanation of this position. Saussure marks off language, which belongs to a reversible (synchronic) time and belongs also to the structural (syntactical) side of language, from speech, which belongs to a nonreversible (diachronic) time.[71] Myth, as explained by Lévi-Strauss, actually belongs to some third level midway between language and speech, for myth, although it refers to events that occurred long ago and continue through time (that is, it is diachronic), has a timeless value and is equally operational for explaining the future (that is, it is synchronic).[72] Myth seems to mediate between these two orders. It is the area of culture in which *traduttore, traditore* has hardly any value; that is, the mythical value is preserved despite poor translation. Edmund Leach claims: "Common to all the symbolist writers is the view that a myth can be understood as 'a thing in itself' without any direct reference to the social context in which it is told; the meaning can be discovered from a consideration of the words alone." This is simply another aspect of the arbitrariness of the symbol applied by Lévi-Strauss to the notion of mental structures in anthropology. Any functionalistic interpretation of the social relations in any given society, on the structuralists' supposition that social facts are symbols, could be a misunderstanding of the way that symbols interact in society. For the structuralist, a symbol is not an expression of the particular context in which it appears, relative only to that society.[73]

On these grounds, Lévi-Strauss rejects the functionalism of Malinowski and the notion of "structure" employed by Radcliffe-Brown, and even the idea, advanced in the work of Montesquieu and Spencer, of the "spirit" governing the laws of certain societies.[74] Again, on the same grounds that a myth can be understood without any direct reference to the context in which it is found, Lévi-Strauss rejects any analogy between his "structures" and Jungian "archetypes." The Jungian idea that a mythological pattern (the archetype) would possess a certain meaning is really equivalent to the old philosophies of language notion (dispelled by Saussure) that different sounds possess a natural affinity with their meaning—for example, that the liquid semivowels are connected with water; the open vowels with things that are large, loud, or heavy; and so on. On the contrary, the mental structures that language mirrors exists in an aggregate form called the unconscious, which (unlike the collective unconscious of Jung) is nothing in itself. It is as empty or alien to mental images as the stomach is to the foods that pass through it. It simply has a function that is symbolic; it functions among all men according to the same laws; it is the ensemble of these laws.[75]

According to Lévi-Strauss, then, one must distinguish the subconscious, which is individualistic and can be considered as full of recollections and images collected over the course of a lifetime, from the unconscious, properly speaking, which imposes structural laws upon unarticulated elements that come from elsewhere—drives, emotions, representations, memories. The subconscious is the individual lexicon containing an accumulated vocabulary of one's personal history: that vocabulary only becomes significant to the extent that it is structured according to the laws of the unconscious and, thus, is fashioned into a discourse. What is significant is that these laws are the same for all individuals, under all circumstances. The structure is the important part, the vocabulary the unimportant. A myth, whether it be recreated by an individual subject or borrowed from a collective tradition, is a collection of representations that is variable, yet the structure always remains the same. It is important to note that the number of such structural laws is finite; therefore, though a compilation of known stories and myths would be vast, yet they could be reduced to a small number of simple types.[76]

The method of this reduction, as expressed in the *Structural Anthropology* chapter entitled "La structure des mythes," is as follows: the structures of the diverse myths will be discovered only when each version of myth is reduced to its constituent patterns, which, linguistically, Lévi-Strauss called "mythemes." These constituent units of myth presuppose the other constituent units of language—phonemes, morphemes, and sememes—but must belong to a higher degree of complexity, since myth is not confused with any other kind of speech.[77] The mythemes must exist on the sentence level and, to discover them, one should use as a guide the principles of all structural analysis: (1) economy of explanation, (2) unity of solution, and (3) the possibility of restructuring the whole from only a fragment and later stages of development from the actually developed stages. The first principle is the usual scientific one known as Occam's razor; the second presupposes that the structures of the mind are finite and that the myths could even, conceivably, be reduced to one myth.[78] In reference to the last principle, it should be noted that Lévi-Strauss is considering structural analysis as similar to the method that one would employ when carefully watching the playing of a game of cards whose rules were unknown. Even if one had never seen a playing card, one should be able to reconstruct, through careful observance of the plays, both the rules of the game and even the composition of the deck of cards.[79]

The ethnologist is, according to Lévi-Strauss, like an observer at a spiritualist's séances. As the ethnologist knows something of the various cultures from which his myths appear, the observer knows something of the spiritualist's clients: their sex, physical appearance, social status, and such. He listens to and records the séances and later makes comparisons among them. To return to the earlier example, it is mathematically possible for the observer-ethnologist to reconstruct the nature of the deck (either fifty-two or thirty-two cards), composed of four sets of the same units, one feature alone varying: the suits. It is apparent that Lévi-Strauss is dealing, in this last principle, with the power of the mind to employ transformations—that is, the reversibility of its synchronic structures. Since all meaning accrues to a symbol only because of its place in a system, that is, by its opposition to the other symbols, the transformational structures of the mind can appear only through a process of revealing permutations or links among the different stages of the myth.

The technique for discovering the mythemes (which must exist at the sentence level) consists in breaking down each myth into the shortest possible sentences and writing each sentence on an index card bearing a number corresponding to the unfolding of the story. Each card will be seen to reveal the assignment of a predicate to a given subject. In other words, each mytheme is a relation.

Two questions immediately arise. First, how do mythemes differ from phonemes, morphemes, and so on—from all the constituent units of linguistics—for all refer to relations? Second, since the story is unfolded diachronically (and all cards follow this order), we have dealt only with one aspect of myth. Yet myth is *both* diachronic and synchronic, or nonreversible and reversible. The latter aspect remains unexplained.[80]

To account for the synchronic order, Lévi-Strauss postulates a new hypothesis: that the true constitutive units of myths are not the isolated relations but "des paquets de relations," and only as such can they produce a meaning.[81] Such bundles of relations can mean only one thing: Lévi-Strauss, like Lacan and the other structuralists, is saying that the unconscious is an ensemble of analogical relationships. Catherine Backes correctly notes Lévi-Strauss's position when she writes that the differences between the myths "are situated at levels which one can call analogical: the same function is discovered, from myth to myth, but the code differs."[82] The metalanguage [83] (the mythemes) in which Lévi-Strauss can speak of the language of myths represents a triumph of syntax over semantics insofar as meaning comes from syntactical groupings. Mental operations are subject, herein, to determined laws; "everything is syntax there"; yet, in another sense, the mythemes are words, and "everything is vocabulary"—the bundles of relations are like musical notations.[84] For music can also be read both diachronically (from left to right, from the tops of pages to the bottom), and synchronically (in reversible time), in its recurring musical arrangements of notes. It is the latter that provide the harmony in music. Music, then, is read on two axes: one horizontal (diachronic) and the other vertical (synchronic), the latter according to bundles of relations among the notes.

According to Lévi-Strauss, one can read myths similarly, along two axes. After recording every sentence of each version of the myth on a different index card, with a number corresponding to its position in the narrative of the story, we read these cards along the first (diachronic) axis in something like this sequence:

1, 2, 4, 7, 8   2, 3, 4, 6, 8,   1, 4, 5, 6, 8,   1, 2, 5, 7   3, 4, 5, 6, 8.

Arranging these as myth would be spoken (or read on a printed page), they would be structured:

$$1, 2, 4, 7 \quad 8$$
$$2 \quad 3 \quad 4 \quad 6 \quad 8$$

$$1 \quad 4 \quad 5 \quad 7 \quad 8$$
$$1 \quad 2 \quad 5 \quad 7$$
$$3 \quad 4 \quad 5 \quad 6 \quad 8$$

But if our task is to situate them so that all the patterns that are alike are considered not in succession but as a whole—that is, as the myth might be understood—then the result is somewhat different:

$$1 \quad 2 \quad\quad 4 \quad\quad\quad 7 \quad 8$$
$$2 \quad 3 \quad 4 \quad\quad 6 \quad\quad 8$$
$$1 \quad\quad\quad 4 \quad 5 \quad\quad 7 \quad 8$$
$$1 \quad 2 \quad\quad\quad 5 \quad\quad 7$$
$$3 \quad 4 \quad 5 \quad\quad\quad\quad 8$$

According to this argument, the synchronic structure is slowly appearing when the units are arranged in columns.[85]

Lévi-Strauss has simply presented the myth in the conception of the two general arrangements of linguistic terms given by Saussure, and then combined these (like Lacan) with a fresh interpretation of the Freudian unconscious. For Saussure the distinction becomes even more complex. The relationships of linguistic terms develop on two levels, corresponding (as in Jakobson) to two forms of mental activity.[86] The first is "syntagmatic," that is, discourse as a combination of signs; it is linear and irreversible. Each term receives value from being in opposition to that which precedes it and that which follows it; the analytic activity applied to it is continuity; its terms are united *in presentia.* This type of mental activity is, clearly, close to what Saussure termed *la parole,*[87] and it is also what we have seen Jakobson discuss as "metonymy." The second level is that of "associations." Since Saussure, this level is most often spoken of as the paradigmatic, or as the systematic; it is very close to *la langue.* The analytic activity applied to it is classification. Its terms are united *in absentia* (this level was seen above, in the analysis of the *Fort Da* in Freud's *Beyond the Pleasure Principle*). Paradigmatic relations are called "correlations" by Hjelmslev, "oppositions" by Martinet, and "similarities" by Jakobson; they are the source of "metaphoric" order in Jakobson and of "bundles of differential elements" in Lévi-Strauss.[88]

The two axes corresponding to these two levels of language are called the axis of *combinations,* which is diachronic, and the axis of *selections* or of *substitutions,* which is synchronic. The relationships between these two axes are linked by Saussure in an image that recalls the number groupings shown above. Each linguistic unity is like a column of a Greek building. The column is linked in a relationship of contiguity with the other parts of the building (for example, with the cornice), and this is its "syntagmatic" link. But it is also, let us say, a Doric column, and thus it evokes the other types of Greek architectural columns, the Ionic and the Corinthian: one could virtually (though perhaps not actually) be substituted for another. This interchangeability is its paradigmatic link. A myth is, for Lévi-Strauss, a combination of all such columns.[89]

Applying this methodology to a particular recurring myth, the story of Oedipus, Lévi-Strauss reinterprets in a structural fashion the various versions—including Freud's rendition, the Oedipus complex, as well as the Sophoclean account—and shows that the next step in structural analysis of the myth is an attempt to arrive at the meaning common to each bundle of relations (or column) in the set. In this way he reduces each column to its unifying factor; he then sets about showing the relationships between the columns. Each column (fortuitously) turns out to be an assertion of the opposite of at least one other column. In the Oedipus example, there are four columns (eight in the above pattern). Columns

1 and 2 are binary opposites, and columns 3 and 4 are binary opposites; therefore, he can establish a relationship of analogy among the four columns: column 1 is to column 2 as column 3 is to column 4. It becomes evident that the myth is simply an attempt to mediate by establishing a relationship of analogy among a series of binary oppositions. For Lévi-Strauss, myth affords a logical model by which the mind can avoid unwelcome contradictions; it makes them less final and, therefore, more acceptable. In this way, his analysis of the Oedipus myth shows that it concerns a problem of patrilinear descent: how to immortalize fathers in their sons without the intervention of women (that is, how to believe in autochthonous descent). To do so is, of course, impossible, but, in the myth itself, the impossibility is eliminated through the mediating power of the ambivalent sphinx, which is both male and female.[90] The mediation of logical structures in Lévi-Strauss is always between the basic binary oppositions of nature and culture. Oedipus kills his father and marries his mother. These unnatural acts must be mediated, and are, in the killing of the Sphinx (Oedipus's correctly answering the riddle of the Sphinx), a legitimate destruction of an unnatural being and, consequently, a reaffirmation by Oedipus of bisexual generation.[91]

The same mediatory power reconciling nature with culture appears in the four volumes of *Mythologiques*. In *Le cru et le cuit*, there are two natural elements, meat and fire. Meat—the raw—is mediated by fire—the natural way to cook. In such a myth, fire transforms nature into a cultural product: the repast.[92] In *Du miel aux cendres,* the opposition is again between the natural and the cultural, or between the raw and the cooked, or between honey, which is "infra-culinaire," and tobacco, which is "meta-culinaire," but the opposition is the inverse of that in the myths of *Le cru et le cuit*. Here, instead of going from nature to culture, the myth goes from culture to nature. That is, the myth refers not to the origin of culture from nature but of culture's fall toward nature, first, insofar as smoking (tobacco) is an attempt to absorb a cultural product as if it were natural and, second, in the confusion that exists in honey between its being food (the bees are driven off by fire, and so the honey is cooked and is therefore cultural) and also excrement (of the bees, so that it is natural).[93] Fire, here again, mediates as natural and cultural.

In *L'Origine des manières de table,* the voyage of the sun and the moon in the mythical boat of the heavens provides a new equilibrium between day, as conjunction of heaven and earth, and night, as disjunction of heaven and earth. The sun is the fire of the day, the moon the fire of the night. Through various permutations, the transformational powers of the myths are brought to light from the Bororo myth of reference onward, until the unity of the myths becomes evident.[94]

Lévi-Strauss finishes his long article on the structure of mythology by drawing three important conclusions. First, there is obviously much re-duplication and repetition in the unfolding of any myth. Its function, consequently, is that it exists in order to make the synchronic structure apparent. Second, none of the layers of meaning within the myth (which appeared by organizing its diachronic sequences but reading them syn-chronically, along the columns) are ever rigorously identical. Since the purpose of myth is to provide a logical model to overcome real or lived contradictions, which are themselves infinite, an infinite number of these synchronic repetitions, each slightly different from the preceding ones, can be produced. In this way a myth grows like a spiral. Its growth is continuous, but its structure is discontinuous. In this way it stands midway between language (*la langue*) and speech (*la parole*). Finally, and most importantly, Lévi-Strauss concludes that the mental structures of primitive peoples who create such vast, complicated, and rigorously scientific mythologies are as advanced a form of thought as that of the modern natural scientist. In short, he agrees with Piaget, Bruner, and the other structuralists that the power of analogical thinking is an ad-vanced accomplishment, for it is the capacity to recognize invariance across transformations in the appearance of things; hence, it opens the door to knowledge of proportion, or a knowledge which cannot be ostensibly pointed to, since a proportion is a relation of two variables. From this, all the higher forms of thinking result, for example, the idea of logical necessity, which depends, according to Piaget, upon a process of dealing not with concrete experience itself but with the nature of propositions themselves. In this way, the mind transcends the material properties of concrete events "just as mathematicians operate upon the language rather than upon what the language refers to." For Lévi-Strauss, there cannot then be any great distinction between "primitive" thought and scientific thought. The working processes of the two are the same; their difference lies in the objects to which they are applied. Human nature has evolved only peripherally, with regard to the circumstantial objects that it encounters, but in itself, it remains identical for all men of all times and climes.[95]

The Repudiation of the Cartesian Starting Point

The contribution of structuralism to psychoanalysis is that, much as in the work of Mauss,[96] the natural drives (governed by the Freudian pleasure principle) are considered to be intersubjective modes of exchange or ways of communicating between men, clans, and so on, on an analogy with linguistic systems. Lacan, for example, claims that the unconscious gives birth to language at the stage of development in which the basic narcissistic drives are overcome by the formation of an unconscious structure (the Other). In such an occurrence, reality is denied or displaced entirely at the whim of the pleasure principle. The latter completes itself only by suppressing the intersubjective demands of the Other into an unconsciously structured logic of transformations.[97] Thus, all cultural accomplishments depend upon repression and sublimation of egotistic natural drives into intersubjective cultural drives, and this repressive function gives birth to the power of metaphorical thinking—mana, among the "primitives." Such metaphorical thinking is rigorously scientific because, on the level of the linguistic, it assumes the same role played by the variable in algebra: it represents the mathematics of exchange.

The repressed dialogue that regulates our conscious thoughts is contained in a language that is in the subject but not spoken by the subject.[98] Ideally, the subject should say, "It is speaking," in lieu of saying, "I am speaking"—that is, the unconscious, the id, speaks through me. Lacan expresses this idea by saying, "The unconscious is the language of the Other." This "displacement of the source of language" is, of course, a major revolution effected by Freud in the tradition of Western philosophy from Descartes onward (according to the structuralist psychoanalysts). The Cartesian identification of the subject with consciousness is questioned, and the phenomenologists' equation of (phenomenal) experience with reality is denied.[99] Lapouge writes: "Each of us is a subject operating in ways unknown to himself. Lacan expresses this in the telling phrase: 'I think where I am not; I am where I do not think.' Rimbaud, that solitary genius, had already hit on the formula 'Je est un autre.' "[100]

These themes arise from the milieu and mostly from the pen of Claude Lévi-Strauss. The basic starting point of all structuralist thought is, then, the repudiation of the Cartesian starting point and the subsequent embrace of the collective. Lévi-Strauss writes on the last page of *Tristes Tropiques*: "The self is not only hateful: there is no place for it between *us* and *nothing*." [101] It is this restoration of the collective that provides the ground for the Lévi-Straussian enterprise.

4 ☸ *There Are No Privileged Societies*

The Primitive Mind: A Scientific Mind

We have already seen that one traditional interpretation of the mind
of the primitive—one vigorously opposed by Lévi-Strauss—was attuned
only to its apparently erratic behavior. From ritual to dream to play to
fantasy, and so on, the savage's mind never seems to be able to concentrate very long upon any one object. He has thus, in his mental pre-
occupations, been regarded as a sort of primitive child, unable to restrain
his natural capriciousness and unable, consequently, to manage very well
in a highly organized, highly restricting technological culture. According
to this perspective, primitive peoples manifest a "prelogical" mentality,
which is quasi-mystical and highly "participatory" in the way it regards
the surrounding universe. The latter point seems to mean that the primitive cannot really make mental distinctions or think logically. This view
of the primitives' mind is usually associated with the name of Lévy-
Bruhl,[1] and this also seems to be the interpretation of the primitive
mind held by Sartre.[2]

But is this fluidity, forever condemned to "participations,"[3] the true
mark of the primitives' mind? If, on the other hand, we could show that
there, where man most readily seems to be a useless passion, there in the
mind of the primitive, we find not infinite possibilities but finite de-
termining structures of a limited number,[4] then we could prove that
mind, where especially it was thought to be chaotic, contingent, and
"condemned to be free," is everywhere determined and necessitated.

Lévi-Strauss believes he can do just that, can show that man's mind
is one with the sociohistorical world and is patterned according to a
series of finite structures.[5] As a result, this aspect of structuralism, what
we have called the "turning-to-the-world," veers away from idealism

toward a biological naturalism. In fact, a consequence of structuralism should be, as Lévi-Strauss has written, "to rescue associational psychology from the discredit into which it has fallen." [6] He concludes that the mistake of associationism [7] was that it did not recognize that the contours of this original logic, which it had itself drawn, were a "direct expression of the structure of the mind (and behind the mind, probably of the brain)," rather than the product of the environment as it works upon "an amorphous consciousness." Another way of expressing this point is to say that this logic explains the laws of association and not the reverse. [8] What is this logic that, for Lévi-Strauss, constitutes the laws of association, and how is it expressed in the life of the primitive? We have already seen it demonstrated in primitive mythology and briefly in the marriage cycle of certain primitive peoples. Now let us examine it in his explanation of the anthropological phenomenon of totemism.

The Scientific Value of the Primitive Mind

Recall that Lévi-Strauss rejects Lévy-Bruhl's assumption of the mystical mentality of the primitive and asserts, on the contrary, that the primitive's intelligence is highly structured and deeply scientific. Ultimately, this postulate of a similarity in mental processes between those of the native and those of the nuclear physicist is a denial by Lévi-Strauss of an evolutionary theory of human intelligence and of historical meliorism. One can see these aspects of Lévi-Strauss's thought in his discussions of totemism.

Totemism offers a good example of the "participatory" mind of the savage, for through it, as everyone knows, a place is assigned to man in the animal kingdom. [9] In lieu, however, of an example of the nonanalytic character of primitive thought (Lévy-Bruhl's interpretation), Lévi-Strauss maintains that Boas and Taylor were on the right track when they saw that "the formation of a system, on the social level, is a necessary condition of totemism." By way of clarification (among many different cases), Lévi-Strauss presents an example of totemic classification drawn from the Nuer tribe. These people say that twins are both "one person" and also not persons at all but "birds." The reasoning seems to be the following. Twins are manifestations of spiritual power and as such are "children of God," but God dwells in the heavens; therefore, they are "persons of the above." But birds are of the above, and, therefore, twins are assimilated to them. Yet twins are still human beings; therefore, they are relatively "of below." To account for this contradiction, another distinction is made. Some species of birds fly higher than others; hence, birds may also be divided according to above and below. Thus, twins are often called by the names of "terrestrial" birds, such as the guinea fowl, the francolin, and so on. Lévi-Strauss is attempting to show here that the mind of the savage is capable of making some very subtle distinctions and of building up, by means of these distinctions, a concrete analytic logic uniting the social world with the animal world.[10]

Lévi-Strauss acknowledges a debt here to Bergson, for Bergson recognizes the classificatory power of totemism and thus becomes the first of all thinkers (philosophers as well as anthropologists) to see its true meaning.[11] He sees it as a means of exogamy, that is, a way by which the members of one clan (represented by an animal totem) express a difference in blood from the members of another clan and therefore marry outside their own clan.[12]

Lévi-Strauss rejects one part of Bergson's thesis: Bergson maintains that exogamy itself is the effect of a natural instinct, but Lévi-Strauss repudiates this idea by saying that "if such an instinct existed, a recourse to institutions would be superfluous." Even Bergson tempers his position by acknowledging that there is no "real and active" instinct warning against consanguineous unions. Instead, he says that nature supplies for the lack of such an instinct by means of "intelligence." Lévi-Strauss's own position is that exogamy (and totemism that follows it) is a cultural entity, not a natural one. In other words, "the category of class and the notion of opposition" inherent in totemic classification establishes systems of communication among the different clans.[13] For example, a member of the bear clan is different from, and therefore able to contract marriage with, a member of the eagle clan; here, systems of communication are established by marriage.

Bergson's "correct" solution to the riddle of totemism is ultimately contrasted with Durkheim's "faulty" one. Although Bergson was the philosopher of the unstable and Durkheim the founder of the science of sociology, yet Bergson saw that the classificatory nature of totemism establishes culture (through exogamy), whereas Durkheim spoke too often as if intellectual classifications were merely functions of the social. The distinction is very important: Lévi-Strauss sees culture and civilization as established by the intellect itself (which, in its very logic, functions through systems of binary oppositions). Durkheim adopted a functionalistic notion of mind—that mind is a function of its environment. For Lévi-Strauss, the intellect (through the power of the collective will exerted in the unconscious) establishes society. For Durkheim, society establishes the intellect.[14]

The reason for Bergson's success in unraveling the meaning of totemism, Lévi-Strauss claims, is Bergson's philosophy of creative continuity; that is, Bergson's metaphysics sustains a cosmos composed of two aspects of reality—the "continuous and the discontinuous." This is also the picture of reality substantiated by structuralism, and Lévi-Strauss approvingly cites Bergson's passage in *The Two Sources* in which the philosopher summarizes his metaphysics.[15] Indeed, this is, perhaps, the clearest metaphysical recitation of the world as totemically conceived, or of the world as the so-called mystical [16] or totalizing intellect of the native conceives it:

> A great current of creative energy gushes forth through matter, to obtain from it what it can. At most points these stops are transmuted, in our eyes, into the appearances of so many living species, i.e., of organisms in which our perception being essentially analytical and synthetic, distinguishes a multitude of elements combining to fulfill a multitude of functions, but the process of organisation was only the stop itself, a simple act analogous to the impress of a foot which instantaneously causes thousands of grains of sand to contrive to form a pattern.

The "creative energy" that ties the discontinuities together in civilization is, for Lévi-Strauss, the collective. In another passage he has called the collective the "order of orders." It imposes its will upon the individual through the (collective) structures of the unconscious. Here, the collective links the self with the other in a continuous unity, as continuity of the discontinuous.[17]

But Lévi-Strauss maintains that Bergson had a philosophical predecessor who also, a full century before Bergson, solved the problem of totemic classification. It was Rousseau, according to Lévi-Strauss, who was the author of "the first anthropological treatise in French literature": the *Discourse on the Origin and Foundation of Inequality among Mankind.* Rousseau, he states, discovered the true significance of totemism in this treatise insofar as he realized that, when man accrues unto himself the characteristics of animal and vegetable species, he is undertaking the very first "logical operations," the beginnings of a "social differentiation which could be lived out only if it were conceptualized." Indeed, Rousseau envisaged the primal problem of anthropology: "the passage from nature to culture." In Rousseau's *Discourse*, when man passed from the state of nature into that of civilization, his mode of labor, because of demographic increase, was diversified, and his relations with nature were multiplied. But such diversification and multiplication in society should lead to social and technical transformations, and these can only be achieved if man makes his diverse relationships with nature into objects of thought. Another way of framing this idea is to say that the importance of symbols originates in their enabling us to experiment with reality without actually becoming immersed in it. In still other words, the advent of culture coincides with the birth of the intellect, for, to live in society, man must possess both "foresight and curiosity"; he cannot, like the beast, abandon "himself solely to the consciousness of his present existence." At this stage, at the moment of the passage from nature to culture, the intellect is born, and with it, language. Language, for Rousseau, was originally, primally, figurative affective emotional communication, because the primary passion of man out of which all language and intellect are born is compassion—a primal identification of the self with the surrounding natural (animal and vegetable) world.[18]

Three important observations should be made about Lévi-Strauss's study of totemism. First, his adoption of Rousseau's position that man originally identifies with his fellow man and the entire surrounding world of nature puts Lévi-Strauss, as he states it, "as far as may be imagined from Sartre's existentialism, which on this point returns to Hobbes' view." [19] Second, Lévi-Strauss's adoption of this position reveals his adaptation of Mauss's concept of "totalisation" and his ability to relate it to what Rousseau termed "compassion" (and later to a third element: Marxian dialectical reason).[20] "The total apprehension of men and animals as sentient beings, in which identification consists, both governs and precedes the consciousness of oppositions between, firstly, logical properties conceived as integral parts of the field, and then, within the field itself, between 'human' and 'non-human.' " [21] Thus, Lévi-Strauss maintains, in relation to the primitives' logic, that continuity (Lévy-Bruhl's "mystical mentality") is ontologically prior to a more analytical logic. The collective, then, is in some way ontologically prior to the individual.

Third, the importance of figurative language, or of *tropes,* again appears. Lévi-Strauss shares Rousseau's contention that the origin of language lies in emotions and that the first language must have been figurative, meaning metaphorical. It is metaphor that links the self with all the levels of unconscious meaning, or with all the levels of the Other within the self. In Lévi-Strauss's own words: "Metaphor, the role of which in totemism we have repeatedly underlined, is not a later embellishment of language, but is one of its fundamental modes. Placed by Rousseau on the same plane as opposition, it constitutes on the same ground, a primary form of discursive thought." [22] That Lévi-Strauss's statement of the scientific character and value of the primitive mind has a basic affinity with the thought of Rousseau is, of course, indicative of Lévi-Strauss's intellectual heritage, but that affinity is also indicative of his position as a moralist. This observation is fundamental to an understanding of his works on kinship systems.

5 ✿ Rousseau and Lévi-Strauss

Reason and the Collective Will

Lévi-Strauss recounts a tale in the first part of *The Elementary Structures of Kinship* that, in itself, sums up the entire theoretical exposition of structuralism. In some of the lower-priced restaurants in the southern, wine-growing areas of France, where wine is surrounded by a certain mystical aura and is, because of its value to the community, "rich food," there is a ritual, trifling only in the expenditure of energy, that attests to the power of exchanges or reciprocities in man's life.

Wine being included in the price of the meal, each customer has a small bottle in front of his plate on the communal table. Each bottle is identical to the others, as are the portions of food. If there should be the slightest deviation in the service or in the size of the portions from table to table, each occupant will bitterly complain as an *individual*; but it is quite different when one comes to the wine.

Each person, as it were, eats for himself. The food serves to assuage the nature. But the wine is a cultural entity. If a bottle is insufficiently filled, its owner will appeal to his neighbor's judgment, and the proprietor will face a complaint not just of an individual but of the group. The *plat du jour* is a personal acquistion; the wine is a social commodity and, thus, something to be shared by the totality. Even if the little bottle contains only one glassful, its contents will be poured out, not into one's own glass, but into one's neighbor's. And the neighbor will reciprocate by pouring the contents of his bottle into one's own glass. But what has been exchanged? "What has happened? The two bottles are identical in volume, and their contents similar in quality. Each person in this revealing scene has, in the final analysis, received no more than if he had consumed his own wine. From an economic viewpoint, no one has gained and no one has lost. But the point is that "there is more in the exchange itself than in the things exchanged." [1]

We are, with this remark of Lévi-Strauss's, at the very core of structuralism's intersubjective unconscious: in itself it is nothing; it exists only in the dynamic interchange among its parts. It is unconscious precisely because it is always intersubjective, collective.[2] The inspiration for the collective side comes partially from the General Will of Rousseau.

The connection between Lévi-Strauss and Rousseau is of consequence. According to Lévi-Strauss, Rousseau was "the most anthropological of the *philosophes*." He possessed a keen interest in peasant customs and thought. But, contrary to a common interpretation of Rousseau's writings on the primitive, Lévi-Strauss holds that Rousseau did not conceive the state of natural man as separate from that of cultural man. "Natural man did not precede society, nor is he outside it." [3]

His own *Tristes Tropiques* is itself written in the genre of the eighteenth-century philosophical traveler who journeys to foreign lands and there, eventually, finds the most "native," in the sense of "natural," of all peoples.[4] But Lévi-Strauss finds at the end of his journey, like his master Rousseau, that there are no primitive peoples: that man, by his very "nature," is a being of logic, and if of logic, of culture, and if of culture, of society. Rousseau had, on this journey, led the way: "Rousseau never fell into Diderot's error of idealizing natural man. He is never in any danger of confusing the natural state with the social state; he knows that the latter is inherent in man, but that it leads to evils; the only problem is to discover whether these evils are themselves inherent in the social state. This means looking beyond abuses and crimes to find the unshakable basis of human society." A brief explanation of what this "unshakable basis" (*base inebranable*) of human society may be is in order.[5]

It is not difficult to interpret Rousseau as claiming that man does seem to have dwelled in some Arcadian paradise, a state of pure nature in which man is not antisocial, as in Hobbes, nor asocial, as he appears in Locke, but simply extrasocial. For Hobbes, man seems to exist with his fellowmen in a naturally bellicose state; to counter these antisocial tendencies, man enters through fear into a social contract with his fellowmen, in order to sculpture the anatomy of the state. For Locke, on the other hand, man in the state of nature lived completely free of all social restrictions, but as he began to amass property he realized that, for retention of his rights and of "life, liberty, and the pursuit of property," he would have to band together with others into society, so that there might be (1) a public law, (2) an impartial judge of dispute, and (3) a judge who could exercise power and force in the support of rights.[6]

By way of contrast, in Rousseau there is no opposition between the natural man and the social man, but there is a change of emphasis. The transition from natural man to social man, from nature to culture, comes about with the introduction of intersubjective exchanges. Rousseau explains in his *Discourse on the Origin and Foundation of Inequality among Men* that the state of nature held sway as long as savages remained content with their individual industries; with their clothes made of animal skins; with their simple adornments of feathers, paints, shells; with their rustic huts; and so on—in short, with those accomplishments that a single person, alone, could bring about. But as the complications of civilization increased and as the diversification of skills multiplied, as man became dependent upon his fellowman and constructed systems employing exchanges of some talent or special commodity in return for those some one else could provide (with the "division of labor"), then equality disappeared, private property was introduced, and work became indispensable.[7]

Since society and its forms of culture are necessary, according to Rousseau, to the growth of intersubjective rapport, the problem of reconciling the constraints of society with the individualistic freedom he finds in the natural man arises. He holds in the *Discourse* that, upon the introduction of diversification of skills, goods, and private property, there began a certain self-alienation in which the worker was forced to imprint his image upon a recalcitrant natural environment, if he were to foster the growth of his own private properties and subsequent complication of exchanges. For Rousseau, this type of alienation is the very opposite of freedom: it is slavery, for the worker is forced into a constant round of exchanges of property, labor for more property, and subsequent barter. Here, there is no free gift of oneself or of one's goods: "To alienate means to give or to sell. Now a man who becomes a slave of another does not give himself. He sells himself for bare subsistence, if for nothing more." [8]

By the time he wrote *The Social Contract* (1762), Rousseau had seen that life in society imposed some bonds upon the individual and that these fetters could not be avoided, for to evade them meant a life divorced from the dialogue between subjects—a condition that was, for most men, perhaps for all, an impossibility. Hence, his purpose in *The Social Contract* is not to free man from the chains that bind him but to discover a way in which man may be free in the midst of the limitations placed upon his liberty by society. As Lévi-Strauss has correctly observed, Rousseau never advocated a return to some primitive state of nature; this might be the position of Diderot, but never of Rousseau. Rather, he sought a reconciliation of nature with culture. The famous opening lines of *The Social Contract* accent this sentiment: "Man was born free, and everywhere he is in chains. Many a one believes himself the master of others, and yet he is a greater slave than they. How has this change come about? I do not know. What can render it legitimate? I believe that I can settle this question." Clearly, his goal was not to free men from society, but to tell them how they might legitimately remain in their chains and yet, at the same time, be free. His answer to this perplexing problem lies in his concept of "the general will." [9]

The purpose of this important concept is to show that the fulfillment of man's duty to abide by the general will is, at the same time, the action that makes him free. In being free, man will be *de-naturé* insofar as his liberty is guaranteed not by nature but by reason—by the logic that appears as soon as one communicates (exchanges) with one's fellowman. "Whoever refuses to obey the general will shall be constrained to do so by the whole body; which means nothing else than that he shall be forced to be free. . . ." [10]

Although, in the supposition of a state of nature, men can, perhaps, be considered as not having entered into any transactions and hence as equal, nevertheless, they cannot be considered as being free. Under the social contract, each individual, instead of yielding his rights to a particular sovereign in the usual accepted sense of the word, yields them to the community as a whole. The equality of the "natural" (individualistic) state is retained insofar as each individual surrenders these rights under equal and common restrictions. Freedom is added to the individual's bounty, however, for, in giving oneself to all, one gives oneself to no particular person. This liberty is the opposite of that alienation which Rousseau felt transpired when a laborer was forced to work for a particular other. [11]

Our textual excursion into the general will of Rousseau affords the centerpiece in Lévi-Strauss's triptych of Freud, Rousseau, and Marx, for the general will becomes the keystone in the systems of reciprocities which, for Lévi-Strauss, form the logic of the unconscious. Primitive peoples—the object of his lifelong studies—most strongly reflect the general will, for they are always most careful to purge any divisions in their ranks from their midst. For example, frequently, before taking a political vote, they will hold an athletic contest to eliminate individual sentiments from their ranks, in order that the group as a whole may make the decision. This act of unanimity portrays the operations of Rousseau's general will, which Lévi-Strauss characterizes as follows: "The General Will is not, in Rousseau's view, the will of the whole, or of the majority of the population, expressed on particular occasions; it is the latent and continuous decision whereby each individual agrees to exist as a member of a group."[12]

The role of the general will of the group takes on a new dimension because, in the work of Lévi-Strauss, it is combined with the notion, coming from Marcel Mauss, of the "total social fact." The "total social fact" is an attempt to view a social phenomenon in all its relations with all the spheres in which society operates—to define the social itself as a reality. The reality of the social is, in Lévi-Strauss's thought (as in Rousseau's), none other than the collective exchanges, which, as we have seen, function through an unconscious logic. This logic composes what Lévi-Strauss calls "the innate structure of the human spirit." The reality of the social, however, in Rousseau, Mauss, and finally in Lévi-Strauss, is in no way a "filled" reality; it is in no way a "substratum" in which its symbols would reside. Rather, it has no more reality than a language has; and a language is real only insofar as it is exchanged among speakers. "Like language, the social is an autonomous reality. . . . The symbols are more real than that which they symbolise. . . ." As the individual, for Rousseau, only becomes an individual insofar as he is a cultural member of the group, so, in Lévi-Strauss, it is the gift, seen as a system of reciprocities, that constitutes the individual-within-the-group. All aspects of life—birth, initiation, marriage, position, sickness, and so on—are moments for gift-giving and are viewed as a constant round of exchanges within the group.[13] The story recounted by Lévi-Strauss of the wine exchanges in the French restaurant is, for him, an illustration of the "total social fact"—whose implications are social, psychological, and economic.[14]

Further, the basic opposition between nature and culture that forms the groundwork for the enterprise of both Rousseau and Lévi-Strauss rests upon the question of reciprocities in life, and nature, the area of the universal and the instinctual, also moves to a double rhythm of giving and receiving; it is characteristic of nature that it can give only what it has received. *Natura non facit saltum.* Heredity well expresses this continuity. The individual, however, always receives more than he gives and gives more than he receives; this is the place of culture. We call the receiving education, the giving invention. There is, then, for cultural phenomena, this double disequilibrium not found in nature. Biological phenomena, for example, manifest a certain stability, whereas one can say of cultural phenomena only that they remain in a state of "dynamic synthesis." [15] In the cultural state, the individual is never simply a thing-in-itself, apart from all others. He is a member of a group, an ordered and dynamic whole, which is more than simply the sum of its parts.

Culture is the realm of true reciprocities; the individual becomes a free individual ("dynamic synthesis") only insofar as he is wrested out of nature by culture. Culture is not simply juxtaposed with, nor super-imposed upon, life but, in a sense, substitutes for it and, in another sense, transforms it in order to bring about a synthesis of a new order.[16] This new order is that of the group, in which the chance selections of nature are transcended by cultural organization. In place of heredity, descent, and natural consanguinity, culture substitutes alliance. Among primitive peoples, he who is not a member of the group is against it; there are no neutral relationships, and it is utterly impossible for prim-itives to conceive of the existence of no relationship. They know only two ways of classifying strangers: either "good" or "bad." A "good" group is one to which hospitality is immediately given, along with the most precious gifts. A "bad" group is one from which one expects suffering or death and to which one promises the same. In short, with one there exists exchange and, with the other, fighting. Exchanges peacefully resolve wars, and wars are the result of unfortunate transactions: "The prime role of culture is to ensure the group's existence as a group, and conse-quently, in this domain as in all others, to replace chance by organiza-tion." [17]

Just as Rousseau realized that there really exists no absolutely natural precultural man, so, too, Lévi-Strauss emphatically denies the existence of any precultural or prelogical, totally natural level of man.[18] If a do-mesticated animal, such as a dog, cat, or farm animal, is lost or isolated, one can expect that it will return to the natural behavior of the species prior to domestication. One cannot expect this behavior of man; the species has no natural behavior to which an isolated individual can return. What is fascinating about man, then, is that, if he is a domesti-cated animal, he is the only one who has domesticated himself. "A bee,

Voltaire said, having roamed far from the hive, which it can no longer find, is lost, but for all that, has not become more wild." [19]

The collective, in this view, becomes a system of rational reciprocities, insofar as it is brought into being by the transcendence of the individual's natural instincts toward the collective. It becomes the arbitrator of individual wills. Man freely (meaning rationally) surrenders his "rights" in order that equality of rights may prevail. The general will is nothing in itself but simply the multiple exchanges of interdependent parts (as the collective unconscious, for Lévi-Strauss, is nothing in itself, but, like the linguistic unconscious, exists only through exchanges). We uncover here analytic reason (which Lévi-Strauss lauds), which, in the action of Rousseau's general will, enables the individual to analyze himself away into those collective structures that constitute both his self and his "freedom." In this action, nature is surpassed yet emerges transformed into culture. Rousseau does not oppose the natural man to the social man so much as he contrasts the natural man (who would not be a man, because he would dwell at a prelogical level) with the simultaneous birth of both logic and man.[20]

In Ernst Cassirer's neo-Kantian interpretation, the community of man is not for Rousseau founded simply upon instinct, for neither the instinct of pleasure nor that of sympathy would have been sufficient to afford an entrance into society for the "natural man." Rather, society is founded upon the idea of freedom and the consciousness of law. This interpretation is revealing. Cassirer, of course, grants the existence of the romanticist Rousseau and his famous "sentiment," but he notes that his romanticism is "rooted in his nature-understanding and nature-emotion," and "from these roots it rose into a new world: it pointed the way into the 'intelligible' and found its true fulfillment only in that realm." The "great principle of Rousseau's work can be considered to be enunciated in the first sentence of *Émile* and expressed again later in his *Rousseau juge de Jean-Jacques*: 'That nature has made man happy and good, but that society depraves him and makes him miserable.' Nevertheless, it must be understood that, if society is the source of evils in man, it must also be, for Rousseau, the agent of his salvation." Explaining how this therapy is to be achieved is the goal of *Émile*. [21]

According to Cassirer's interpretation, the apparent contradiction in Rousseau between, on the one hand, his praise for society and subordination of the individual to the general will in *The Social Contract* and, on the other hand, his attempt in *Émile* to separate Émile from society is overcome when one admits that Rousseau is using the concept "so-ciety" in a twofold sense. Society means, for Rousseau, both empirical reality—that is, the society of Émile's times, with all its mores and habits, "its preferences and its prejudices"—and also what society can and should be. The empirical society will change only when confronted with a cate-gorical duty, a will to renew itself that is absolutely unconditioned. The individual is kept away from this parochial empirical society in order that he may know what it is to be a man—not just a man in a particular society bound by particular, provincial customs:

> Rousseau therefore excludes the cooperation of *societas* precisely
> for the sake of *humanitas,* for he separates most sharply the universal
> significance of humanity from its mere collective significance. He
> renounces the collectivity of men in order to found a new and truly
> universal humanity . . . for every individual is capable of discover-
> ing within himself and by his own power the original pattern of
> humanity and of shaping that pattern out of his own self. . . . the
> universal can be discovered only when every man follows his own in-
> sight and recognizes, in and by virtue of this very insight, a neces-
> sary solidarity between his will and the general will . . . that step
> is . . . the distinctive mark and privilege of reason.

According to this interpretation, Rousseau clearly affirms that the indi-vidual instinct by which man aligns himself with all other men is not sentiment but reason. Through reason, man can view himself as human, and only through reason can man work for the establishment of the kindom of ends, by treating humanity itself as the end of all one's ac-tions.[22]

Lévi-Strauss's interpretation of Rousseau is somewhat different from Cassirer's.[23] He accepts the twofold sense of the concept of society in Rous-seau (leading to the distinction between *societas* and *humanitas*). But he has never entertained the notion that Rousseau placed the unifying power of the self with the other in reason. For Lévi-Strauss, this adhesive force is found in Rousseau's comments upon the quality of pity. Rous-seau, claims Lévi-Strauss, recognized that all men and animals are feeling beings. In this sentience, their identification consists, and it long antedated man's awareness of his difference from all other beings.[24] Such a sentiment impelled Rousseau, for example, to wonder· if man should imprison in zoos some of the African and Asiatic great apes, first being imported in his day into Europe. For they could very well, he warned, turn out to be humans with a language as yet unknown to us. This instinct of pity becomes in Rousseau (Lévi-Strauss claims) a reverence for all life, enshrined more in Oriental religions than in Western ones. Rousseau's account of coming to consciousness after having fainted, in which reemergence he was filled with an overwhelming wonder for all living things, is the culmination of this feeling of pity, which, for Lévi-Strauss, rewards us with a reverence for just "being alive." [25] This instinct of pity was the source behind Rousseau's idea that all language was originally figurative, for metaphor is that "in which one object is contained in several others."

"Pity" is also the message behind *The Social Contract,* in which man is bidden to seek the society of nature (that is, *humanitas*) in order to meditate on the nature of society (that is, *societas*). Because we have lost this notion of pity, man has, from the Enlightenment with its emphasis on reason onward, turned in exploitation upon his fellow living things. Especially in our own century, men, seeing even further differences instead of likenesses between themselves and other men, have separated themselves from and turned upon other human beings as well.[26] Here we observe an interesting facet of Lévi-Strauss, which he ascribes to Rousseau also: he is an antihumanist, in the most basic meaning of the term. He sees man as neither the center of the universe nor the end or purpose of it all. He is just a peripheral phenomenon in the much larger stream of the life principle, frequently called by savages "mana."

The principle of "confessions" must enervate every true anthropological treatise (as it does Rousseau's own *Confessions* and Lévi-Strauss's *Tristes Tropiques*). In confessions, "the observer uses himself as his own instrument of observation," and so he must look at himself at a distance, as if he were another person. And, in fact, he does observe another—the other who is within himself. We are drawn back again to the notion of Lacan's *l'Autre* ("the Other"). The Other that he finds within himself when he thus evaluates himself becomes "an integral part of all the observations he carries out in the field on groups and individuals and the *other* within them." [27] Again, we return to the mutual convertibility of the transformations that Lévi-Strauss calls "structures" and to the theme of the anthropologist as psychoanalyst. For it is in the mutual convertibility of the transference of patient to analyst and of the counter-transference of analyst to patient that the analysis itself appears. And it appears, as I have explained earlier, through an analogy of being.

Consequently, Rousseau frequently speaks of himself distantly as *he*, and eventually he breaks down the *he* into the "famous formula 'the me is another.' " The anthropologist strives for the same disinterested glimpse of himself and then proceeds "to show that other people are men like himself, or in other words, the other is me." [28] And so, the psychoanalyst and the anthropologist must both themselves be analyzed before embarking on their analyses of others.

Rousseau, perhaps, might even have been the founder of the analytic method, as Lévi-Strauss states that he was "the great innovator of the concept of unconditional objectivity." His aim was "to study the modifications of my soul and their sequels," which resulted in the "astonishing revelation" that "there is a third person 'he' that thinks within me." Lévi-Strauss sees this as a total repudiation by Rousseau of the *cogito* of Descartes. [29] The self is not the center of the universe; the Other is the center of the self: the universe is within the *I*. Rousseau's "concept of unconditional objectivity" also, for Lévi-Strauss, serves as a rejection of the notion of "transcendental subjectivity" that dominates Husserlian phenomenology.

Finally, it is the concept of pity in Rousseau, that, according to Lévi-Strauss, rejects the Cartesian dualism of mind and matter. The three subjects that so dominated Rousseau's thoughts—language, music, and botany—are good illustrations of this unifying function of pity. In each of the three—all human pursuits—there is an uncompromising unity of spirit and matter. In language, a sensible word carries an immaterial meaning. In music, "a transfer occurs in the relationship between mind and matter since the music actually *lives* within me." In botany, there exists a unity of "sensitivity and intellect," a "chain of relationships" presented by nature in "perceptible objects." Additionally, language and music, at least, reveal to the self the Other within and, in so doing, repudiate Descartes's "I think, therefore I am." Language, as discussed above in the section on Lacan, was originally, according to Rousseau, metaphorical, simply the language of identification of self with other; in music, "a transfer occurs in the relationship between the self and the 'he' in us; since I listen to music I hear myself through it." [30] This constant emphasis on pity and identification prior to distinction creates in Lévi-Strauss a strong desire to function as a moralist in the manner of the moralist-anthropologist Rousseau. We turn now to Lévi-Strauss, the moralist.

Lévi-Strauss as Moralist

Lévi-Strauss approaches his work of anthropological investigation with Rousseau as his guide. He, like Rousseau, wishes to construct the ideal society by finding "the unshakable basis of human society." Anthropology can contribute to this discovery in two ways. First, it shows us that to seek this foundation in our own society would be to succumb to our own parochial, and therefore limited, horizons—as if they were universal for all mankind. Second, by trying to distinguish patterns of civilization common to all society, we may, through anthropological research, construct that ideal model of humanity itself.[31]

Lévi-Strauss calls Rousseau the author of "the first anthropological treatise in French Literature." He, of course, had never dissociated theoretical sociology from the necessary field or laboratory researches. But Lévi-Strauss recognizes that, for Rousseau, natural man does not predate society and is not outside society. Rather, the model of the ideal society of man is eternal and universal. There is a risk involved here, of course, and Lévi-Strauss is well aware of it: the structural anthropologist may underestimate the reality of progress, for if, as structural anthropology (and its predecessor, Rousseau) teaches, "men have always and everywhere undertaken the same task, and assigned to themselves the same object; all that has differed is the means employed," then "the zealots of progress" run the risk of knowing too little about the immense riches that our race has stored up on either side of the narrow furrow upon which they train their eyes.[32]

Yet, if any age were to come close to this ideal model, declares Lévi-Strauss (echoing Rousseau), it would probably be the neolithic, because then man had already constructed most of the inventions necessary for his security: agriculture, stock-raising, pottery, weaving; for the last eight or ten thousand years, all we have done is to improve upon these skills. One should note that history here takes on a cyclic character, rather than one of steady progression.[33] As in *Émile*, if we are not to be victims of the prejudices and perspectival point of view of our own society when we attempt a construction of this (hypothetical) and ideal model of the natural man, then we must disentangle ourselves from the mores and interests of at least one society—our own.[34]

In *Race and History*, Lévi-Strauss attempts to show that we tend to regard some cultures as "cumulative," that is, as societies in which all developments in science, art, and similar areas have added up to "a lucky combination" (an "advanced" civilization), because there is something in their development that corresponds to our own culture. When viewing another culture from such an interested perspective, we act like older persons who think that the history being made by a younger generation is relatively stationary, whereas history, when they, the older people, were young and active, was actually moving. When we take this *engagé* perspective (involved as we are in our own customs), the history of a culture other than our own depends upon the number and variety of our interests and not upon its intrinsic qualities. On the other hand, if we disentangle ourselves from all "heteronomous" norms and look at the culture in question as if it were an end in itself, then "to the extent that so-called primitive societies are very distant from our own, . . . we can discover in them those 'facts of general functioning' of which Mauss spoke, which stand a chance of being 'more universal' and 'more real.' " One of the principal themes of *Tristes Tropiques* had been the brutal method by which Western civilization in attempting to "reform" and "civilize" the primitive tribes and Indian natives of the New World actually destroyed their culture (and eventually the natives) in lieu of amalgamating them into the West.[35]

In calling for a disengaged attitude [36] before a system of culture other than our own, Lévi-Strauss is, of course, breaking with that broad tradition that has been dominant in French existentialism, first rejuvenated in the twenties by André Malraux, the tradition of the author who is committed to a position: *l'homme engagé*. This is best exemplified, perhaps, by Sartre's position in *Qu'est ce que la littérature? (What Is Literature?)*. Here, the prose writer is the man who is the extreme utilitarian. His task must be to take a position, to be *en situation* (as the existentialists are fond of saying), and to change that situation. The author is that man who cannot view a situation without changing it. In Sartre's world, the other, through looking at me, puts "facticity" into my very being, as the author, by his glance, structures his object.[37]

As is clear from what I have said already, Lévi-Strauss is diametrically opposed to Sartre's *engagé* theory of the author. The concept of confessions, which he employs in his own approach to writing and which he borrows from Rousseau, decrees that the anthropologist-analyst "look at himself objectively and at a distance as if he were another person," in order to observe "the other within them," that is, within the primitive peoples.[38] Distance and commitment—the commitment of the glance of Sartre's author, which intends and creates the object that it sees—are opposite attitudes toward authorship.

The anthropologist (psychoanalyst) must be disengaged before a culture that is alien to his own, notes Lévi-Strauss, in order to avoid imposing the conscious cultural representations stemming from his own culture upon those of the natives. Eventually, he will come to recognize that the collective unconscious whose structures are progressively discovered is atemporal and leads to a humanity whose outlines are everywhere, and in all ages, the same. This recognition the exponents of progress and the evolutionists miss, missing especially the fact that the powers upon which our ancestors drew are "also present in us." Lévi-Strauss calls for an anthropological retreat to the structures of Rousseau's natural man, an idealized humanity reunited in its scaffolding with the natural sociohistorical and physical world that surrounds it,[39] from which (physical) world man's mechanical and technological civilization have separated him.[40]

In *The Scope of Anthropology* and in the *Conversations with Claude Lévi-Strauss*, he returns to the theme of an idealized humanity through the door of his celebrated distinction between "hot" and "cold" societies.[41] Primitive societies are "cold" and function like mechanical machines—like clocks—because they can theoretically operate indefinitely on the energy that was theirs from the very beginning. "Hot" societies, in contrast, are like thermodynamic machines, which, like steam engines, function on a difference of potential between their parts; indeed, societies first began to appear in different parts of the world following the neolithic revolution..

The "cold" societies (called thus because their internal environment reads "zero" on the scale of historical temperature) seek to escape, as it were, from history, or, at least, to resist strongly any structural modification. Their exploitation of the environment guarantees them a modest standard of living; their marriage rules reveal to the demographer the common function of maintaining a low and constant fertility rate. Their political life is based on consent: all decisions are communally agreed upon. Personal lives are marked by order and organization. Looking at them only in comparison to our own societies (that is, without an air of *dégagement*), we see only lack of historical progress (diachronic development) and will likely miss their synchronic level.

On the other hand, the "hot" societies are clearly historical. They operate, however, upon a foundation of slavery and class/caste distinctions in order to extract a quantum of energy. They produce what physicists call "entrophy"; that is, they produce an enormous amount of "progress" and work, but all the while consuming their source of energy and destroying it progressively. In short, they are marked by disorder and decay.[42]

It is here that Lévi-Strauss's Rousseauist dream of an idealized humanity and a new morrow begins. The picture is not all dark for modern humanity, for, although slavery and caste systems sprang up after the neolithic revolution among the great city-states of the Mediterranean Basin and the Far East, yet they served to produce culture at a rate undreamed of until that time. In a similar fashion, the industrial revolution of the nineteenth century, although built "on the same abuses and the same injustices," yet enabled the transfer to culture (through advances in man-made machines) of the dynamic, historical function first assigned to society. If the anthropologist were to predict the future of humanity, then he would conceive of an integration of the "cold" and "hot" models of society. He would dream the old Cartesian dream of placing machines, like automatons, at the service of man. This is the event we can remotely glimpse through the recent advances in information theory and electronics—the conversion of a type of civilization in which men were machines into one in which machines were men. At this point the anthropological distinction between society and culture is fundamental. Culture would have assumed the task of manufacturing progress, whereas society would be freed from the thousand-year curse that has forced it to enslave men in order that progress might exist. History ("progress") would now make itself by itself. Society, now divorced from history, would exhibit once again that organization and those crystallike structures that the primitive societies presently being preserved by social anthropologists show us are not alien to mankind.[43]

In short, Lévi-Strauss's vision of an idealized humanity (society freed from history) corresponds to Rousseau's idea of the *noble savage*: the individual freed from the corruptions of historical progress, which is the object of the education of Émile. As in *Émile*, if society is the source of evils in man, it must also be the font of his redemption. It will become the latter, as Cassirer pointed out, if the castes, prejudices, and preferences upon which society presently breeds are filtered out, and a new society—*humanitas*—reigns in its place. This reign of *humanitas* is accomplished in Rousseau by the general will, in which each individual recognizes in himself the pattern and laws of humanity.[44] Briefly, as Lévi-Strauss writes of Rousseau's idealized humanity: "Nothing is settled; everything can still be altered. What was done but turned out wrong, can be done again. 'The Golden Age, which blind superstition had placed behind [or ahead of] us, is *in us.*'"[45]

It may be appropriate to recall here that Kant's ethics became a transition, in the minds of many, between two great conceptions of man and his culture as related to nature. The first was the eighteenth-century notion that man is part of nature and subservient to her laws; the second is that of the later romanticists (Herder and others) who stressed the autonomy of man above nature and made him a law unto himself. In his ethics, Kant attempts a combination of both views. Lévi-Strauss tends toward the former view, the existential movement toward the latter. In the eighteenth century the Newtonian laws that proved the uniformity of nature were anthropomorphized by Kant into his ethics and joined with what he admitted was his favorite rationalistic argument for God, the argument from design, into the ethical "kingdom of ends," that kingdom which man alone by his free, rational acceptance of his duty can create. Lévi-Strauss's passion for architectonics (similar again to Kant's) anthropomorphizes the eighteenth century's argument for God from design and argues for an ideal humanity existing in all times and in all climes—an unchanging human nature—the laws of whose logic are transposed in the physical world as the laws of mathematics, physics and all the natural sciences.

In another way, the ethics of Lévi-Strauss is the opposite of Kantian ethics. For Kant, the world is the creature of man in one area only, that of human freedom, in the creative act of the will, which establishes the Kantian "Kingdom of Ends." In Lévi-Strauss, on the contrary, the world always creates man, as is well illustrated by the ethics in vogue among primitive peoples and especially by totemism, which exemplifies the notion that for primitive peoples the self is a projection of the world, and not vice versa (the usual attitude of the nineteenth-century romanticists, including Kant). Lévi-Strauss makes the different views quite explicit in the final chapter, "La morale des myths," of *L'Origine des manières de table.* The primitives, he shows, through the rules of etiquette, manners, customs, mores, and such, show that they have long recognized what we, in Western technological civilizations, are just now beginning to realize: that man pollutes and changes the environment, and not the environment, man. Our morality has long enshrined the Cartesian primacy of the subjective; the primitive morality represents the primacy of the objective, of the world, which apart from man is pure and unsullied. Even our table manners illustrate the difference: we use table utensils, eating rituals, and so on to protect the diner from infection; they use utensils, rituals, and such to protect the world from the diner.

"In place of protecting, as we think, the internal purity of the subject from the external impurity of beings and of things, good manners serve the function, among primitive peoples, of protecting the purity of beings and of being from the pollution of the subject." [46]

Lévi-Strauss's search for idealized humanity can be seen throughout his discussion of kinship systems, particularly of the Avunculate and the chiefs of the Nambikwara.

Kinship Systems and the Collective Will

It is well to recall that, for Lévi-Strauss, the idealized state of primitive nature in which the individual supposedly once dwelt is not divorced from society but, rather, exists in the internalized group—the general will that each individual carries with him as a human. Ultimately, it exists for Lévi-Strauss in the "ground plan," or basic transformation patterns, into which all the structures of all the different groups, tribes, nations, and so on of mankind can be welded. De Gramont writes: "Modern linguists agree that there is a 'ground plan' for all the languages of the world. . . . thus Lévi-Strauss says, 'just as the discovery of DNA and the genetic code led biologists to use a linguistic model to explain a natural phenomenon, I use a linguistic model to explain cultural phenomena other than language.'" The form that these patterns take is the ultimate source of the demands imposed by the group upon the individuals composing that group. To be meaningful is to have a position in a system. "Form imposes its own necessities." [47]

The problem of the source of the prohibition against incest has been a particularly vexing and especially interesting one for both anthropologists and philosophers of culture. Is it an instinct innate to man? Is it a formal stricture built into the fabric of societies? In point of fact, this prohibition against incest is a good illustration of the way in which Lévi-Strauss's "everyday materialism" combines both materialism and formalism, so as to unite the laws of nature with those of culture by unifying material exchanges (in the case of kinship systems, of women) with laws of the mind governing such reciprocities. Scheffler writes: "Kinship is a socializing, integrating or communicating agent, and as the basis of a mode of exchange, as Lévi-Strauss well knows, has its roots in both nature and the human mind. . . . One of the themes of *La pensée sauvage* is the extent to which the content of verbal categories may be constrained by the nature of the real objects or events which are being categorized." Furthermore, a study of this prohibition seems to be most important if one hopes to construct a universal model of mankind—a ground plan for all the groups of the world—in that this prohibition seems to be found everywhere, in all times and in every region of the world. In other words, the prohibition against incest is the most universal law of the structures of cultures.[48]

In addition, the prohibition against incest seems to be one of those universal cultural mores that, by their very existence, repress certain natural instincts (in this case, the sexual instinct). To this degree, the prohibition seems to possess a decidedly negative aspect. But Lévi-Strauss approaches the incest-prohibition quite positively. And though it is both cultural and natural at the same time, the prohibition against incest is also the negative side of a positive rule that establishes social life: "sexual life is one beginning of social life in nature, for the sexual is man's only instinct requiring the stimulation of another person." In this view, the prohibition is merely the negative side of the rule of exogamy, which is an essentially positive rule, for the prohibition forces a man or a woman to marry out of his or her kin group, and thus establishes relationships of exchange between groups. Such relationships, in turn, literally establish intersubjective communication among groups, and thence society itself. "It is no exaggeration, then, to say that exogamy is the archetype of all other manifestations based upon reciprocity, and that it provides the fundamental and immutable rule ensuring the existence of the group as a group." [49]

In the case of the incest-prohibition, the natural drive toward sexual intercourse is repressed by the group will taking precedence over the individual, or, if you wish, by the will of that ideal humanity whose structures Lévi-Strauss strives to expose over the particular. Incest is a thwarting of the principle of reciprocity within society. Its outcome is actually the stabilization of all exchanges, and, if it were allowed by the collective, it would ultimately lead to the destruction of the collective itself. The final foundation upon which all societal groupings rest is "the atom of kinship," or that minimum set of relationships that can be the basic components of a kinship system: "a system of communication based on the exchange of women." It should be noted that, although the prohibition forbids sexual relations between a man and his daughter or his sister, neither this unit nor that of a man, his wife, and their children could compose the "atom of kinship." Rather, in a primitive society, a man receives his wife, and through her his daughter, from another man and in exchange for his own sister. The basic unit of exchange (and, therefore, the binary oppositions that compose society) must be, then, the sets of relationships brother/sister, mother/child, husband/wife, and sister's husband/wife's brother, established by men through exchanging their sisters or exchanging the sister of one for the goods of another. The way in which Lévi-Strauss shows that the group demands subordination of the individual in the cultural systems established by the incest-prohibition is revealing.[50]

Lévi-Strauss distinguishes between the prohibition against incest as it works in modern societies and the prohibition as it works in primitive societies.[51] In a modern society with its immense and vast population proportions, it is sufficient simply to forbid marriage between near relatives. Complicated systems of exogamy are little needed in modern societies. Indeed, simplicity appears to be the rule: modern societies allow for the widest possible freedom in choosing mates. Families are kept in continual flux, and there is a constant "mix-up through intermarriage," ensuring "well-blended social fabric."

But in primitive societies, some with very few members and very little ability to contact other societies, complication within the marriage systems is necessary in order to ensure that "the diminutive size of the group and the lack of social mobility be compensated by widening to a considerable extent the range of prohibited degrees." In such societies, the rules of kinship assume the proportions of "a kind of complicated game." A mathematics of kinships systems is devised: "Apparently ignorant and savage peoples have been able to devise fantastically clever codes which sometimes request, in order to understand their workings and effects, some of the best logical and even mathematical minds available in modern civilization." These complicated systems are artificial rules of culture, as artificial as are the rules of a game.[52] For example, some of the systems consist of the rules of cross-cousin marriage and its variations, or of those of the *leverate* and of the *sororate*, or of those of unilineal descent (by which children receive their status through either their father or their mother but not both). Yet "all these distinctions . . . are fantastic at first sight because they cannot be explained on biological or psychological grounds."

> There is no natural ground for the custom [of the incest-prohibition]. Geneticists have shown that while consanguineous marriages are likely to bring ill effects in a society which has consistently avoided them in the past, the danger would be much smaller if the prohibition had never existed, since this would have given ample opportunity for the harmful hereditary characters to become apparent and be automatically eliminated through selection: as a matter of fact this is the way breeders improve the quality of their subjects. Therefore the dangers of consanguineous marriages are the outcome of the incest-prohibition rather than actually explaining it.

Most importantly, if the prohibition were based on a universal, instinctual psychological or biological foundation—the "horror of incest" theory held by Westermarck and Havelock Ellis, principally—then there would be no sense at all to the numerous proscriptions against incest universally found among all peoples in all ages; for what is instinctively universal does not need to be indicated by rules: "There is no point in forbidding that which would not happen if it were not forbidden."[53]

Since, according to Lévi-Strauss, there is no natural explanation for the incest-prohibition, its rationale is cultural. Analogous to the "principle of sexual division of labor," [54] which establishes an interdependency between the sexes, forcing a perpetuation of the race from sexuality and the foundation of a family, the prohibition of incest establishes interdependency among families, forcing them to create new families. Most important of all, in this "artificial framework of taboos and obligations . . . there, and only there . . . we find a passage from nature to culture, from animal life to human life. . . . To put it in other words: what makes man really different from the animal is that, in mankind, a family could not exist if there were no society." [55]

This citation is important, for it exemplifies very powerfully Lévi-Strauss's views of the group as establishing its own norms for the individual. The group brings its own demands (as the general will of Rousseau) and places them upon the shoulders of the individual. The group thus establishes the individual, and not vice versa. Since the structures of the incest-prohibition have been shown to be cultural and thence artificial, not natural, we might well say that Lévi-Strauss's work on kinship systems underlies that dictum which links together all structural analysis. Form imposes its own necessities. For Lévi-Strauss the principle of division of labor, an artificial structure of culture, which establishes the family, is dependent upon the incest-prohibition, which, in turn, establishes systems of familial relationships, or society. Marriage is not a natural demand, but a cultural one, since, "among most people . . . the social set-up provides for many opportunities [that is, for sexual intercourse] which can be not only external to marriage, but even contradictory to it." The bonds of marriage were the result of the cultural need for division of labor, which establishes the family; the incest-prohibition provides for the proliferation of families, establishing thereby a homogeneous and well-knit society.[56]

Culture, here, is seen to systematize natural drives through exogamous kinship systems, always basing these systems upon reciprocal exchanges. In short, the group (and here the Marxist overtones become apparent) equalizes the inequalities of nature. As Lévi-Strauss writes: "Let us add that, even if there were as many women as men, these women would not all be equally desirable . . . and that, by definition (as Hume has judiciously remarked in a celebrated essay), the most desirable women must form a minority. Hence, the demand for women is in actual fact . . . always in a state of disequilibrium and tension." [57] The principle of reciprocity lies at the most elementary level of any structuralistic system, based on binary poles of opposition.[58] The prohibition against incest appears as simply the negative side of Marcel Mauss's theory of reciprocity.[59]

What should also be clearly recognized in Lévi-Strauss's discussion of kinship systems is that "a kinship system does not consist in the objective ties of descent or consanguinity between individuals. It consists only in human consciousness; it is an arbitrary system of representations, not the spontaneous development of a real situation." [60]

Radcliffe-Brown, influenced by Montesquieu and Spencer, stands out among Anglo-Saxon thinkers for his introduction of the notion of structure into anthropology. He wished to treat society as a social organism, as a system of interdependent parts, looking for "analogous structures among diverse groups." However, he could never divorce his research from the English empiricist tradition. Consequently, he thought the structure was "of the order of fact; it is given in the observation of each particular society." Thus, he sought to combine a structural approach with a functional one. A functionalist attempts to understand how the life of the culture that is studied fulfills "the biological and psychological needs of its members." In a functional approach, society is not viewed as suprapersonal; it is "the mere sum of individual social relations at a given moment." Hence, the "structures" discerned by Radcliffe-Brown were always identical with surface phenomena. The Durkeimians rejected this view, for the models employed by anthropology must, they claimed, be remote from surface phenomena.[61]

Lévi-Strauss rejects any naturalistic atom of kinship, for example, the elementary family, consisting of a man, his wife, and their children (as Radcliffe-Brown would have it),[62] and, in its place, substitutes the only elementary family that would allow exchange to function in society, one resting upon four terms (brother, sister, father, and son) linked by two pairs of correlative oppositions in such a way that in each of the two generations there is always a positive relationship and a negative one. What one should notice here is the central role played by the term *brother* among the four terms; for the relationship between "brothers-in-law is the necessary axis around which the kinship structure is built." This is the famous *avunculate, l'oncle maternel*, upon which all kinship systems, as modes of exchange within the collective, are built. One could not, incidentally, substitute the female for the male in these four terms (sister, her brother, brother's wife, and brother's daughter) and establish the sororate as the foundation-term of all kinship, because in kinship systems, quite simply, "it is the men who exchange the women, and not vice-versa." In other words, exchange in marriage is based upon the prestation of a man obtaining a woman "from another man who gives him a daughter or a sister." The disequilibrium in one generation between the group giving the woman and the group receiving her is balanced by counter-prestations in following generations. Thus, all kinship structures must exist both spatially (atemporally, or on a synchronic level) and temporally (diachronically).[63]

The relationship between brothers-in-law is the elementary structure upon which all kinship systems are built. It is, then, a relationship as real as any of the terms related. It is a discourse that is a direct result of the universal incest taboo. And the relationship upon which this discourse is constructed is the avunculate: "Thus we do not need to explain how the maternal uncle emerged in the kinship structure: He does not emerge—he is present initially. Indeed the presence of the maternal uncle is a necessary precondition for the structure to exist. The error of traditional anthropology, like that of traditional linguistics, was to consider the terms, and not the relations between the terms." [64]

Before leaving Lévi-Strauss's analysis of the incest prohibition, we should further note that, just as his conception of totemism as a function of exogamy can be traced to both Rousseau and Freud, so, too, his views on the incest-prohibition are quite analogous to views expressed by both Marx (and Marxist writers) and Freud. For Freud, after the revolt and killing of the primal father by his sons in order that they might enjoy sexual relationships with his wives, the taboo against incest was eventually imposed by the group upon itself (after an initial period of sexual licentiousness among the sons and the wives) in order that the group might expand through exogamy. Repression of natural biological energy into cultural energy is, in Freud, the basis of exogamy and the cornerstone without which the collective would disintegrate.[65]

The same view—that "repression" is "a condition for stability in social life"—has been anticipated by Engels and can be held to represent Marx's view. In *The Origin of the Family,* he postulates that the earliest and most fundamental form of sexual relationships are the "group marriages" in which "all the women of one totem belong sexually to the men of another." Of course, some repression is needed even here, since a male cannot mate with a female of his own totem, and, additionally, since all the women of an opposite totem are potential wives for all the men of an appropriate totem, the individual men are forced to repress feelings of jealously within each gens. However, prior even to this period of group marriages (between corresponding gentes), there was, according to Engels, a period of unrestricted sexual intercourse. But this stage, without the guidance of structures of exogamy, could not be viewed as organized around the intercourse of men, only that of beasts. In Engels's own words: "All the forms of the group marriage known to us are accompanied by such peculiarly complicated circumstances that they of necessity point to a preceding form of sexual intercourse, and hence in the last instance to a period of unrestricted sexual intercourse corresponding to a transition from the animal to man." [66]

The affinity between Marx's (here Engels's) and Freud's views on marriage systems is well expressed by Osborn:

We can quite easily correlate the views of Engels and Freud. The period of "unrestricted sexual intercourse" to which the former refers is paralleled by the period succeeding the slaying of the primal father, wherein unrestricted satisfaction of sexual impulses became possible. And as Engels notes that "mutual tolerance of the young males" was necessary to stabilize society, so Freud remarks that the brothers, to live together, had to erect the incest barriers. And, finally, the group marriage is equivalent to the first totem grouping wherein mutual antagonisms and jealousies are repressed and sexual desires satisfied outside the totem group or gens.[67]

Accordingly, in his explication of totemism, the incest-taboo, and exogamy within society, Lévi-Strauss has built upon the Marxist-Freudian as well as Rousseauist base. He would, most assuredly, agree with Engels that repression of personal desires into mental structures of exogamy marks the transition from the bestial to man and the birth of reason.[68] We have already seen how repression contributes in the Freudian-Lacan view to the development of the unconscious, the locale of fantasy, the place of metonymy, metaphor, and symbolism, and "the language of the Other." Lévi-Strauss adds to the theory of repression an explication of the logical structures of this reason born through repression, and he finds that they rest, as far as the exchange of women in society is concerned, upon a rational relationship among brothers-in-law—a relationship that is both formal and yet concretely symbolized in material (sexual) intercourse. Finally, he finds such kinship structures to be the creatures of the collective, guarding it against the self-interest and desires of its individual members. All such elements of Lévi-Strauss's thought can be seen in his actual anthropological research.

One concrete example of the power of the collective is offered by Lévi-Strauss in the position of the Nambikwara chiefs. Political power among the Nambikwara is not hereditary. Rather, as a chief grows old or ill, he picks a successor, who must be acceptable to the majority of the people. Lévi-Strauss records that few, if any, actively seek the job, because the position of the chief seems to be that of the *servus servorum Dei*. He records a story told in 1560 to Montaigne, in Rouen, by three Brazilian Indians brought back to France by some early explorer. Montaigne asked them what were the privileges of the king of their company. One of them, himself a chief, replied that he was the first man to march into war. Astonishingly, in *Tristes Tropiques*, Lévi-Strauss recalls receiving the same answer to the same question. The Nambikwara word for chief, *Uilikande*, itself seems to mean "the one who unites or binds together." And Lévi-Strauss remarks that "the etymology suggests that the native mind is aware of the phenomenon I have already emphasized, namely, that the chief is seen as the cause of the group's desire to exist as a group, and not as the result of the need for a central authority felt by some already established group." In short, the chief of the Nambikwara, according to Lévi-Strauss's narrative, has no function as chief outside of the one that is all-important: he is the hub around which revolve the different spokes of the Nambikwara wheel. Lévi-Strauss relates various ways in which the chief is really the servant of the people: he has no powers of coercion over the governed without the consent of those governed, and he seeks to keep popular opinion on his side by prudent generosity and the dispersal to the tribe of all personal gifts made to him.[69]

Finally, as some sort of reward for his service to the body politic, the chief alone of all the men of the village is allowed to practice polygamy (since there is a chief wife, the others are really secondary wives or concubines.) The tribe is very small; therefore, the polygamous privileges of the chief foster difficulties for the life of the group. It means that some of the younger men must either remain single for years or take widows or older women who have been deserted by their husbands. This *quid pro quo* exchange, in which the group as a group grants the chief the privilege of polygamy (and thus gives up some of its rights to a wife for every man) in return for the collective security it receives from authority, is an example of the social phenomenon that Rousseau chronicled in "the renunciation by individuals of their particular independence in the interest of the general will." The notion of reciprocity flows from the mutual contract signed and sealed between the group and the chief. He has duties and must give them gifts; they in turn must give him wives from their collective midst. Between them, there is a constant adjustment and search for equilibrium. Their life is a constant round of prestations and counter-prestations.[70]

The primacy of this consent and contract theory over the lives of the individual members of the collective, as individuals, shows that Rousseau and his contemporaries were profoundly correct, states Lévi-Strauss, when they realized that the elements of culture that are summed up in the words *contract* and *consent* "are not secondary creations," as Hume and their adversaries maintained, but rather "the basic material of social life. . . ." Again, we find Lévi-Strauss stressing the primacy of the collective over the individual and breaking radically with the egocentricity of the Cartesian *cogito*: "The prime role of culture is to ensure the group's existence as a group, and consequently, in this domain as in all others, to replace chance by organization."[71]

6 ❀ Lévi-Strauss and Marx

Lévi-Strauss's Science of Superstructures

In *Tristes Tropiques,* Lévi-Strauss proudly asserts that he rarely pens a line of structural anthropology without first reading a page or two of Marx, preferably of the *Eighteenth Brumaire of Louis Bonaparte* or of *The Critique of Political Economy.*[1] The work of Marx, he explains, like geology and Freudian psychoanalysis, shows, first, that understanding consists in reducing one type of reality to another and, second, that "true" (*vraie*) reality is never the most evident of realities, which is manifest by the care it takes to avoid our detection. The problem concerns the relations between reason and sensation and the goal of all structural investigations, which is always "a sort of *superrationalism,* which will integrate the first with the second, without sacrificing any of its properties."[2]

We know that the base of all society in Marxist analysis is economic. The superstructures are the forms of social life that follow upon the economic foundation; or, as Engels expressed this idea, before the pursuit of politics, art, science, religion, and so on, mankind must first eat, drink, and have clothing and shelter. For Marx, social existence determines the individual consciousness, and not vice versa: "Does it require deep intuition to comprehend that man's ideas, views and conceptions, in one word, man's consciousness changes with every change in the conditions of his material existence, in his social relations and in his social life?" It follows that the superstructures of society (such as art, literature, political life) are built upon the economic structure of society; thus it is not the consciousness of men that determines their being but their social being that determines their consciousness. The relations of production, which form men's social being and, in turn, determine their consciousnesses, are relations into which men must enter and which are conceived by Marx as "indispensable and independent of their will." "The historical event . . . may again itself be viewed as the product of a power which works as a whole unconsciously and without volition." "We have learned from Marx, that the diachronic can also exist in the collective. . . ." [3]

The relations of production correspond to a definite stage of development of men's material productive forces. The sum total of these relations of production is the economic structure of society. But at a certain point in the social development of mankind, the material productive forces of society come into conflict with the existing relations of production. Thus begins an epoch of social revolution, when the relations of production turn into the chains of the productive forces (in lieu of their means of development). The existing relations of production are, for Marx, private property relations. With the change of the economic foundation, there is a corresponding transformation of the huge superstructure. [4]

When Lévi-Strauss attributes the creation of the monogamous family to the collective through the division of labor, he is following the fundamental doctrine of Marx and Engels, which views all the superstructures of society (including the family) as standing on an economic base.

In the materialist conception of history, the tribe and monogamous family (which was patriarchal) succeeded a prehistorical stage of man's development in which the "gentile organisation" (from the Latin *gentes*, "tribe or nation") had predominated. When productive forces began to improve (for example, metal tools replaced stone tools), a diversification of labor arose. Agriculture, handicrafts, and so on became the rule. With these went the production of surplus commodities (that is, more than their producer could consume himself) and a concomitant exchange of commodities. The gens and the tribe then dispersed into separate families, which assumed their individual roles as separate producers and forces in the economic base of society. Each family represented, at this stage of history, a private economy, and the role of dominance in the family unit passed from the hands of mothers (who controlled the tribal unit in the days of the gens, when the fatherhood of individual children, because of the communism of the primitive community, remained uncertain) to the fathers, who arranged and controlled the division of labor within the monogamous family. [5]

It is, as we have seen, to a science of the transformations that exist between the economic and social structure and the superstructures that

Lévi-Strauss dedicates his enterprise. If, as in Marx's view, infrastructures and superstructures are composed of various levels, and the transformations themselves are varied and multiple, then, disregarding content, we should be able to characterize different types of societies according to the transformations occuring within them. The transformations within society between the economic structure and the superstructures are, for Marx, of a dialectical nature, as they ultimately are for Lévi-Strauss. The social anthropologist, working from Marxist theory, replaces a complex model with a simpler one that each society unconsciously employs to resolve its inherent contradictions (or, at least, to conceal them).[6] Understanding is seen as reducing one type of reality to another.

But true reality is never the most evident of realities. In *Structural Anthropology,* Lévi-Strauss distinguishes between social relations, which consist of the materials out of which the models composing the social structure are built, and the actual social structure, which can never be reduced to a simple ensemble of the social relations of the particular society. The mistake of those who confuse the two[7] is the failure to distinguish between observation and experimentation. The former consists in detailing and describing all the facts, whereas the latter includes experimenting on the models, that is, observing how a given model will react when subjected to change, by comparing models of varying types. It is especially important that the model being observed be an unconscious one, because the primitives' conscious representations, although they are important as part of the facts to be observed and recorded, may be just as far removed from the unconscious reality as any other representation.[8]

The very same distinction between social relations and unseen social structures exists in Marx's *Capital.* A visitor to capitalist Victorian Britain, for example, might have asked an inhabitant about the meaning of English words like *price, salary,* and so on. But a description of the world of appearances, even by an intelligent informer, would not have conformed to the structure of the real system. For instance, *salary* might not, in reality, have meant total pay for total work at all. More importantly, in Marx, the hidden structure must always be the diametrical opposite of the visible structure, for it is this internal conflict that accounts for Marxist historical dialectic and the class struggle. As a result, the informant's interpretations of his social structures are not to be trusted as true accounts. Lévi-Strauss agrees that the very Marxist notion of a science of history depends upon this contradiction, for all science would be superfluous if the appearance and the essence of things were confused.[9]

Marxist Praxis in Lévi-Strauss

The Marxist notion of praxis forms the core of all economic bases of society for Lévi-Strauss. However, he adds to that notion the idea that, between praxis and *les practiques,* there always intervenes a "mediator" in the form of a conceptual scheme (the structures of society). He considers this addition a contribution to the theory of superstructures.[10]

The word *praxis* means action of some sort. Briefly, it signifies that, for Marx, "life determines consciousness," and not vice versa. By this, Marx signified a change of the philosophic point of departure from the Hegelian and neo-Hegelian concept to the empirical notion of life: "The premises from which we begin are . . . the real individuals, their activity and the material conditions under which they live, both those which they find already existing and those produced by their activity. . . . They begin to distinguish themselves from animals as soon as they begin to *produce* their means of subsistence." Marx's basic idea here is that, whereas the animal is one with its activity, man makes his life activity an object of his will and his consciousness. As a result, the individual man becomes conscious of himself as part of the species. To emphasize this point, Marx calls man a "species-being." [11]

Alienated labor activity that does not see its own image imprinted upon the product of its activity reverses the natural relationship of activity. Instead of his life activity being his *being,* the alienated laborer's activity becomes only a means for his *existence.* Hence, on the deepest level, Marx appears as a shrewd analyst of mankind's psychological (as well as economic) woes. Psychologically, the alienated begin to confuse being and having: they think that they *are* what they possess. Since all activity produces an object (that is, culture), man is related in a double way to his products: first, he realizes himself in them, and, second, he loses himself in them. Loss without realization is alienation. Economically (that is, in the class struggle of history), alienation comes about when the human laborer (the proletariat class) becomes an artificial commodity or merchandise because private property has turned the laborer into the quantity of products he can make: he is the amount of gold (capital) that he can bring in to his management-owner (the bourgeois class). Integra-

tion (wholeness) is brought about by conscious struggle to free the proletariat, so that, in the last analysis, Marxist praxis becomes revolutionary
activity.[12]

Marxist praxis is a materialization of the Hegelian notion of formative
activity, perfectly expressed in the dialectic of master and slave in *The
Phenomenology of Spirit*.[13] The section of this work, so important in the
history of ideas, that is crucial for our argument comes toward the end
of the dialectic. Here, Hegel begins to reveal a shift slowly coming to
pass in the relationship of slave to master, which corresponds to Marx's
stage of integration achieved by revolutionary praxis.[14]

The slave, who has lost in the initial struggle and is now reduced to
a state of servile fear, works upon matter, preparing it for the service of
the master. Slowly and laboriously, the slave molds the material element,
impregnating it all the while with his own image. But through this formative activity, a surreptitious reversal of the relative positions of master
and slave is taking place, for the master is dominant only over the slave.
Thus, he is conscious of himself (as master) only because of the slave's
mediating position between him and the material element. On the other
hand, the slave is slowly becoming aware of himself as he impresses his
own image upon the matter. The slave no longer displays the stubborn-
ness of the downtrodden but, rather, a real mind of his own. Both master
and slave exist through a process of *dédoublement,* of split representation, with the distinction that the master's self-consciousness is mediated
by the slave's consciousness of him. The slave is liberating himself from
bondage to nature by his formative activity.[15]

The Bororo Village and Marxist Principles

These same themes are evident in Lévi-Strauss's analysis of the Bororo
village structure. This and his study of the Caduveo are, he tells us,
"some attempts to interpret native superstructures founded upon dialectical materialism.[16]

He begins with a description of the village structure, not of the Bororo
(South American Indian), but of a Winnebago (North American) tribe,
given by Paul Radin. What is strangely interesting about the description
of the village outline is that two distinctly different village structures
were described by the elderly folk who were Radin's informants. One
group explained that the tribe always formed a circular village plan and

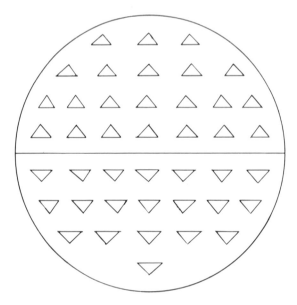

Figure 1. Diametric Structure

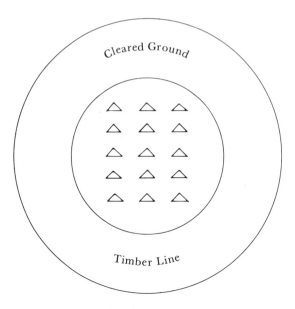

Figure 2. Concentric Structure

that the circle was divided into two halves, with lodges scattered throughout by an imaginary diameter running northwest and southeast (see
fig. 1). Others denied this arrangement, however, and claimed that the
homes of the chiefs of both halves were in the center and not on the
periphery. By this description, in place of the diameter cutting the circle
into two halves, a smaller circle appeared within a larger one. In the
inner circle, the lodges were all grouped together, whereas the outer
circle was a buffer zone of cleared ground separating the lodges from
the virgin forest surrounding the whole ensemble (see fig. 2). Furthermore, the first pattern was described by those who belonged to the upper
half of the first figure; those who belonged to the lower half always
denied the existence of the first figure and described instead the second
one.[17]

Lévi-Strauss proceeds to offer other examples of village groupings of
both types from other societies around the world. For example, he mentions Malinowski's village plan of Omarakana in the Trobriand Islands,
which possesses a concentric structure. The two circles are composed of a
series of binary oppositions. At the very center of the village, for instance,
stands the plaza, which seems to be the "sacred" part of the urban environment, the scene of many religious rites and festivals. The rest of the
village Malinowski called the "profane" part. Only the bachelors may live
in the center ring; the huts of the married couples are grouped all around
them. Raw food is stored in the center (in yam storehouses), and the cooking and consuming of food may take place only in the outer ring. Finally,
the central circle is aligned with the male, the surrounding street with the
female.[18] Other examples from Indonesian and Chinese village structures
follow, but at this point Lévi-Strauss offers a hint of the direction in which
he is leading the reader by mentioning that, in his opinion, the two types
of village structure encountered (diametric and concentric structure) are
not two different organizations. Rather, they are two different ways of
formalizing one organization which is so complex that each half described
it in a manner appropriate to its position in the social structure.[19]

At first glance, that is, when we examine the apparently obvious plan,
the village of diametric structure seems to be based upon a series of reciprocal exchanges, and, thus, the village structure seems to be the outcome of a balanced dichotomy between social groups. By this description,
Lévi-Strauss means simply that, when a village is divided in this manner
into halves that service one another, the relationship between the halves
would always seem to be symmetrical; in fact, however, they are asym-

metrical, insofar as they are represented by binary oppositions—for example, of superior and inferior, elder and younger, noble and commoner.
Since the nature of villages of this type seems to be "steeped in reciprocity," there seems to be a contradiction in their very structure, in that
most diametric structures, in apparent contradiction to their nature,
present an asymmetrical character. Concentrically structured villages are
always asymmetrical, or hierarchically related, in that the two elements
are arranged respectively toward the center: one of the circles is, of
course, closer to this center than the other one. The problem is, then,
threefold: (1) to explain the nature of diametric structure, (2) to explain
the nature of concentric structure, and (3) to explain how most diametric
structures present both a symmetrical character (through reciprocal exchanges of the two halves) and an asymmetrical character, so that they are
midway between absolutely symmetrical societies and the asymmetrical
concentric forms.[20]

In order to reach a solution to this threefold problem, Lévi-Strauss
turns his attention upon a society that seems to be both diametrically
and concentrically structured—the Bororo of South America. The society
is concentrically structured: at the center is the men's house, out of
bounds to the women (the punishment for transgression is death). Then
comes a circle of uncultivated scrub-bush land. Finally, there is a peripheral circle of family huts, surrounded, in turn, by the forest. The basic
opposition here is between male and female, since the men control the
center of the village and the women control the encircling family homes
(descent being matrilineal and residence matrilocal).[21]

But the society is also diametrically structured. It is divided into two
halves by an east-west axis separating the eight clans into four clans that
ostensibly are exogamous. This axis is, in turn, cut by another one, perpendicular to it and running north-south. This axis corresponds to the
stream beside which the villagers like to build, and it separates the eight
clans into two other groups of four, called the "Upper" or the "Lower,"
depending upon their position in relation to the stream (that is, up-
stream or downstream). This perpendicular axis, in actuality, divides the
village into three matrilineal sections: an Upper, Middle, and Lower.
Since Uppers may marry only Uppers, Middles only Middles, and Lowers only Lowers, Bororo society is actually reduced to three endogamous
groups, each in turn divided into two exogamous halves.[22]

We should recall here that the real structure of the village (as opposed to the apparent one) is always that structure upon which exchanges,

or reciprocities, function. Thus, the operational reality of the village is discovered in the triadic, asymmetrical organization, and when the Bororo mention dyadic structure to the ethnographer, they are celebrating a "dyadism" (and symmetry)—a hidden desire for equality, which exists only in their minds. The dyadic formal arrangement of the Bororo village is a partly cultural artifact, existing only in the villagers' own minds but betraying their deep wish for symmetry within society. The implications here, one should note, are Marxist: namely, the proletariat, although existing in a state of inequality (a caste system), yet yearns for the equality that lies at the core of man's exchanges; also, the most obvious structures of the village are not the real ones. Figure 3 illustrates the arrangement.[23]

In figure 3, we can observe that the classes (Upper, Middle, Lower) are arranged symmetrically, so that the two semicircles are joined at one end by the two *U*'s and at the other by two *L*'s. Lévi-Strauss concludes that one half is really the mirror image of the other. This arrangement corresponds to the mirror image of the unconscious that is central to structuralism (as the *dédoublement* of the self). It highlights the existence of an unconscious dyadic structure that says men are equal and opposites, as in a mirror, yet this structure exists only in the mind. Lévi-Strauss writes, "From this remarkable arrangement it appears to follow that despite its circular form the natives do not conceive of the village as a single entity susceptible of analysis into two parts, but rather as two distinct entities joined together." [24]

Another strange and interesting fact appears. In the two halves, two clans occupy a special position, since they represent the two great cultural deities of the Bororo, Bakororo and Itubori, guardians of the East and West. Figure 4 represents a further experimentation upon the models: clans 1 and 7 represent Itubori, and 4 and 6 represent Bakororo.[25] Lévi-Strauss chooses these clans because they are the only ones contiguous to both axes: 1 and 4 with the east-west axis, standing at two ends and on the same side, and 6 and 7 with the north-south axis, standing at the same end but on either side of the axis.

Changing figure 4 by even further experimentation upon the models from a diametric structure into a concentric one, we come up with a still different representation (fig. 5). [26] To turn this diagram back to the diametrically structured one (fig. 4), we would first open the inside circle at the south and straighten the line out, while shifting it northward; then,

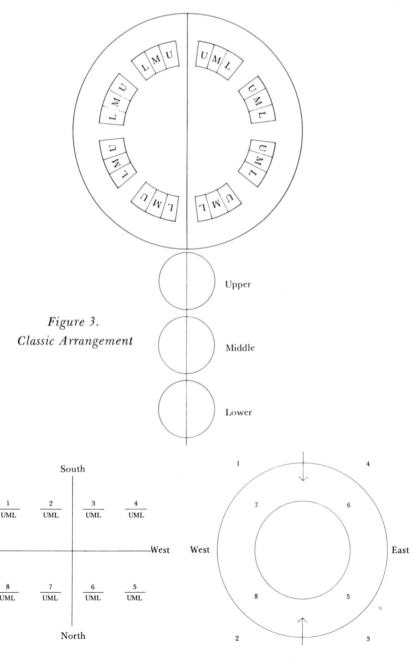

Figure 3.
Classic Arrangement

Upper

Middle

Lower

Figure 4

Figure 5

opening the outside circle at the north, we would (after straightening the line out) shift it southward.

We may then draw the following conclusions from Lévi-Strauss's analysis, chiefly Marxist in character:

1. As in dialectical materialism, the apparent structure of the Bororo village is not the real one: that is, the apparent triadic asymmetrical structure of Upper, Middle, and Lower serves only as a mask for a hidden dyadic symmetrical structure, since the village is halved so that Uppers only marry Uppers, Middles marry Middles, and Lowers marry Lowers. The two halves of the village dyadically serve one another: "to live and breathe each through and for the other." They exchange women, goods, and services; they intermarry their children and bury one another's dead. Their cultural life, in short, mediates the inequalities of their natural existence.[27]

2. As in dialectical materialism, understanding consists in reducing one type of reality to another. With further experimentation upon the models (that is, by a system of transformations), we can transform the classical arrangement into a concentric dualistic structure, which combines both the dyadic structure and the concentric one.

3. Again as in dialectical materialism, the hidden structure is always the diametrical opposite of the visible structure. Lévi-Strauss expresses this relationship by stating that one half of the village is really the mirror image of the other half.

The Bororo and the Master-Slave Relation

The parallels between Lévi-Strauss's analysis of the Bororo and the Hegelian analysis of the master-slave relation reveal still further the depth and character of the importance to his thought of the notions of Hegel's mediation or Marx's praxis. The reduction of the dyadic structure to the concentric dualistic structure introduces such notions. That is to say that it introduces the Hegelian triadic dialectic (the in-itself, the for-itself, the in-and-for-itself), which is transformed in Marx's praxis into the triad of truth, going beyond (alienation), and integration.[28] The three last movements that, according to Lefebvre, characterize every aspect of Marx's thought correspond to the three structures we have just seen in Lévi-Strauss: the triadic one (*vérité*—only in the sense of apparent), the dyadic (*dépassement*), and the concentric dualistic (*désaliénation*), what I have called "integration."

Basically, for the Bororo villages, consciousness of self must be mediated through consciousness of the other. Recall that the relation of master-slave is similar. The master initially triumphs over the slave, but, at this dialectical moment, is immediately related to himself (*Ich bin Ich*) and mediately related to both the thing (matter) and the slave who works upon the thing: to the thing through the mediation of the slave, to the slave through the mediation of the thing. But, in point of fact, the master's "immediate" relation to himself is also "mediate," for it is possible only through the silent mediation of the slave. But to be master, the master must be recognized as master by the slave. At this point of the dialectic, it becomes clear that the master's self-consciousness is exterior to his own self; that is, it resides in the slave.

Conversely, the master cannot recognize the other who recognizes him, because to grant the slave recognition would be to admit a certain dependence on the slave. But without recognizing the slave, the master cannot be truly free, for to be free (that is, to be master, not slave), one must acknowledge that the other, in whose eyes one is free, is first worthy of bestowing that freedom upon oneself. Clearly, the master is caught in a web of impotence. Kojève succinctly summarizes this impasse. On the other hand, the slave begins to liberate himself by his "formative" activity, in Hegel's terms, or "praxis," in Marx's phrase. His selfhood is not mediated through the master, but is immediately seen as imprinted on the material with which he works. For Hegel or Marx, this is a process of humanization (the third moment [*désaliénation*] in the triadic moment of praxis).[29]

The mediatory power of the concentric dualistic structure forms a perfect similitude of this moment in the master-slave dialectic, because, for the primitive to regard his own half of the village as the central circle and the other half as the peripheral, it is only necessary for him to reverse the directions.[30] The concentric dualistic structure of the Bororo represents, on the one hand, the freedom that accrues to the slave and, on the other, the bondage that is becoming the lot of the master. The slave, becoming free, can change the direction of the village structure by recognizing the master as master (through his service to him), but the master cannot recognize the slave (for recognition would be a form of service).

Clearly, we return here to the profound notion of gift-giving as reciprocal. Lévi-Strauss notes that, among primitive peoples, gifts are always exchanged for counter-gifts; goods are never just economic commodities but vehicles for realities that transcend the material, such as influence, sympathy, power, status. Primitives are engaged in a constant chess game in which the players do not give each other the pieces that they alternately move forward on the board, but move only to provoke a counter-move, that is, in order to gain security through alliances and rivalries. We are carried back again to Lévi-Strauss's analysis of the most dominant structure of human cognition: "the synthetic nature of the gift," exemplified by the learning process of taking turns that every child must undergo. We return here to the basic structural notion that what gives the object any value at all is the 'relation to the other person.' " Hence, for Lévi-Strauss, "the desire to possess is essentially a social response. . . . Beyond the intrinsic value of the thing given, there is the gift itself as a sign of love, and beyond that, the gift as a sign of the fact of being worthy of love." [31]

The most heinous of human fates has befallen the master in the Hegelian dialectic. He has lost the power of giving, of communicating. He is mute and trapped in an impasse of his own creation; this loss of language constitutes that impasse. Yet, in the concentric dualistic structure of the Bororo village, since all inequalities are obviated no matter from which direction the primitives view the village structure and their position in it, Lévi-Strauss has discovered *yet another language* as potent in their lives as their phonetic code and their own rules of marriage exchange. Culture, for Lévi-Strauss, through a dynamic synthesis (that is, the concentric dualistic structure) symmetrizes the inequalities of nature.[32]

The analogy is instructive. Cross cousins belong to families that are in a state of "dynamic disequilibrium" in relationship to each other, which is then mediated by their marriage and alliance (as opposed to the relationship of parallel cousins, who are in a relationship of static equilibrium to each other). In an identical fashion, concentric dualistic (village) structure is the mediator between diametric dualism and triadism because the transition from the asymmetric triad to the symmetric dyad takes place through the agency of concentric dualism—which is asymmetric like the former but dyadic like the latter. Like parallel cousins, diametric dualism is static; but concentric dualism is dynamic and contains an implicit triadism. In other words, concentric dualism provides the area of "Thirdness" in which the linguistic unconscious dwells. The implicit triadism appears analogically in the conscious terminology of the natives. The ternary nature of concentric dualism arises because the system is not self-sufficient and its frame of reference is its environment. The binary opposition, in the Bororo village, of cleared ground to wasteland has need of a third element, the brush or forest (that is, virgin land), which both circumscribes the binary whole and extends it, "since cleared land is to waste land as waste land is to virgin land." Analogy again enters our exposition.[33]

This complicated analysis can be finally rounded out with the reintroduction of the fundamental Lévi-Straussian distinction between apparent and real structures—which reappears here in the notion of the north-south axis. Since the north-south axis (or upstream-downstream axis) of the village structure actually divides what was the apparent triadic asymmetrical structure into a dyadic, symmetrical structure, it is the sole agent, as it were, in the Bororo urban environment, of the Bororo society itself. Without that axis, Bororo society itself would not exist. Thus, it can be characterized as a "zero-value" (as mana was a zero value), because it divides the village into two halves, enabling one half to exchange reciprocally with the other. Its sole function, consequently, is to allow a concentric dualistic structure to exist. What else, then, is the concentric dualistic structure (and consequently its cause, the north-south axis) but a pure variable, allowing each native to conceive of the village as both triadic (that is, concentrically structured and hence invariable) and, at the same time, dyadic (that is, variably dynamic)? We return, with the notion of the zero-value of the north-south axis, to the original concept of the linguistic unconscious as that area in which the self is distinguished from the other in order to be reidentified with the other in language. The zero-value is not dependent upon the society in which it is found (like other social institutions), for it itself establishes society. It is *society itself in act*. It is pure Marxist praxis. The zero-value of society is a constant theme in Lévi-Strauss and is fundamental to his understanding of the history of Western philosophy.[34]

7 ❁ Some Issues and Criticisms

Analytical versus Dialectical Reason

Let us recall that the purpose of experimenting upon the models by utilizing various transformations of the same myth is precisely an attempt to bring out the underlying meaning by deliberately injecting change (through transformations) into a given structure, and then observing how it functions under such permutations; only through permutations (interchanges) will the hidden structure appear, as it does scientifically through the interchanges of psychiatrist and patient, or of ethnologist and natives.[1]

Let us also recall that Lévi-Strauss conceives of the mind as necessarily operating according to absolutely determined laws, which probably have their foundation in "a bio-chemical substratum." [2] The result is that the apparently creative, free outsurge of the mind, expressed in areas that at first seem to be quite arbitrary, even chaotic (such as marriage rules, mythology, and so on), "presuppose laws operating at a more profound level." Lévi-Strauss thus concludes that the mind is as much a material, structured entity as DNA or the material particles of the atom—although, unlike such "entities," the mental structures do not describe any particular entity so much as they predict the way genetic inheritance, on the one hand, and the atom, on the other, will act under given circumstances. The mind is conceived as a totally material entity, a thing among the other things of the world.

Combine with these observations the recollection that the division of labor within society is, for Lévi-Strauss, as it was for Marx, innate: it is based upon the exchanges functioning in each society, indeed, it is nothing other than these exchanges. In turn, the exchanges are mathematically, natively ordered according to structures which Lévi-Strauss claims are finite and which, although unconscious, appear consciously (although in a contradictory or mirrorlike fashion) in the conscious activities (praxis) of each society. Ultimately, then, the mental structures are society itself in act. This aspect of Lévi-Strauss is, as we have seen, his living Marxism.[3]

The importance of these observations is that the methodology of structuralism is analytic; that is, its purpose is not to constitute man but to analyze him into the constituting structures: "the final end of the human sciences is not to constitute man but to dissolve him." Lévi-Strauss's structuralism reapproaches scientific positivism from a new light. It remains an "everyday materialism," for its purpose is to "reintegrate culture into nature, and finally, life into the ensemble of its physico-chemical conditions." And it is also a *superrationalisme*, for, approaching the Marxist science of superstructures from a linguistic point of view, it employs analytical reason to reduce the individual to (synchronic) collective structures. The aim of a science of superstructures, as Marx wrote, is to show that "the human being is not an abstraction inherent in an isolated individual. In reality, it is the ensemble of social relations."[4]

We should note that in neither Marx's nor Lévi-Strauss's conception can the individual escape the primacy of the collective. For, *qua* individual he does not exist; *qua* member of a collective he works out his individuality within the collective structure.

True, structuralism is analytic. Yet, in a very real way, Lévi-Strauss all along has been dealing, through structural analysis, with the dialectical function of the human mind. The savage mind in its "participatory mentality," as he has explained it, totalizes the entire universe: in its affirmation *homo sum, nihil humanum alienum est mihi*, "dialectical reason discovers its true root." Consequently, dialectical reason and analytical reason are, for Lévi-Strauss, only two sides of the same coin. Dialectical reason is not seen as something other than analytical reason, but simply as something additional in analytical reason. Dialectical reason is that aspect of analytical reason which, when roused to action, constantly tries to transcend itself. By making dialectical reason simply an aspect of analytical reason,[5] Lévi-Strauss implies that basic doctrine of all positivism: that life can always be reduced, ultimately, to nonlife. He conceives of the gap between the two as only a temporary one that science will eventually resolve. Eventually, science will discover the link between the two, even showing that mind is not distinct from matter but just a slightly different aspect of matter.[6]

Lévi-Strauss is a total scientific determinist; there is no room in his

thought for any doctrine of free will ("illusion of freedom"). He characterizes all those who opt for the primacy of dialectical reason and the
individual totalizing *cogito* (particularly Sartre) as those whose thought
is agonized by transcendence and who find in historicism the last refuge
of a transcendental humanism. His own scientism he terms an agnosti-
cism,[7] whereas Sartre calls it a "positivism of signs." In point of fact, it
is precisely this notion of symbol, to which Sartre here alludes, that enables Lévi-Strauss's structuralism to be a positivism, finding in matter
the attributes of mind. Symbols are both quasi-material and quasi-intel-
lectual. We have explained in great detail the way that symbols, for Lévi-
Strauss, transcend and combine the best of both worlds, so that in structuralism nature is not (to use a favorite saying of John Dewey) either
rational or material; rather, it is intelligible (read "structural"). Hence,
Lévi-Strauss most properly characterizes his conception of reality as neither an idealism nor a total materialism, but a realism.[8]

Since it now becomes quite evident that Lévi-Strauss sees all cultural
superstructures as reducible to the physicochemical process of the brain,
the original Lévi-Straussian distinction between culture and nature is
seen in a new light. Culture is never divorced from nature but is simply
a nature transformed by an unconscious element. This becomes the basis
for an "une psychologie non intellectualiste," a "qualitative mathematics"
in which relationships are established between classes of individuals
distinguished from one other by discontinuous values, in which the
discontinuity becomes one of the essential characteristics of qualitative
sets in relation to one another. All that is needed for such "qualitative
mathematics" is a finite number of categories and definite relationships
among the categories. We have seen how mana provides the latter, as a
variable, enabling man to categorize his world mathematically.[9]

But, is there any unifying factor in the world of Lévi-Strauss, or is the
totalization of dialectical reason completely subordinate to analytical
reasoning? The answer is that the structures are subordinate to the human
spirit: "And if it is now asked to what final meaning these mutually sig-
nificative meanings are referring—since in the last resort and in their
totality they must refer to something—the only reply to emerge from this
study is that myths signify the mind that evolves them by making use of
the world of which it is itself a part." The structures and the human
spirit that is their constitutive base—"In my view dialectical reason is
always constitutive"—are completely empiricized. Earlier we termed this

the "turning-to-the-world" in Lévi-Strauss.[10] It is thus that the goal of ethnological inquiry is, as in Kant's first *Critique*, to establish higher and higher syntheses so that the empirical diversity of cultures is absorbed into the unity of a general humanity, which is reduced to the unity of a universal human spirit, in turn being absorbed in the conditions of all physicochemical possibilities, so that ultimately culture is reintegrated into nature.[11]

Structuralism: The Death of Man?

This Lévi-Straussian "psychologie non intellectualiste" is actually a mathematics of secondary qualities for Lévi-Strauss and the *novum organum* of the social sciences of the twentieth century. For the first time the strictly qualitative, that is, the secondary qualities (Lévi-Strauss hopes even the quality of scents), which have been so long considered to be ineffable and belonging to the realm of the individual, are shown to belong to the collective and to be mathematically ordered. Thus, one commentator contends that Lévi-Strauss's greatest accomplishment is having shown that one can reject the metaphysical idea of a human nature while yet accepting man as subject to a universal code, accepting, that is, that man is a part of nature. The structuralist's celebrated "death of man" is an important movement in modern thought.[12]

For Michel Foucault (*Les mots et les choses*), the Lévi-Straussian dissolution of man can mean only one thing: the death of man, following the Nietzschean death of God. Foucault envisions man as concerned for centuries with decoding the message of God's word (and the secrets of nature that mirrored it). Once this theocentric universe disappeared, it was succeeded by a historical one. Like the hands on a clock, the hand that once pointed upward gradually moved to a horizontal plane—and pointed to man, the creator of history. But as man the subject of history became the object of scientific study, he seemed to appear more and more to be composed of structures that transcend the individual: those of life in Freud, those of work in Marx, and those of language in phonological linguistics. Thus, the social sciences themselves are dissolving, since their object will no longer be man but those forces that create him. The hand on the clock now points downward toward the unconscious structures. *Man is dead.*[13]

Lévi-Strauss versus Sartre

We are thus brought face to face with the underlying question in Lévi-Strauss: is structuralism unalterably opposed to humanism? The affirmative answer to this question forms the core of the rejection of structuralism by both existentialists and by some neo-Marxists.[14] Consider, for example, the antihumanist, even scientifically pessimistic, overtones of such typical Lévi-Straussian comments as this: "The world began without man and will end without him. The institutions, morals and customs that I shall have spent my life noting down and trying to understand are the transient efflorescence of a creation in relation to which they have no meaning. . . ."[15] These implications cannot be reconciled with the obvious humanistic tendencies of existentialism—with, for example, the absolute freedom of the Sartrean *pour-soi* in his early philosophical work.

The constituting ego of *Being and Nothingness* is not itself simply a creation of an underlying collective but, rather, is the source of all potentiality and of all constitution.[16] It is this Sartrean "immediate sense of one's self" that exudes not a "pessimism, but the sternness of our optimism," a sternness based upon a "consistently atheistic position" (the "death of God"). The individual never leaves the center stage of the Sartrean world.[17]

The primacy of analytical reason in Lévi-Strauss leads him to reject the freedom of the *pour-soi* transferred from *Being and Nothingness* to the freedom of the constituting dialectic in Sartre's *Critique de la raison dialectique*. At the heart of Sartrean individualism (even when it is clothed in the garments of Marxism in the *Critique*) stands Sartre's embrace, which he has never abandoned, of the loneliness of the Cartesian individual *cogito*.[18] For this brand of individualism, Lévi-Strauss reserves his sharpest barbs: "He who begins by steeping himself in the allegedly self-evident truths of introspection never emerges from them." The introspectionists are, in guise of arriving at a knowledge of man, actually only working their way to a knowledge of individual man. Sartre becomes, according to Lévi-Strauss, the prisoner of his *cogito*. Lévi-Strauss contends that Sartre has betrayed even his master Descartes. For, whereas Descartes made it possible to reach universality "conditionally on remaining psychological and individual," Sartre has sociologized the *cogito* so that each individual's group and epoch are now the center of consciousness, in lieu of timeless consciousness.[19]

Finally, in insisting upon Lévy-Bruhl's gratuitous distinction between the primitive (the nonhistorical) and the civilized (the historical), Sartre simply repeats the fundamental opposition between self and the other that first appeared in *Being and Nothingness*. "Descartes, who wanted to found a physics, separated Man from Society. Sartre, who claims to found an anthropology, separates his own society from others." The principle of reciprocity that Lévi-Strauss finds at the core of all societies obviously destroys, in its very concept, the individualism of Sartre. And this is the heart of Lévi-Strauss's ethics: "The moral immanent in myths takes the opposite position from that we profess today. It teaches us that a formula about which we have made a great deal—that 'hell is others'—does not constitute a philosophical position, but an anthropological witness to our civilisation. Because they have accustomed us from infancy to fear pollution from without." [20]

Consequently, perhaps the "man is dead" theme of structuralism does not prevent it from being a form of humanism. Sartre charges that structuralism is a form of positivism and that its forerunner was Auguste Comte. Since structure, for him, is a part of the practico-inert,[21] it can never be a humanism, because it is out of the control of man's creative freedom; it is simply "la chose sans l'homme." Yet, in a way, all of this misses the very real point, the lesson taught by the distinctive table manners of modern and primitive peoples: impurity infects the universe from the subject, from the individual man, and not vice versa. This ethic [22] enshrines a new humanism ("un nouvel humanisme"),[23] a hope for a day that will come when society will be separated from the class systems and the orders of slavery imposed upon men by individuals on behalf of individual technological, cultural progress ("to spread humanism to all humanity"). In short, "a well-ordered humanism doesn't begin with itself, but places the world before life, life before man, the respect of other beings before self-esteem." [24]

The Self in Lévi-Strauss

Through the processes of reciprocal intelligibility, obtained through progressive transformations, the operation of the ethnologist's mind finds its form in the operation of the primitives' minds, and vice versa. The structuralist term for this process is *dédoublement*. Through it, the progressively more intelligible structure of the human mind—"regardless of the identity of those who happen to be giving it expression"—is made manifest by "the doubly reflexive forward movement of two thought processes acting one upon the other." [25]

In *The Savage Mind*, Lévi-Strauss uses the Sartrean term "progressive-regressive" to refer to the *dédoublement* but adds that it is progressive-regressive "two times over" ("elle l'est deux fois"). For Sartre, the progressive-regressive method is linked to the freedom of the individual, his existentialist transcendence of whatever he is at any one moment. It is progressive in that it is an aspect of one's comprehension of the project of another—the way in which one objectifies the work of the other; the other's work betrays his *projet*, or his going always beyond himself toward something. It is regressive in that, simultaneously, one grasps the original condition of the other, that condition that initiated his *projet*.[26]

In Lévi-Strauss the method is doubly employed because there is a *dédoublement* in the person of each individual in the dialogue. The two find their link in the area of the unconscious. We have here not two terms to the discourse, but three: the unconscious is the area of thirdness. Consequently, analytical reason takes over the progressive-regressive method in place of dialectical reason. Jean Pouillon expresses this metamorphosis in his article on Lévi-Strauss and Sartre:

> For Sartre . . . the dialectic is constitutive. For Lévi-Strauss, . . . reason is always constituted. In the first case, the link to the real is before me and the real is contemporaneous with me; in the second case, this link is behind me, and the real is less an object that I think than the condition of the fact that I think. In the first case, the link is established by praxis; in the second case, it is revealed by structure.[27]

However, we have already seen that Lévi-Strauss, contrary to what Pouillon seems to say, also believes that dialectical reason "is constitutive." [28] But it is constitutive only in an initiating fashion. It places in the hands of the human sciences an initial reality, a *totalization*, to use the word employed by Malinowski and, in his *Critique*, by Sartre. In a totalization, the anthropologist attempts to understand culture in all its aspects; he must merge his initiatives in "a feeling of solidarity with the endeavors and ambitions of these natives." Of course, Lévi-Strauss believes that the totalizing power of dialectical reason must begin the anthropologist's work. In Chapter 5, we discussed how he aligns this synthetic stage with "pity" in Rousseau. In a revealing interview with Sartre, given at the beginning of the seventies, the interviewer mentions to

Sartre that "the subject who speaks never totalizes linguistic laws by his words. Language has its own intelligibility as a system which appears heterogeneous to the subject." Sartre is then asked, "Can . . . 'totalization' ever account for the emergence of ordered social structures. . . ?" His reply is clear:

> But there is totalization in language. You cannot say a single sentence which does not refer, by its elements, to opposites. Thereby the whole of language, as a system of differential meanings, is present in its very absence, as linguists themselves admit. Every sentence is a levy on the entire resources of speech, for words only exist by their opposition to each other. There is thus certainly totalization in language.[29]

On the other hand, for Lévi-Strauss, scientific explanation begins only when the object is constituted by a totalizing empathy. The proper scientific endeavor itself consists in decomposing and then recomposing on a different level. It is this view of the proper scientific endeavor (the *dédoublement*) that Sartre cannot accept. In order to keep consistency, in his rejection of this science, with his firm belief in the Marxist dialectic, Sartre distinguishes between science in Freud and science in Marx. He feels that psychoanalytic theory is a syncretic and not a dialectical thought—that is, there are "interpenetrations without contradiction"; one reality is reduced to another level of reality. Therefore, every subsequent relationship in an individual's life is referred in psychoanalysis to a primal, unforgettable, yet forgotten, relationship between father and mother. He acknowledges that there might be some truth in this interpretation; for example, the fixation of a young girl for an older man may refer to her relationship to her father. But this new relationship should also be autonomous and irreducible, whereas, in historical dialectical theory, each of the configurations of reality is conditioned by the previous one, but each later dialectical reality preserves and supersedes the former ones. The latter stage cannot be simply reduced to its predecessor. Hence, Sartre can accept Marx but not Freud. Moreover, the main theme of Sartre's *Critique* is the way in which, through progressive dialectical totalizations, a fundamental homogeneity between the individual and history—through worked matter, the group, the series, the practico-inert, and collectives—is achieved.[30]

All this may seem to be excessively extenuated and simply a dusty academic debate. However, involved in this question are allied ones: whether one can present a doctrine of individual freedom and economic determinism (as Sartre does); whether Marx's vision of history is the first one, or simply one particular mythic version; and whether Sartre favors one version of history (the Western one) to the detriment of all others. On the other hand, Sartre's criticism of Lévi-Strauss implies that structuralism's emphasis on the synchronic is just another excuse for maintaining the status quo and plays into the hands of the reactionary forces in history. Perhaps even more fundamental to this entire discussion is the different attitude of both men to human relationships. The question lurking on the horizon is whether Sartre's attitude toward psychoanalysis simply repeats his celebrated view of human personal encounter with another human. In *No Exit* and in, of course, the interesting section of *Being and Nothingness* called "The Look," he characterizes it as one looking through a keyhole into a room and seeing an eye gazing back at him from the other side of the door. In this respect, Sartre's entire life work has opposed "a therapy of reciprocity" in favor of "a therapy of violence." [31]

Perhaps René Girard's thesis that both Sartre and Lévi-Strauss are still totally influenced by the philosopher who dominated French philosophy at the time both were Sorbonne undergraduates—Henri Bergson—is the explanation of this most fundamental opposition. Bergson's *élan vital*, "disguised by the Germanic terminology" (that is, of Hegel and Heidegger), becomes the flux of Sartre's *pour-soi*, becomes Sartrean freedom. We have already noted Lévi-Strauss's appropriation of Bergson, in his remarks on totemism.[32] But Girard believes that Lévi-Strauss, influenced by the modern discovery of the genetic code, becomes a Bergson in reverse. The *élan vital* principle of undifferentiation becomes an *élan différentiateur*, or an *élan codificateur*. The primacy of intuition becomes the dominance of analytic reason. Although still unalterably opposed to psychoanalysis, Sartre has, at least, broadened the role of the early *pour-soi*, which he now calls a "rationalist philosophy of consciousness," to account for "the stress of neurosis" and for "those processes which are 'below' consciousness and which are also rational, but lived as irrational." He now speaks, in place of the *pour-soi*, of "lived experience" that is always "simultaneously present to itself and absent from itself." [33]

For Sartre, self-consciousness and consciousness of things are revealed in historical praxis. But for Lévi-Strauss, the truth of self-consciousness is always functional; it never apprehends only itself, either in reflection or in praxis. This self is entirely an activity (praxis), but the activity of being aware of an object; the self, then, is dissolved into that object by its awareness, and the object, in turn, is dissolved into its constituent symbols. In this way the self is actually an object among other objects, a thing among things, a thing in the world. In short, for Lévi-Strauss, it is nonexistent: "my ambition being to discover the conditions in which systems of truth become mutually convertible . . . the pattern of those conditions takes on the character of an autonomous object, independent of any subject." [34]

From this basic difference between Sartre and Lévi-Strauss, the existence or nonexistence of the self, all other differences between them flow. First, for Sartre, freedom is an individualized affair; for Lévi-Strauss, one is "free" exactly as much as one is free in Rousseau's *Discourse on the Origin of Inequality*; that is, by giving myself to all I give myself to no one and consequently am free, only within the collective. Second, for Sartre, the individual is marked by ambiguity, which is a sign of his freedom; for Lévi-Strauss, also, the individual is marked by ambiguity, but it is a sign not of his freedom but of his being determined, for the mind is ambiguous only because it is metaphorical, which, as we have seen, means rigorously scientific (that is, ambiguous in the message, but isomorphic in the code). Third, for Sartre, absurdity rules man's unconditioned freedom (that is, there are no meanings intrinsic to the individual); for Lévi-Strauss, nothing is absurd, and everything is meaningful, for if there is meaning anywhere, there is meaning everywhere. This omnipresence of meaning suggests that Ricoeur is correct when he calls Lévi-Strauss's view of the self "a Kantianism without a transcendental subject" but one that is homologous to nature, even *is* nature itself.[35] Lévi-Strauss acknowledges the similarity of his work to some sort of nontranscendental Kantianism.[36]

Principal Criticisms

The commentators on and critics of Lévi-Strauss fall into three basic categories.[37] Their arguments can be outlined, but it would be impossible to recount Lévi-Strauss's detailed replies. Whenever possible, however, I will indicate the direction in which his replies travel.

Perhaps the most common criticism is the Marxist critique, leveled especially against Lévi-Strauss's notion of the synchronic. Basically, it is maintained that Lévi-Strauss neglects history and reduces evolution and progress to mere chimeras. It has been best formulated in detail by

Maxime Rodinson in a 1955 article in *La Nouvelle Critique*. The essence of the criticism is the following: since Lévi-Strauss has taught that the human spirit (mind) is everywhere the same, then all societies are basically equal. But this argument must be viewed as a denial of the concept of social evolution. Just prior to Rodinson's article, a variant of this critique appeared in an article by Roger Caillois. His position is the same as Rodinson's but arises from a different base (that is, a non-Marxist one). Caillois's strategy is to attack Lévi-Strauss insofar as the latter's synchronic structures would deny the supposed superiority (supposed by Caillois, that is) of the European races over other peoples.[38]

But the usual criticism takes the form of that leveled by Rodinson. It occurs in works of Marxists and in Sartre.[39] The main tenor of Lévi-Strauss's replies is that he is not unfaithful to the tenet of Marx that "the history of all hitherto existing society is the history of class struggles." On the contrary, he is quick to point out that this dictum does not state that class struggle and humanity are coextensive and that the Marxist ideas of history and society can be applied only from the time the class struggle first appeared. Marx and Engels quite frequently stated, he asserts, that the so-called primitive societies are directed by "blood-ties" (kinship systems) and not by economic relationships.[40] And if these cultures were not destroyed from without, they might endure indefinitely.

Nor, insists Lévi-Strauss, has he ever sought to disparage the idea of progress; rather, he has merely sought to put it into proper perspective. The objection voiced by Rodinson is that the Lévi-Straussian denigration of the idea of progress would drive Billancourt (that is, the French working-class—it is a name taken from the huge Renault plant in this Parisian district) to desperation. Lévi-Strauss compares this objection to that of the capitalists, who, in order to discourage social change, also argue that atheism would reduce the working class to desperation.[41]

And, further, one must agree with Ricoeur when he says that Lévi-Strauss does not simplistically oppose synchrony to diachrony, as this first objection tends to imply. There is, as Ricoeur points out, a subordination in structuralism of the diachronic to the synchronic; it is not an opposition. Both Lévi-Strauss and Jakobson carefully distinguish the synchronic from the static.[42]

The Marxist sociologist Henri Lefebvre was not convinced by defenses of Lévi-Strauss. In a critique, he calls the reader's attention to an almost "maniacal, almost schizophrenic" emphasis upon the motionless, in which consists the New Eleaticism of Lévi-Strauss. Lefebvre charges Lévi-

Strauss with being a covert disciple of the Parmenidean "One." According to this critique, the core of the structuralists' approach to reality is nondevelopmental and rests on the simple assertion of Parmenides, the greatest of the pre-Socratic philosophers, that "It is." Parmenides himself was a materialist, but his thought and his emphasis upon the unchangeability of Being contains, according to Stace, the germs of idealism. The same statement might analogously be made by a Marxist criticizing Lévi-Strauss. Structuralism becomes the tool of "a capitalist ideology" attempting to eliminate historical development as "a counterrevolutionary defense of the status quo." [43]

Perhaps this criticism of structuralism is best reserved for Louis Althusser, instead of Lévi-Strauss. Althusser, who teaches at the Ecole Normale Supérieure in Lyon, has attempted to do for Marx what Lacan did for Freud, that is, to find out what Marx wanted to say, which is different from what he actually did say. Lacan's return to Freud, according to Althusser, is a return to the maturity of Freud, not to his formative stage and not, then, to the period of the not yet scientific psychoanalysis, "the period of the relations with Charcot, Bernheim, Breuer, up to the *Studies in Hysteria*—1895." Althusser praises Lacan for having defended the irreducibility of psychoanalysis to any other preceding philosophy, to "the primitive experience of the Hegelian struggle, of the phenomenological for-others, or of the Heideggerian 'gulf' of being," or to its own "childhood." "Lacan's first word is to say: in principle, Freud founded a *science*. A new science which was the science of a new object: the unconscious." [44]

Althusser builds upon Gaston Bachelard's concept of an epistemological break. A change (*coupure épistémologique*) took place in Marx's thought between 1845 and 1850. The pre-1845 writings, and in particular the *1844 Philosophical Manuscripts,* are all relegated to the prescientific state of Marx's thought. It was not until the appearance of volume one of *Capital* (1867) that the foundations of economy as a strict science were established. However, even there some Hegelian influences remained. The *Grundrisse* of 1857–58 are tainted with the Hegelian notion of alienation, and only the *Critique of the Gotha Program* (1875) and the *Marginal Notes on Wagner* (1882) are totally free of Hegel's influence. Marxism is not primarily a philosophy but a methodology for explaining social facts. Dialectical materialism is really a science about sciences. One is reminded here of Lévi-Strauss's notion that his four-volume *Mythologiques* is itself a myth: simply the myth (that is, science) of mythology.

Up to 1845, Marx, according to Althusser, pursues a humanist pseudo-philosophy received through Kant and Fichte via Feuerbach. In this period the Hegelian concept of alienation is of paramount importance, and Marx's writings are influenced by such concepts as essence, subject, meaning, history, and finality. After 1845, beginning with *The German Ideology,* Marx thinks in terms of objects and form and structure. Rather than seeking meanings, he looks for structures.[45]

Althusser criticizes two chief Hegelian concepts: that of totality and that of contradiction. *Totality* refers to the notion that Hegel's essence (the world *spirit* in *The Philosophy of History*) is expressed in every level; it permeates world civilizations. That structural Marx rejects this view of totality and favors the relative autonomy of each level of structure. He sees contradiction as the mover of history, the tension that leads to change. In Hegel, it is associated with the Idea, and the source of contradictions in society becomes men's failure to realize the Idea. Causality is, then, an idealist notion in Hegel. In Marx, causation is fixed within structures as their very interiority. Contradictions within a structure cannot be located simply at one level; each contradiction is complicated by contradiction at every other structural level. This complication is called by Althusser the "overdetermination" of contradiction, and he follows Lévi-Strauss's lead in explaining this "overdetermination." And Lévi-Strauss follows Freud. The term *overdetermination* is used by Freud in *The Interpretation of Dreams* to express the way one dream image may contain several unconscious desires, through condensation of several dream thoughts into one image. And, conversely, many images may express the same dream thought. When utilized by Althusser, *overdetermination* means that "the contradictions of capitalism and imperialism are never simple but multi-dimensional and over-determined." [46]

The dialectical method is, in the later Marx, a structural method. There is no role for real individuals as the subjects of production. The real subjects of production are the relations of production, existing at many different levels—economic, political, ethical, aesthetic, ideological. The basic unit of history is neither an individual subject nor absolute consciousness, as in Hegel. Structures, in the later Marx, are totally objective, and men merely their bearers. Individuals may labor to make money and spend it; but money actually uses man to maintain itself, and not the opposite. One is reminded of Lévi-Strauss's kinship systems in which women are the unit of exchange among the levels of structure. Only on the question of the dominance of the economic structure over the others does Althusser, perhaps, exceed Lévi-Strauss, who seems to regard each level as equal in force. In any case, in no way can Althusser's Marxism be considered a humanism.[47]

Nor can it be regarded as a historicism. In Hegel, history is the continuity of time and has the task of "periodizing moments of the Idea." History is always contemporary. There is a gradual unfolding of an innate developmental potential. But in Althusser's view of history as expressed in Marx, "different levels of the totality are . . . considered to have their own time-scale related to their relative autonomy. . . . The relationship between one social formation and the one that follows it is to be understood in terms of displacement rather than the gradual unfolding of an innate developmental potential." We are dealing here with a unity of different and separate histories. The individuals forming a group (as in Sartre's *groupe-en-fusion*) are not the subject of structural history. Rather, Etienne Balibar and Althusser in their 1968 *Reading Capital* claim, borrowing a term from Lévi-Strauss, that change in structures occurs through *bricolage* ("puttering-about"). The *bricolage,* without out a human *bricoleur,* puts together bits and pieces from the trash heap of the previous structure, like a junk dealer, a tinkerer working with pieces of used material. Gradually, a new structure emerges, but with contradictions, since it is not perfectly designed but is constructed of remnants. Praxis (action) is futile because structures are relatively autonomous and because ideological interests (that is, interpretations and individual significations) always distort praxis. Marx cannot be viewed as an ethician, for he was not concerned with the immortality of inhuman relations (as in a capitalist system), since all relations are truly inhuman. Nor would he wish, then, to change those inhuman conditions. In short, "history," according to Althusser and Balibar, "is to be interpreted as an axiomatic and self-sufficient system without any axiological or teleological basis." In the "Foreword to the Italian Edition," reproduced in the English edition of *Reading Capital* in 1970, Althusser attempts to separate his views from the structuralist terminology and ideology; elsewhere in the book, he tries particularly to separate his ideas from those of Lévi-Strauss.[48]

However, in her work comparing the views of both men, Glucksmann correctly rejects Althusser's divorce-attempt and his criticism of Lévi-Strauss, showing, in the process, many more similarities than differences. For Glucksmann; "Despite his denials, Althusser is just as much of a structuralist as Lévi-Strauss in the respects he wishes to deny. . . . He

[Althusser] has a tendency to change sides depending on his audience so as to maintain his superiority over all of them." In any case, it is clear that Althusser's structural Marxism and its antecedents in Lévi-Strauss's structural interpretation of Marx represent a radical departure from the more humanistic and historicistic interpretations that are usually based upon a Hegelian insight into Marx (and, textually, upon the *1844–1845 Philosophical Manuscripts*). Consequently, Roger Garaudy, Henri Lefebvre, and Sartre himself must be ranked as opponents of this view. And, drawing the parameters of the issue even more widely, the reading given Marx by Lukács in his celebrated 1923 *History and Class Consciousness* and those given by Erich Fromm and Herbert Marcuse as members of the Frankfurt School, located from 1923 to 1934 in Germany and afterward transferred to America, would also take issue with a less humanistic interpretation.[49]

The second major objection to the Lévi-Straussian enterprise asks, in general, whether it is legitimate to apply a linguistic method to the entire sphere of culture. Behind this reservation lies a deeper critique, coming from the phenomenological-existential camp. The question is first broached by Handricourt and Granai, and Lévi-Strauss's reply is contained in the fifth chapter of *Structural Anthropology*. Ricoeur raises this same question again in a discussion with Lévi-Strauss, Axelos, and others, which was published in *L'Esprit* and which provides perhaps the best statement of the linguistic critique. Ricoeur points out that phonemes are manipulated unconsciously in language, whereas myths (especially the biblical ones) have a sense that transcends an unconscious one; this sense is manifest and remains irreducible to the hidden sense. Especially in Semitic and Indo-European cultures (about which Lévi-Strauss says very little), content has, as it were, determined the structure, and not vice versa, as in the cultures he has selectively studied. This content (theologically called a "deposit of faith") has structured whole new areas in architecture, literature, philosophy, and other disciplines. Ricoeur's notion of the *kerygmatic* is here being opposed to Lévi-Strauss's structural.[50] Lévi-Strauss, Ricoeur notes, has opted for "syntax over semantics," and for this reason Ricoeur calls the founder of structuralism an exponent of "l'agnosticisme moderne," a man who is in despair of any real meaning: Ricoeur claims that Lévi-Strauss might discover meaning, but it is the meaning of nonmeaning ("le sens du non-sens"), a syntactical arrangement of a discourse that says nothing. This is a telling consideration and, putting it in the simplest and most colloquial of terms, really asks; after all is said and done, what do you have when you have it? Are Lévi-Strauss's investigations anything more than fascinating and flashing displays of Olympian chess games,[51] brilliant displays of logical forms? [52]

Ricoeur is working from the perspective of his hermeneutical philosophy. *Hermeneutics*, as he defines it, is "the theory of the operation of understanding in its relation to the interpretation of texts." The key word in this "working definition" is *interpretation*. Hermeneutics most often arouses mention of the name of Dilthey, who conceives of life in the pluralistic fullness of its experiences as the proper subject matter of philosophy. By *life* is not meant the narrower conception advanced by the empiricists—ultimately only discrete, atomic sense data or, at the most, ideas mechanistically constructed out of these data. Rather, for Dilthey, we feel the blue Monday, we see the lovely girl, we hear the angry thunder; we do not infer a depressing mood into the day, we do not reason to loveliness in the girl, nor do we argue to anger in the thunder. "Life appears as a dynamism that structures itself." From this fusion of dynamism and structure Dilthey's hermeneutical methodology grows. To understand a human expression, one must understand, Dilthey proclaims, the context in which it appeared. Thus, understanding involves immersion in the social conditions that are the context of the object of understanding. And understanding demands a grasp of the cultural conditions that determine a particular cultural expression. Before we can grasp the meaning of a movement in an unknown game, we must know the rules of the game.[53]

The hermeneutical approach is antithetical to the structural approach to understanding. The structural approach, which, as was pointed out in Chapter 5, is a variation on the Freudian interplay between transference and counter-transference, allows that one who has never seen playing cards, or a game of cards, ought to be able to "reconstruct," by the play of the cards, both the rules of the game and the structure of the deck. Contextual, environmental, temporal, societal, and cultural differences matter little in a search for synchronic harmonies. But in hermeneutical understanding there is still a primacy placed upon individual understanding of ordered wholes. There is a primacy placed upon intuition or upon " 'internal connection' or 'inner connection' by which the life of another person lets itself be discerned and identified in its manifestations." The transition from Dilthey's hermeneutics to Husserl's phenomenology and the various "structured wholes" of transcendental eidetic intuition is discernible. Ricoeur writes: "Spiritual life fixes itself within structured wholes capable of being understood by another person. From 1900 on Dilthey depended upon Husserl to give consistency to this notion of 'interconnection.' Husserl at that time was establishing that psychic life was characterized by intentionality, the property of intending a meaning capable of being identified." Hermeneutics, according to Ricoeur, comes down strongly on the side of subjectivity and the development in Husserl's work of the Cartesian *cogito*. This attitude, perhaps, leads Ricoeur into his linguistic critique of Lévi-Strauss, who appears to stand for *reason* as opposed to *life* philosophy.[54]

Ricoeur thinks that the generative grammar of Chomsky offers the necessary correction to the "taxinomies, closed inventories, and already settled combinations" of structuralism. Ricoeur feels that (non-Chomskyan) structuralism has overemphasized *la langue* (the system of a language) and has ignored *la parole* (the individual speech acts)—to use Ferdinand de Saussure's original distinction (given in his *Cours de linguistique générale*).[55] For Ricoeur, structural linguistics (dealing with *la langue*) only prepared the way for Chomsky's problematic "production of new sentences." Speech as discourse and the work of Humboldt (Chomsky's predecessor) in the field of the *production* of speech are invoked. Chomsky's distinction between *competence* and *performance* ("related, respectively, to *langue* and *parole*") are employed as the tools for the "conversion" of structure into "event." *Event*, for Ricoeur, signifies what *encounter* usually means in an existentialistic context. For Ricoeur, the subordination of "event" to "structure" means something similar to the subordination of "encounter" to "transference" for the American existential psychotherapist Rollo May: "the concept of transference can undermine the whole experience and sense of reality in therapy; the two persons in the consulting room become 'shadows,' and everyone else in the world does too. . . . What has been lacking is a concept of encounter, within which, and only within which, transference has genuine meaning. Transference is to *be understood as the distortion of encounter*." [56] What propels Ricoeur toward reading Chomsky as the linguist who will save "event" in a structural approach seems to be the emphasis that Chomsky has always placed on the creativity or "open-endedness" (Chomsky's phrase) of language. This means that "the theory of grammar should reflect the ability that all fluent speakers of a language possess to produce and understand sentences that they have never heard before." Any language consists of an indefinitely large number of grammatically correct sentences, but only a small fraction of these have ever been or ever will be uttered. In Chomsky, a *generative* grammar is one in which the grammar generates "all the sentences of the language and does not distinguish between those that have been attested and those that have not." Ricoeur seems also impressed by Chomsky's invocation of Descartes and the Cartesian rationalist linguists of the seventeenth century. Ricoeur writes: "Chomsky continually opposes a generative grammar to the inventories . . . taxinomies favored by the structuralists. And we are led back to the Cartesians [Chomsky's latest book is titled *Cartesian Linguistics*] and to Humboldt. . . ." [57]

However, it seems quite a dubious enterprise to invoke Chomsky as a corrective to structuralism. Culler rejects Ricoeur's denomination of structuralism as "taxinomies" and claims that generative grammar is still primarily concerned with *la langue*. He admits that Descartes cited animals' inability to use language creatively as proof that they were mechanistic, nonthinking beings. But he immediately claims that a generative grammar "makes even the creation of new sentences a process governed by rules which escape the subject." This he states after citing the structural-sounding utterance of Heidegger: "Language speaks. Man speaks only in so far as he artfully 'complies with' language." [58]

John Searle, in his masterful exposition of Chomsky's thought, attacks the notion that Descartes, while holding a doctrine of innate ideas, also felt that "the syntax of natural languages was innate." In fact, the opposite seems to be the case. According to Searle, even though Descartes held that "the creative use of language distinguishes man from the lower animals," yet he also maintained that only concepts were innate; language was arbitrary and acquired. "He thought that we arbitrarily attach words to our ideas." And then there is the unconscious, which Searle thinks Chomsky needs: "Furthermore Descartes does not allow for the possibility of unconscious knowledge, a notion that is crucial to Chomsky's system." Finally, Searle clearly disagrees with Ricoeur about Chomsky's position in the question of intentional versus structural approach to language. Searle faults Chomsky with not seeing sufficiently clearly that competence is ultimately "the competence to perform," with not seeing that "making a statement to the effect that the flower is red consists in performing an action with the intention of *producing in the hearer the belief* that the speaker is committed to the existence of a certain state of affairs, as determined by the semantic rules attached to the sentence." In short, Searle feels that Chomsky misses the "intentional" character of "speech acts." [59] Searle maintains that Chomsky has also (as much as Lévi-Strauss) ignored the performative aspect of language. He has overlooked the fact that (in the words of the dictum attributed to Merleau-Ponty) "Every attention is an intention and every intention is an 'I can.'"

Another aspect of the objection against applying linguistics to ethnology and the structure of the mind is offered by Edmund Leach in his "Telstar et les Aborigènes ou 'La pensée sauvage.'" [60] Very briefly, Leach does not care for the adoption of the notion of binarism from phonological linguistics, because, according to Leach, humans think in terms of more or less, as well as yes or no, and binarism, although able to deal with the latter mental structure, cannot handle the former.[61] I do not feel that this objection is entirely cogent, for, as I have tried to show, the digital computer of the brain (as Lévi-Strauss envisages it) can handle analogies adequately, though not, perhaps, with as much precision as Leach would wish.

This objection does, however, lead to one that is perhaps wider in scope and is quite common.[62] It charges that Lévi-Strauss is an absolute rationalist attempting to transform lived experience, which in some way escapes reason, into mechanical and static rationalistic structures. In short, Lévi-Strauss wants to transform life into a Leibnizian *mathesis universalis*. Lévi-Strauss's main reply to this type of objection—which parallels, obviously, Kierkegaard's celebrated polemic against Hegel [63]—is that it entirely misunderstands his notion of a qualitative mathematics, which entails the retention of both form and content in structure, and therefore misunderstands the intermediary role (between thing and idea) of symbols. Additionally, the objection seems to misunderstand the notion of Marxist praxis he employs.[64]

But we cannot dismiss this objection out of hand, since it really concerns one of the major lacunae in Lévi-Strauss's structuralism: the role of the individual in the creation of language. At this point, Leach's criticism of binarism and Ricoeur's hermeneutical critique come together. Binarism certainly provides a very convenient methodology for the analysis of a text. The most heterogeneous elements can be tied together in antithetical fashion, and the basic homology of $A : B : X : Y$ seems to be capable of indefinite extension. However, it is precisely this capability that makes one wonder if the *mathesis universalis* is not too universal. Lévi-Strauss argues, by way of illustration, that although sun and moon by themselves cannot be used to signify anything whatsoever, once they are placed in contrast, in mythology, there may be no limit to the contrasts they convey.

One is led, then, even beyond Leach's doubts about universal binarism to the criticism of mechanism (and behaviorism) voiced by Merleau-Ponty, in that the meaning of the whole is not produced by an inductive summing up of the meanings of the parts. Rather, only in light of a hypothesis about the meaning of the whole can the meaning of the parts be defined. Furthermore, does not Lévi-Strauss himself employ a hypothetico-deductive method? Of course he does, as he himself affirms. But the problem then involves the question of the formation of hypotheses. Leach fears that Lévi-Strauss "unconsciously" selects his evidence to fit his theories. Consequently, if he has, for illustration, by volume 2 of the *Mythologiques*, made reference to 353 different myths, there certainly "is a great deal of other, rather similar stuff which he might have used, and we have to take it on trust that it really all says the same thing." Leach's verdict is that it probably does say the same thing, but the suspicion arises basically because Lévi-Strauss's "mathematics of manipulated sensory objects [is] too systematic." He does not allow, according to Leach, enough leeway for the fact that the symbols of primitive thought are heavily loaded with "taboo valuations . . . psychological factors such as evasion and repression. . . ." This disregard of Lévi-Strauss's for the emotionally nonneutral in favor of the "emotionally neutral" Leach attributes to his binarism. I would attribute it, rather, to his "everyday materialism," which, after all, is the most basic hypothesis of the system. In his system, Lévi-Strauss writes, "when the mind is left to communicate with itself and no longer has to come to terms with objects, it is in a sense reduced to imitating itself as object." The mind (*l'esprit*) is simply "a thing among things." Even the unconscious (if this is the meaning of *l'esprit*) is nothing in itself, is as unrelated to its contents as the stomach is to the things in it. And whereas the real *locus* of myths (and musical scores) is in the unconscious, the *locus* of this unconscious is, in a very real sense, nowhere (*de nulle part*). Because the myth comes from nowhere, it is usually given a supernatural origin.[65]

Actually, Leach's judgment is less ethnographic and more existential than even he may suppose. It does seem that, to use Kierkegaard's phrase, there are some situations in experience in which "truth is subjectivity." There may well be some circumstances in which a reality would not exist as an object of experience for me unless I am willing, first, to take a stand toward it. Pascal's injunction to the atheist that, if he wishes to believe, he need only bend his knee and Rollo May's insistence that, at the outset of the psychoanalytic therapy, the patient (or, better, "client") accept that his cure lies in his own, not the analyst's, hands—these are but two of many such situations that come to mind. Perhaps Lévi-Strauss's own hypotheses in his hypothetico-deductive method are themselves illustrations of such subjectivity.

It seems that the essence of the phenomenological-existential critique of structuralism lies in the existential indictment of the assumption really underpinning all of Lévi-Strauss's enterprise. This supposition is the Freudian homeostasis principle, and not even Marxist praxis can save Lévi-Strauss from his subservience to this principle. For Freud, the pleasure principle retreats to its underground lair, and the unconscious is formed because the general tendency of life is to avoid change (the sources of unpleasure) and to seek "the peace of the inorganic." In Lévi-Strauss, the myth performs the same unconscious function: it mediates the (painful) contradictions found in nature. Thus, in Lévi-Strauss, as in Freud's *Beyond the Pleasure Principle*, the inorganic, thanatos, is the goal of the organic. From this starting point he derives his *mathesis universalis* and his emphasis upon synchrony. On the other hand, the existential approach stresses that man does not seek a tensionless state but "rather the striving and struggling for some goal worthy of him." It may even be, argues the existential therapist, that the value connected with striving would lead one to seek, as in Binswanger's celebrated case of Ellen West, the ultimate contradiction: when the organism, in order to fulfill its existence, needs to destroy itself.[66] Interestingly, the traditional Marxist critique (such as Lefebvre's), examined above, coincides here, in its unwillingness to accept a structuralist subordination of the diachronic to the synchronic, with the phenomenological-existential one.[67]

Some of the earliest opposition to incipient psychoanalysis in its turn-of-the-century Viennese days was written by that *enfant terrible* of contemporary Viennese society Karl Kraus. He blames psychoanalysis for destroying the sources of creative fantasy by equating them with neuroses. But to Kraus, most of all, psychoanalysis is the disease for which it proclaims itself the cure. As a self-enclosed system, it is simply another religion, seeking to replace the traditional Judaeo-Christian mythology with its own mythology. And like any self-enclosed religious system, it is impervious to criticism from without. If one accepts the premises, one accepts the conclusions. Kraus's judgment is summed up in the oft-quoted remark "Psychoanalysis is that spiritual disease of which it considers itself to be the cure." [68]

Kraus seems to have anticipated some of the firmest reservations against Lévi-Strauss's structuralism. They coalesce about what I would like to term the *empirical* critique. The core of the empirical resistance to Lévi-Strauss lies in the question of falsifiability. Pettit, who has most recently dealt with it, acknowledges that the degree to which one hypothesis "may be criticised in terms of another . . . is under debate in contemporary philosophy of science." However, he continues his account of Lévi-Strauss's *Mythologiques* by defining a "weak" sense in which a hypothesis must be falsifiable: "a hypothesis must be such that when it is faced with the data it is possible that no fit may be found." He continues by judging Lévi-Strauss's "transformational hypothesis" nonfalsifiable for several reasons. First, the transformational hypothesis is very vague. By this, Pettit indicates that the vaguer the parameters of the transformations become, the less the theory rules out of its extension. For example, in his structural analysis of the Oedipus myth, Lévi-Strauss includes even the Freudian use of it in the Oedipus complex as simply another variant of the myth. The broader the theory's extension, the less its comprehension. Consequently, the less the theory (hypothesis) rules out, the fewer possible falsifiers it has. Furthermore, Lévi-Strauss in his referent analysis of the Oedipus myth uses a descriptive procedure arranging the elements of the myth in columns (which, as I mentioned earlier in this book, "fortuitously" consist of columns of binary oppositions). Since he imposes no limit on the abstractness of the description, the number of elements that could slide under any of these columns is always "indefinite." And Lévi-Strauss himself acknowledges the "inexhaustibility" of myth analysis. Unexpected affinities and oppositions can keep popping up.[69]

Pettit seems to be applying Popper's criterion for the scientific status of a theory. That is, it must be empirically falsifiable; for it to be a truly scientific theory, there would have to be an empirically observable state of affairs that, if it occurred, would refute the theory. A single contrary instance would suffice. Of course, the more a theory rules out, the greater its possible falsifiers. And, according to Popper, the greater, then, is its actual empirical content. On such grounds, Lévi-Strauss's hypotheses have very little empirical content and would not be, in this respect, scientific. There is, however, one other possible rubric under which they might dwell. It would have to be the instrumental criterion holding that theories of unobservable entities may be admitted as scientific if they are understood not as descriptions of realities but as rules of inference by which one observable state of affairs may be predicted from another. In this way, they have no more reality than the meter readings on a yardstick; they predict rather than describe reality.[70]

At certain times Lévi-Strauss sounds as if he were leaning toward such an explanation of scientific theory. For example, he writes that his four-volume *Mythologiques* is itself a myth, the myth of mythology, for it is simply a compendium of mutual translatabilities. Elsewhere, he proclaims that the subject of one of the four volumes is to have no subject, that the myths are no-where, that the unconscious, the place of the myths, is nothing in itself, and so on. However, his "Kantianism without a transcendental subject," his "everyday materialism," his remark as far back as 1950 that the *necessary* laws of the mind have their foundation in "a biochemical substrate," and finally, his obvious aversion to and derogatory remarks about American pragmatism and instrumentalism in *Tristes Tropiques*—all incline me to reject the instrumental criterion as sufficient to ground Lévi-Strauss's structuralism as a science. At the very least, one can say that his language lends itself to a certain imprecison on this point.[71] The problem of falsifiability in Lévi-Strauss is, from an empirical viewpoint, the same as the problem of a myriad number of descriptions of his *esprit humain*. There is, as Leach puts it, a certain "reckless sweep" of his generalizations. His methods tend to "lead into a world where all things are possible and nothing sure." The problem, as Pettit sees it, is that "you make up the rules as you go along." [72]

Simonis attempts to reply to the empirical critique by distinguishing. He feels that one should realize, first, that every theory is not empirical and to this degree, creates its own scientific object (its "facts"). If one were to create a scientific (chemical) theory about strawberries, then one certainly would not be doing so through the medium of seeing strawberries. And, conversely, one could not verify the relevance of this chemical discourse by eating strawberries. Lévi-Strauss, himself, compares anthropology to astronomy, for both allow the discovery of objects that are extremely distant from us, insofar as they are distant. In fact, it is their distance that affords the perception of their objects. Simonis then deals in the following fashion with Popper's question of falsifiability. He claims that the verification through facts in Lévi-Strauss "takes place before and not after the construction of the theory." A "scientific discourse" is created by applying controls at every step "of the construction of the process of moving away from ethnographic facts." [73]

What are we to understand by this reply to the issue of falsifiability?

The first part (that the verification takes place before and not after constructing the theory) seems analogous to the usual response given when Freudian analysis is attacked as a pseudoscience. It is alleged that the verification of the theory about to be constructed lies in the fact that the neurotic patient can usually "recall" the repressed desire (under hypnosis, or through free association).[74] But this "recall" can be, as Quinton observes, seriously questioned. The first reason that he offers for questioning the factual basis of this recall—that "the supposed recollection is always prompted by the analyst, trying out his interpretation on the patient's symptoms"—is clearly incorrect. Early intervention in the patient's free association processes is strongly disfavored in classical psychoanalysis, and it militates against the disengaged attitude of the anthropologist-analyst that is favored by structuralism. Quinton's second reason for questioning the recall is that, if the postulate of infantile sexuality can be established by "direct observation of children's behaviour," then most adults are neurotic and this proposition is "self-contradictory," in that it robs "neurotic" of any real meaning (as if one were to say that "nearly everyone is much taller than the average"). Again, Quinton's reservations arise from his own confusions. Lévi-Strauss's structuralism (like Freud's psychoanalysis) does conclude the universality of neurosis. This is one of the meanings of the mirror-stage in Lacan and the *dédoublement* and mana in Lévi-Strauss. In the light of structuralism, the meaning of "neurosis" must be redefined.

Quinton's subsequent observations are more to the point. He faults psychoanalysis for "the practice of taking the contrary of what the theory predicts as being as much a confirmation of the theory as its originally predicted opposite," since the unconscious, by its very nature, is deceptive. This criticism is closer to the mark and coincides with Pettit's remark that in structural analysis "you make up the rules as you go along." Finally, as to the controls that Simonis claims are exerted by Lévi-Strauss at each step of the construction of the process of moving away from the ethnographic facts, readers should judge for themselves from Lévi-Strauss's analysis of the Oedipus myth and explanation of the structural method, presented in an earlier chapter. Quinton ends by appealing to Wittgenstein's view that Freud was not a scientist but the proposer of a "new notation"—a new and "poetically exciting way of describing familiar things." [75]

Before leaving Quinton's analysis of scientific theory according to Freud, we should mention that some interesting discoveries about the accuracy of Freud's observations have recently been published by Fisher and Greenberg in their *Scientific Credibility of Freud's Theories and Therapy*.[76] They report that considerable clinical evidence now exists for such Freudian concepts as the oral and anal types, the preoccupation of some paranoids with defenses against homosexuality, and the castration complex. The question of the scientific value of his theories is, however, still open.

Interestingly, Leach seems to arrive at the very same conclusions as Quinton when he examines the scientific verifiability of Lévi-Strauss's structuralism. He remarks that, by 1970, "The whole system seems to have developed into a self-fulfilling prophecy which is incapable of test because, by definition, it cannot be disproved." He gives an example from volume 3 of *Mythologiques* of Lévi-Strauss's assuming an example contrary to the theory's prediction as a confirmation of the theory. Leach then wonders aloud whether the theory can ever be tested if contraries can become "supplementary dimensions" (Lévi-Strauss's phrase). He concludes that the really "valuable" part of Lévi-Strauss's contribution is the truly poetic range of associations he brings to bear in the course of his analysis: "in Lévi-Strauss's hands, complexity becomes revealing instead of confusing." Leach agrees with Simonis's earlier (1968) observation that Lévi-Strauss is, primarily, revealing "the structure of aesthetic perception." [77]

I would like to end this excursus on the empirical critique by recalling Roland Barthes's analogy of the structuralist theory to the construction of a ship that is rebuilt over the years, section by section, piece by piece, until not one piece of the original ship is left. Yet Barthes maintains that the ship still exists, because the system is superior to its manifestations.

The Cartesian Background

We can properly understand Lévi-Strauss's achievement only if we situate him in relationship to the philosopher whose scientific endeavor he replaces—Descartes. Lévi-Strauss enters French philosophy as the antithesis of Descartes, who was its modern founder.

As is generally accepted, the Cartesian enterprise is an attempt to found a *mathesis universalis*, a type of universal algebra that was to be consummated by the linking of mathematical certitude even to metaphysics.[1] There is a twofold supposition in Descartes: that extension, on the one hand, exhausts the essence of material reality, whereas thought (which, as we shall presently see, means both the conceptual and volitional sides of man) exhausts the essence of spiritual reality. In accord with the first supposition, Descartes attempts a reduction of physics to geometry and geometry to mathematics. On 27 July 1638, he wrote to his friend Père Mersenne that "my physics is nothing else than geometry." Furthermore, Descartes states that he will accept no principle in physics that is not also accepted in mathematics. He also asks, if there can be such a correlation between two previously unrelated sciences as algebra and geometry, that is, in the Aristotelian scheme, then why can there not be a similar cooperation among all the sciences? This attempt to found a universal mathematics is the very beginning of that analytical reason which Lévi-Strauss defends so strongly in *The Savage Mind* against the onslaughts of Sartrean dialectical reason.[2]

But Descartes, contrary to the usually accepted reading, does not restrict himself to analytical reason. He does, after all, place a limit upon his own mathematical method, and this limit is found in the area of thought that is conceptual but also volitional, the will not being capable of reduction to *mathesis universalis*. In short, the two entities to which the mathematical method and analytical reason cannot be applied are the self and God.

According to Descartes, man is not "a thing among things" (in the Lévi-Straussian phrase), because man is not pure structure. There is, in Descartes's conception of man, an ineffable core that we call his will. Notice, for example, the volitional phraseology applied to Descartes's definition of his *self*: "But what is it then that I know? A thing which thinks. What is a thing which thinks? That is a thing that doubts, that conceives, that affirms, that denies, that wills, that doesn't will, that imagines also, and that feels." But, for Descartes, man is not alone in the ineffable power of his will. Man's will only mirrors the creative power of the Divine Will,[3] and this Will always transcends the sphere of analytical reason. It is in no way capable of penetration by human intelligence. Descartes feels that his predecessors, the medieval scholastics, with their doctrine of essences (natures) found throughout the material universe, have compromised God's inscrutable power, because these natures, which for the scholastics exist unchanging from all eternity, present an order of intrinsic possibilities inherent in the universe, apart from the creative power of the Divine Will. These intrinsic possibilities mirror God's ideas of his own essence, and they are, for the scholastics, the final cause of all that exists. In their place, Descartes maintains that only the efficient causality of the universe, that is, God's creative Will, can be the object of philosophical discussion. According to the twenty-eighth principle of the *Principles of Human Knowledge*, "It is not at all necessary to examine to what end God has made each thing, but only by what means he willed that it be produced." [4]

The Reversal of Descartes

How does this Cartesian employment of both analytical and dialectical reason fit into our Lévi-Straussian exegesis? To answer this question, we must once again turn to Sartre, for Sartre had radically reshaped Descartes's doctrine of divine and human voluntarism. By accepting the existentialist (that is, Nietzschean and even, to a degree, Hegelian) notion of the death of God, Sartre concentrated all of Descartes's emphasis upon voluntarism in man: Descartes's God becomes Sartre's man, and humanism becomes the center of modern French philosophy. Sartre writes, "It

took two centuries of crisis . . . for man to regain the creative freedom
that Descartes placed in God, and for anyone finally to suspect the following truth, which is an essential basis of humanism: man is the being
as a result of whose appearance a world exists." [5]

And now Lévi-Strauss appears and proclaims the death not of God but
of man. To paraphrase Sartre, Lévi-Strauss proclaims that the world is
the being as a result of whose appearance man appears.[6] Thus, there
has been a progressive constriction of the role of subjectivity in French
philosophy, until human culture is, with Lévi-Strauss, ultimately re-
absorbed into nature. In its way, structuralism is, as Sartre terms it, a
reactionary movement—not because, as he thinks, it is the last effort of
the bourgeoisie to stop the historical class struggle that will eventually
liberate the proletariat, but because it is a reversal of French philosophy
back to an earlier pre-Cartesian stage.[7]

It is, then, entirely appropriate for Auzias to refer to structuralism's
"quasi-Aristotelian distinction between form and content," [8] to talk of
Lévi-Strauss's theory being intellectualistic but not idealistic,[9] and to
mention that there is absolutely nothing of the existentialists' absurdity
or gratuity in structuralism.[10] Lévi-Strauss calls his own system basically
a determinism and a realism. In pre-Cartesian philosophy and in a prehistorical age of philosophy, the hands on the face of the philosophical
clock pointed upward to eternity, to God. In post-Cartesian philosophy
they pointed along a horizontal axis to man. Now, in structuralism, the
hands point downward to those forces that transcend and constitute man.
The question must be asked, if the hands point downward on a vertical
axis, by continuing that axis do we not see them pointing upward once
again? Then, perhaps, Sartre is correct: this other who, in structuralism,
thinks through me—is this not a surreptitious reintroduction of God into
philosophy? [11]

And certainly, the terms employed by Lévi-Strauss can lead us to no
other conclusion than that structuralism is a reemergence of essentialism
in French philosophy, which has been dominated by voluntarism from
Descartes onward. Unlike Descartes, who reserved liberty for the *self*
and *God*, there is absolutely no room for the *will* in Lévi-Strauss's world:
"Starting from ethnographic experience, I have always aimed at drawing
up an inventory of mental patterns, to reduce apparently arbitrary data
to some kind of order, and to attain a level at which a kind of necessity
becomes apparent, underlying the illusions of liberty." When Descartes,
in the second meditation, in the passage on the piece of wax, provided

a foundation for modern science by separating the quantitative (capable of mathematical analysis) from the qualitative (or the primary qualities —figure, magnitude, motion and rest, and number—from the secondary qualities—sight, sound, taste, smell, and so on), he created a dichotomy that has not only enabled modern science to progress but has also remained with modern science, preventing it from entering the realm of secondary qualities. That realm has traditionally been considered too "subjective" and therefore ineffable for mathematical calculation. The triumph of Lévi-Strauss lies in his extending the realm of scientific inquiry even into the area once thought to be the realm of ineffability,[12] by, of course, reducing the subject to a mere abstract illusion. This "new mathematics" of Lévi-Strauss teaches us that, in his own words, "the domain of necessity is not necessarily the same as that of quantity." [13]

Leach correctly sees that the major contribution of Lévi-Strauss lies precisely in this area of the resurrection of an essentialism. He indicates that Lévi-Strauss has taken a step beyond the usual "manipulation" of symbols in the mind, symbols that are thought to represent "things" existing "out there"—beyond the classical interpretation of thinking. Symbols, for Lévi-Strauss, themselves exist "out there" in the environment and "play logical games by themselves without conscious human intervention." According to Leach, through Lévi-Strauss we have now gone full circle. We are back at the age of primitive man, when "out there" was also "in here," when totemic-species categories and food-preparation categories were both things good for thinking and things good to eat. The central paradigm of this monistic union of culture and nature, for Lévi-Strauss, is music. Music, myth, and dreaming are all machines for the suppression of time. Since the repetitions of a musical score depend on the listeners' physiological rhythms, music is natural. But music also operates upon a cultural grid, which encompasses "the hierarchical relations among [the notes] on the scale." We behold in the cultural grid the synchronic totality of the musical work, its internal organization, which catches and enfolds time "as one catches and enfolds a cloth flapping in the wind." Music and myth, according to Lévi-Strauss, appear as conductors of an orchestra of which the listeners are the silent performers. Although music's being is in use, and I listen to myself through it, the real center of the work is impossible to determine. When a myth is repeated, the listeners are receiving a message that comes from nowhere. Music and myth bring man face to face with potential objects of unconscious truths. Lévi-Strauss contends that Richard Wagner was "the undeniable originator of the structural analysis of myths." [14]

In one respect, all of this interpretation recalls, of course, Schopenhauer. The apotheosis of music and the unifying power of music, allowing man to experience both his physiological individuality and his collective (cultural) unity with nature, summon up Schopenhauer's belief that music alone puts us in direct contact with the unificatory power of the universe, lying behind all phenomena—the will itself. Perhaps we encounter here a residue of the tradition of irrationality in French philosophy passing from Schopenhauer to Bergson and thence to Lévi-Strauss. But the unconscious is, for Lévi-Strauss, structured like a language—*is* a language. Hence, the analogy with Schopenhauer begins to break down. It quickly revives if we compare Lévi-Strauss's remarks on myth and music with those of his actual predecessor in this area, Nietzsche. In his first work, the *Birth of Tragedy from the Spirit of Music*, Nietzsche appeals to the German people of his day to pay heed to the union of myth and music being revived at that time by Wagner. In the same work, Nietzsche names the period of pre-Socratic Western philosophy as an age when the aims of philosophy were natural and universal. The pre-Socratic philosophers concerned themselves with *peri phuseos (concerning nature)*, which preoccupation predominated in Greek philosophy and tragedy (Aeschylus and Sophocles) until the rise of Euripides and Socrates. The latter changed the course of Western man's interest from the objective to the subjective by asking the questions of morality, exploring the problems of the individual and his meaning. Nietzsche advocates the rebirth of tragedy for the Germans. It will be there, in the collective *mythos* unfolding through Wagner's resurrection of the pre-Christian Nordic mythology, that the German peoples will find the collective meanings of their newly constituted political unity in the German Empire. Greek tragedy, Nietzsche asserts, began with the choral odes. The audience, originally, was identified with the chorus. When the Greeks attended the theater, they renewed, in their choral repetitions of the collectively accepted mythology, the beliefs underpinning their pre-Christian civilization. This pre-Judeo-Christian spirit Nietzsche terms the Dionysian. It is the union of form and matter in a fatalistic oneness with nature. Man is not a problem to be solved, as he might become in later philosophy, psychology, morality, and religion; he is an object to be dissolved into the natural structures that come together in him.[15]

Again, the Zero-Value

Both the terminology employed by Lévi-Strauss and the definitions given to these terms show us that structuralism, by its extension of science to secondary qualities, is a reversion to a pre-Cartesian stage of philosophy in which the "sacramental character" of the universe [16]—the cosmos as revealing the *vestigia Dei*, a universe in which all things are interrelated [17] and nothing exists without some element of necessity inherent in it—is at the forefront of structuralist thought.

Mana, for example, is the pure variable (the *signifiant flottant*); mana as the zero-value (and the avunculate and the chiefs of the Nambikwara also as zero-value) functions in the same way as the zero-phoneme, which exists in opposition to the "absence" of phonemes. It has in itself no signification but is capable of taking on any signification whatsoever. Mana, then, mediates between signifier and signified wherever a lack between them is revealed. It fulfills the role of the paradigmatic and is exemplified in the metaphorical thinking of the natives. It is the mediating power of the human mind. It is the Hegelian notion that to achieve selfhood it is necessary to be in relation to another. For the primitive, the zero-value, which plays the same role in his world that natural science does in ours, is simply "the subjective reflection of the demand of an unperceived totality." It is a category of thought, not of the real, and having no meaning in itself, being completely neuter,[18] it can become all things; that is, it can take on any value whatsoever, provided that this value remains part of the reserve of floating signifier. The zero-value functions, in Lévi-Strauss, very much like the scholastics' *possible*, in that it provides interior harmony and meaning to the *actual*. Another, more modern analogy to the zero-values will be, it seems to me, the "unaddressed phenomena" of the biologist Adolph Portmann.[19]

Both Lévi-Strauss and Portmann react adversely to evolutionary theory. And their conclusions—the zero-value and the unaddressed phenomena— are exterior manifestations of the interior harmony of the totality, be it the group for Lévi-Strauss or the organism for Portmann. Portmann points out that the functionalistic Darwinian notion of natural selection cannot explain many of the structural phenomena found in nature. A functionalist must maintain that natural structures (the shape and colors of sea shells, animals' fur, animal organs, and so on) must have developed either for cryptic purposes (to hide the animal in his natural habitat) or for semantic purposes (to attract a mate for procreation or another animal of a different species for nutrition). Yet there are still some natural phenomena that cannot be catalogued under these two headings. For example, the beautiful odors and convolutions of some (eyeless) mollusk's shells neither hide them in their surroundings nor attract mates for reproduction or other species for nutrition; the pattern of the pearly butterfly's wings are formed even where the wing is never exposed to light. For Portmann, these natural phenomena can, then, have only one purpose: *display*. Hence, they are called "unaddressed," insofar as they are not themselves patterns of communication.[20]

Mana, as it is used in Lévi-Strauss, also recalls the "MacGuffin" in Alfred Hitchcock's films. The MacGuffin is the device, the gimmick that keeps the plot together, the story line going, and the interest of the audience sustained. It is the glue of the film, the intrinsic possibility of the entire enterprise. But, as Hitchcock explains it, the MacGuffin is totally unimportant in itself. Frequently, a writer collaborating for the first time on a Hitchcock film becomes obsessed with the importance of the Mac-Guffin. For example, in *The Thirty-Nine Steps*, what are the spies after? Why was the woman at the beginning of the film stabbed in the back? What huge secret had she stumbled across? Well, it all turns out that the MacGuffin was simply the formula for constructing an airplane engine. The spies use Mr. Memory's brain to smuggle it out of the country. In *The Lady Vanishes*, the tune that the old lady has memorized, containing some kind of coded message, is the MacGuffin. In *North by Northwest*, it is the "government secrets" that the "importer-exporter" (James Mason) smuggles in and out of the country. Early in the creation of the film, Hitchcock informs the neophyte writer that the MacGuffin is totally irrelevant to the story. In fact, the MacGuffin, he asserts, is "the emptiest, the most nonexistent" part of the film. It is "boiled down to its purest expression: nothing at all." It would be an error for "the logicians" to attempt to "figure out the truth of a MacGuffin, since it is beside the point." All that matters is that the plans, secrets, or documents seem to be of vital importance to the characters. Hitchcock compares his Mac-Guffins with the original ones as they appeared in the novels of Rudyard Kipling. The MacGuffin in Kipling was usually the secret plans that had to be stolen out of a fortress. Particularly interesting here is Truffaut's comment on this matter: "these pictures, hinged around a MacGuffin, are the very ones that some of the critics have in mind when they claim that 'Hitchcock's got nothing to say.' The only answer to that is that a film-maker isn't supposed to say things; his job is to show them." Truffaut clearly understands Hitchcock to be a structuralist film-maker. Behind the sense, there is only non-sense, as Ricoeur insists.[21]

Most Hitchcock films revolve around a central scene, and that central scene around a central object. The scene and the object carry with them the entire import of the film. For example, in *Suspicion*, the central object is a glass of milk, which Cary Grant carries to his wife's bedroom. If she drinks it, her suspicions that he might be a murderer will not have conquered over her love. If she does not drink it, then suspicion wins out, for she suspects that he will poison her that evening. In order to concentrate the audience's attention on the glass of milk, Hitchcock placed a hidden light right inside the milk so that the liquid is luminous. Furthermore, in a Hitchcock film each object receives its meaning from its relationship to every other object, or, at least, every other central object in the film. And objects are frequently transformed into other objects. In fact, one of the means of developing suspense in a Hitchcock film is the fact that nothing ever is as it seems. In *Saboteur*, the Fifth Avenue mansion of a wealthy New York society matron harbors a nest of Nazi spies. In *Psycho*, the demeanor of a quiet, respectable motelkeeper conceals the brain of a homicidal paranoid-schizophrenic. In *Rear Window*, the impersonal façade of a Manhattan apartment building disguises a myriad number of seething emotional conflicts within, including those motivating a hatchet murderer. And so on. The audience learns that what is hidden in the object world is overt and disclosed in the code. The glass of milk in *Suspicion* carries with it the metaphorical import of the entire film. The movie is constructed in the manner of Lévi-Strauss's *bricolage*: one object is transformed into another, and this one into a third, and so on. Hitchcock's early training as an engineer and his rather esoteric hobby of memorizing train timetables illustrate the mental attitude of a director who has the entire film and all the parts of each scene and each day's shooting mapped out in his head before he actually arrives on the set. Truffaut accepts the Eric Rohmer-Claude Chabrol thesis, stated in their (1957) *Hitchcock*, that Hitchcock "is one of the greatest inventors of form in the history of cinema. . . . Here form does not merely embellish content, but actually creates it." What holds the entire world of objects together is the "floating signifier" Hitchcock calls the MacGuffin, which, because it has no signification in itself, is capable of taking on any signification whatsoever.[22]

Returning to Lévi-Strauss, we find that the the zero-value is a pure symbol. It is man himself who, after all, is simply "the place of language" for Lévi-Strauss.[23] Man, then, is the zero-value. And since he is simply a symbol, that is, the area in which the self and the other, through language, are one, Lévi-Strauss can resurrect Aristotelian *hylomorphism* under the name of symbolism and return to pre-Cartesian science: "Our task, then, is to use the concept of the sign in such a way as to introduce these secondary qualities into the operations of truth." [24]

This value, which in itself is *zero* and therefore can become all things, is also reminiscent of the scholastics' philosophical conception of the nature of God, who because he was everywhere was nowhere (in no one physical place), who because he contained all perfection could not be limited or finite in nature, and so on: *qui manet in aeternum creavit omnia simul.* Long before man entered the universe, the "eternal necessities" of God's nature were, for the scholastic, present there *ab aeterno.* Before man knew creation, creation mirrored God's necessary being. The intrinsic possibilities (*possibilia*) of God's nature existed from all eternity, and man only existed when one of these possibles was made into an actual (*actualia*).[25]

We find the identical notion in Lévi-Strauss's writing about the zero-value: "The universe signified well before it began to know that it signified." And again, in a discussion with Ricoeur, Axelos, and others on structuralism: "thought begins before men." For Lévi-Strauss, mana, the "floating signifier," exists precisely because for man there is an over-abundance of signifier in relation to the things signified. Man divides this surplus of signification according to the laws of symbolic thought, so that there may be a complementarity, an equation between signifier and signified. At this stage, language is born as an attempt to relate analogously the different parts of man's universe. The gap between signifier and signified is, in the mentality of the primitive, "reabsorbable only for the Divine Understanding." Man thinks according to analogies precisely because the collective unconscious (the source of language) exists, so that two entities that might be conjoined in the code (and therefore "known" as conjoined or continuous) might be separated in the message. Consequently, there is a distinction for Lévi-Strauss between language and knowledge. Knowledge, the process by which we identify certain aspects of the signifier and certain aspects of the signified in relationship to one another, began very slowly and was marked by continuity. But language, marked by discontinuity, came all in one swoop (that is, man is qualitatively different from the subhuman because of language).[26]

The entire import, then, of mana is that it allows exchange to take place: it is the "something more" in exchange rather than the things exchanged; as is evident from mana, the value of exchange is found in the exchange itself.[27] I submit that the preceding notion of a zero-value and the exchange between men with which it is identified by Lévi-Strauss, is nothing else than a totally empiricized notion of the *analogia entis* prominent in pre-Cartesian scholasticism, through the Platonic notion of participation, and that, in this interpretation, Lévi-Strauss becomes a strange combination of Comte and Aquinas.[28] Gilson writes, "The metaphysics of analogy . . . surely all that would be to fall back into a pre-scientific state of mind and reason in the style of a primtive?" [29] Significantly, Lévi-Strauss explains Gilson's comment in a very rewarding image that illustrates the analogical view of reality:

> The knowledge which it [the savage mind] draws [from the world] is like that afforded of a room by mirrors fixed on opposite walls, which reflect each other (as well as objects in the intervening space) although without being strictly parallel. . . . The savage mind deepens its knowledge with the help of *imagines mundi*. It builds mental structures which facilitate an understanding of the world in as much as they resemble it. In this sense savage thought can be defined as analogical thought.[30]

At this moment, the moment of language, society is born, and man transcends the animal.[31] The attitudes of two people in communication acquire a meaning that they would not possess alone. But man forever dreams of that moment when the law of exchange could be evaded, when man could acquire his selfhood alone, when he could gain without sharing. Of course, these are always dreams, like the Sumerian myth of the golden age,[32] and do not correspond to reality, where one can never "keep to oneself." Involved here is the last and deepest stage of Lévi-Straussian structuralism. Exchange marks the emergence of man from nature, but conversely, Lévi-Strauss wishes to resituate man in nature, by showing that the rules of exchange are universal natural laws. The result is "an impossible situation," since if structuralism were to attain its ends, "all language would have disappeared." Thus, we end in structuralism with "une science 'silencieuse,' " in the sense that Lévi-Strauss explained in the *The Scope of Anthropology*: the golden age when society would be freed (by confining *progress* to machines) from domination by the structures of subordination, and exchange as a surmounting of inequalities would be abolished. We have a foretaste of this golden age, according to

Lévi-Strauss, in music, which, through the natural bodily rhythms by which it operates, lives itself out in the listener, while the listener hears himself through the music. Thus ensues a passage from culture to nature, and from the word to silence. The ultimate goal of structuralism is for man to discover "that he is a natural rhythm." For this reason, Simonis contends that structuralism is "a logic of aesthetic perception" enshrining "an esthetic humanism." We return, then, to "mana" as the source of all esthetic. Structuralism, at least to this degree, is more an art than a science.[33]

Finally, mana is the creative force (Bergson again) that is both the source of Lévi-Strauss's esthetic (his logic of secondary qualities) and the principle of all structures. The work of Jacques Derrida on the role of mana in Lévi-Strauss is, perhaps, particularly enlightening in this regard. Derrida wants us to reevaluate the place of writing and presence in Western philosophy. He claims that the dominance of the voice as the primary means of communication has led to a "metaphysics of presence" which falsely allows us to conclude that through speech we come face to face with objects and reality. But, with the breakup of "logocentrism" (the dominance of the spoken word), writing takes on a new significance. Writing under the dynasty of phonocentrism (the influence of the spoken word) was only secondary, derived from a sound that in turn signified. Logocentrism predominates, for Derrida, in phenomenology, with its emphasis on the presence of the *eidos*, and even in Lévi-Strauss. Derrida utilizes the notion of a decentered structure inherent in Saussurian linguistics. Meaning arises from differentiation (*différence*), or the binary opposition of phonemes, which becomes, for Derrida, an infinite play of signifiers. But to differ is also to defer (*différance* as defer-ment), to postpone, or hold back. By this Derrida intends a rejection of absolute presence in either speech or writing. However, writing brings out this deferment very clearly. In writing, meaning is always only a "trace," an already-happened. In writing, there is always a gap between what it is and what it says. The text and its meaning are never one. From this difference arises interpretation, as an attempt to bridge this gap. A text, then, can have no ultimate meaning, for writing never " 'reproduces' a reality beyond itself, nor does it 'reduce' that reality. In its new freedom, it can be seen to cause a new reality to come into being." [34]

It is important that we consider, for a moment, the Saussurian diacritical function of signs, that is, the concept that they function only by virtue of their differences one from the other and that the link between signifier and signified, in itself, is arbitrary. Jakobson expresses this concept very well, citing Bloomfield: "The phonemes of a language are not sounds but merely sound features lumped together which the speakers have been trained to produce and recognize in the current of speech sounds—just as motorists are trained to stop before a red signal be it an electric signal-light, a lamp, a flag, or what not, although there is no disembodied redness apart from these actual signals." The signifier, in this case the red light, flag, and so on, embodies a signification, only in a particular metaphorical system. It is from the system that its meaning comes, and not from some immaterial realm in which a signification of danger should be tied to a disembodied, archetypal redness. The arbitrary character of the sign—arbitrary, that is, prior to its incorporation into a system—is exemplified by the fact that, as far as the traffic signals are concerned, the group could very well have adopted green to signify danger and red to signify safety. In this case, the colors would become attached to somewhat different semantic functions; green would probably signify venemous, icy—in short, dangerous—whereas red would probably mean warmth, human communication—in short, serenity. Thus, a sign is arbitrary before being created by a particular group, but once created, its function takes on a double relationship to the natural, biological structure of the brain and to the ensemble of other signs, that is, to the linguistic universe, which is systematic.[35]

To offer one more illustration from Lévi-Strauss, he observes that though *fromage* and *cheese* mean the same thing, they do so with slightly different shades of meaning. For him (who is bilingual, having taught during the war in New York), *fromage* evokes a heavy, oily substance, not given to crumbling, and *cheese* evokes a lighter, fresher, slightly more sour substance, more prone to crumble in the mouth, reminding him of the French *fromage blanc* ("cottage cheese"). His conclusion is most important, illustrating as it does the idea that the unconscious is no entity in itself but simply a name applied to the *way* (or system) that different semantical functions interact with one another, brought to being through the exchanges (reciprocities, and so on) of members of a group: "The 'archetypal cheese,' therefore, is not always the same for me, according to whether I am thinking in French or in English." [36]

It is here that the concept of the decentered structure (inherent in the diacritical function of signs) and Lévi-Strauss's mana (which is nowhere but is the intrinsic possibilities of all significations) come together. In an insightful symposium paper given at Johns Hopkins University in the late sixties, Derrida continues to explain his notion of decentering and its relationship to mana. He calls the reader's attention to the fact that Lévi-Strauss's critique of the ethnocentrism of ethnology appears precisely at the time, in Western philosophy, when Nietzsche's critique of metaphysics, Freud's examination of self-presence, "that is, the critique of consciousness," and Heidegger's destruction of metaphysics have all, recently, had their say.[37] By the "critique of ethnocentrism" is meant, of course, the castigation of the idea that Western civilization is the center from which to judge all other civilizations, especially primitive ones. Perhaps Lévy-Bruhl and Sartre would, according to Lévi-Strauss, be most at fault here.

According to Derrida, however, Lévi-Strauss still does not deal with the implications of his own thought, for while exposing the limits of ethnocentric language and concepts, he still uses them as instruments in his method. The distinction between nature and culture that Lévi-Strauss ultimately rejects but preserves as an instrument for his method is offered by Derrida as an example of doing ethnology with the concepts of an already rejected ethnology. But Derrida repeats his observation that there is, in Lévi-Strauss, the roots of a decentered ethnology. It becomes visible in the "Overture" to *The Raw and the Cooked*, in which Lévi-Strauss rightly declares that there exists no end or term to mythical analysis, and no unity can ever be grasped at the end of a work of decomposition. That is, mythological discourse is itself mythomorphic: it has the form of that of which it speaks. If first-order codes are those in which language consists, Lévi-Strauss comments, then myths are second-order codes; his book itself is the draft of a third-order code; and so on. Thus, his "book on myths itself [is] . . . in its own way, a myth." [38]

Here, then, according to Derrida, Lévi-Strauss correctly abandons "all reference to a *center*, to a *subject*, to a privileged *reference*, to an origin, or to an absolute *archè*." Derrida notes that Lévi-Strauss, as early as 1950, in his "Introduction to the Work of Marcel Mauss," spoke of the "super-abundance of signifier, in relation to the signifieds to which this super-abundance can refer," and wrote of mana as a *"valeur symbolique zéro,"* aligning it with the zero-phoneme in linguistics; as early as 1950, then, according to Derrida, Lévi-Strauss foresaw the decentering of the structure. The "disruption of presence" inherent in Lévi-Strauss's work coalesces, Derrida decides, in the concept of "freeplay" (*jeu*) that surfaces frequently in Lévi-Strauss's writings, especially in the *Conversations with George Charbonnier, Race and History,* and *The Savage Mind.* "Freeplay" is "a field of infinite substitutions in the closure of a finite ensemble." It is the concept of "freeplay" in Lévi-Strauss that, according to Derrida, creates structuralism's "tension with history," for historicity has always required "the determination of being as presence." "Freeplay" is, again, "the disruption of presence." Only Nietzsche, Derrida concludes, fully explores "the joyous affirmation of the freeplay of the world . . . without truth, without origin." [39]

I have already explored the conceptual relationship of Lévi-Strauss and Nietzsche regarding their views on myth and music. I think we must return, once again, to Nietzsche to fully grasp the theme of a godless decentered structure in Lévi-Strauss. For it now appears that, like the mind of David Hume, in which there are only players on a stage (passing thoughts), but no stage, there may be in Lévi-Strauss, in a decentered structure in which "God is dead," only divine thoughts (essences, structures) but no divine mind.

Lévi-Strauss as an Essentialist

At this point, mention should be made of the psychohistorical interpretation of Lévi-Strauss given by Stanley Diamond and John Murray Cuddihy. Psychohistory is a variation on the Freudian theme that phylogenesis reproduces ontogenesis. The Bullitt-Freud biography of Woodrow Wilson, portraying Wilson's political troubles as a category of his difficulties with his own masculinity and his need to fail, is a prime example of the psychologizing of history. Psychohistory also appears in Freud's treatment of men like Leonardo and Dostoyevsky.[40]

Anthropologist Stanley Diamond and sociologist John Murray Cuddihy find the framework of Lévi-Strauss's achievement in his "Jewish" preoccupation, expressed or unconscious, in overcoming the "primal antinomy" of Jewish culture, the ancient "Jewish problem" of the "socialization of Jews in the West in the post-Emancipation era—namely, the 'primitive classification' of the world into 'goyim' and 'ourselves.'" All the subsequent binary oppositions of nature-culture, in Lévi-Strauss, are reducible to the primary one, for Cuddihy. In this psychohistorical interpretation, the "return of the repressed" is all-important. The preoccupation with ritual cleanliness, inherited by Lévi-Strauss from his religious forebears and explicitly seen by him in the kosher laws of the dining room of his grandfather (who was the rabbi of Versailles) becomes the basis of Lévi-Strauss's castigation of the West in *L'Origine des manières de table* (and of "Western, modern, Christian civilization") for its belief that impurity comes from outside the self. In this view, Lévi-Strauss is objecting to what Christianity has retained from its Jewish origins. It is not, then, simply a question of distinguishing Gentile from Jew, but one of distinguishing the Jew-Gentile subjectivistic involvement in the individual's purity and its antithesis expressed in the mythological thinking of the so-called savage people, who are really more civilized than we are.[41]

Understandably, then, the basic opposition in Lévi-Strauss is ultimately that of being and nonbeing; the end of *L'homme nu* (1971) and Lévi-Strauss's citation of Hamlet's "To be or not to be" is mentioned. This is seen as "a metaphysicization" of Durkheim's and Mauss's work. At the very least, Cuddihy's explanation sees Lévi-Strauss as a secularized metaphysician, concerned more with Being than with individual beings. In this way, Lévi-Strauss extends the work of relevation begun by Marx and Freud. Marx shows that the economic behavior of the Jews (*Judentum*, a German word standing for both Judaism and, derivately, commerce) is the stuff also of the Gentile bourgeois society. Freud demonstrates that "socially improper behavior can be psychologically normal . . . and socially proper behavior can be truly sick." Lévi-Strauss simply extends and develops the idea of the "founding patriarchs of Jewish intellectual culture in the Diaspora . . . Marx and Freud," by rejecting "the whole idea of social evolution." He becomes ahistorical by a reaction to the historicity inherent in *both* Judaism and Christianity.[42]

Diamond continues the psychohistorical reading by distinguishing in the Jewish tradition between the prophet and the priest. The "prophetic sense" is "existential, concrete, liberating, focusing on the uniqueness of self and others"; it is constantly attempting "to break through into freedom, personal meaning, and socially lived faith." Examples of this sense are the Hasidic movement of the eighteenth century, the derivative theology of Martin Buber, and the interpretations of Heschel. These represent Jewish "authenticity" because these writers choose themselves as Jews and abandon "the myth of the universal man." But the priestly sense reflects a continuous avidity to absorb all nature. It defends, interprets, and falls back upon the ritualized codes. It represents a rationalism and a passion for the universal. It is an inauthentic sense, because, in it, the Jew does not recognize his own Jewishness but tries to reduce, to dissolve himself and all other men into the structures underlying man's experience of individuality and ethnic particularity. Lévi-Strauss becomes, for Diamond, a glaring specimen of the priestly sense in Jewish tradition.[43]

On and on the psychohistorical pattern can be developed. The difficulty with this kind of exegesis is that it becomes itself an instance of what Diamond calls the priestly sense. Too easily it categorizes, and, in so doing, it can fall into a psychological fallacy, losing sight of the uniqueness and "authenticity" of an author's work. There is, however, a certain ring of substantiality to both Cuddihy's and Diamond's arguments. It probably lies in the fact that Lévi-Strauss has revitalized an essentialistic sense of the universe and to this degree does work within a theological, religious, prehumanistic tradition. One is reminded of a certain affinity between Lévi-Strauss and Heidegger. The latter also rejects humanism because it prevents man from going beyond human reality to Being. For Heidegger, man "stands in the clearing of Being." Just as the clearing in the forest makes the forest the forest, so man is the gap in Being that lets Being be. "Because man stands outside of himself, he is open to Being, not just to human being." This is all quite reminiscent of Sartre's remark that the structuralists "will not have any transcendence or at least any transcendence made by men." And so Ricoeur protests any existentialist interpretations of Heidegger and points out that the analyses of care, anxiety, and being-toward-death belong, in *Being and Time*, to a meditation on the "worldhood of the world." These analyses appear, he insists, in order to annihilate "the claim of a knowing subject to be the measure of objectivity" and to reveal "a tie to a reality more fundamental than the subject-object relation." Ricoeur specifies that, in Heidegger, the somewhat existential-sounding problem of Dasein, the either-or, is not primary but is a derivative of Dasein's "being-thrown" in the world.[44]

All of this recalls perhaps a more original link between Lévi-Strauss and the nineteenth-century philosopher we have earlier evoked, Nietzsche. If Lévi-Strauss can be seen as a Jewish theologian *manqué*, then he can be so seen only inasfar as Nietzsche could be seen as an immanentized, this-worldly Christian thinker. Both notions would be acceptable if one always incorporated, in Hegelian fashion, the tradition from which one sprang and to which one might later be opposed. In addition to the analogies between myth and music, between the structural and the Dionysian, with which we have already dealt, there is a certain affinity between Lévi-Strauss's synchronic and the eternal return in Nietzsche. The ethical overtones of the synchronic I have explained in Chapter 5 above. There is a similar nonhumanistic ethics implied in Nietzsche's eternal return. He formulates it in 1882 in *The Joyful Wisdom*: "If this thought were to gain possession of you, it would change you, as you are, or perhaps crush you. The question in each and every thing, 'Do you want this once more and innumerable times more?' would weigh upon your actions as the greatest stress. Or how well disposed would you have to become to yourself and to life to *crave nothing more fervently* than this ultimate eternal confirmation and seal?" [45]

There is a certain proximity of spirit in Lévi-Strauss's "everyday materialism" and his appropriation of pity in Rousseau to Nietzsche's eternal return and its consequent in the notion of the *amor fati*. For Nietzsche, man must learn not just passively to accept his fate but to choose what it is. One always has thrust upon oneself what one resists. Therefore, one must not merely accept one's fate but love and embrace it. In this way, one becomes responsible for the entire world. And then, as in EST ([Werner] Ehrhard Seminar Training), pain and even physical aches disappear as the individual is dissolved into the structures of the collective. The constant refrain of "The Seven Seals" in the third part of Nietzsche's *Zarathustra*—"For I love you, O eternity!"—becomes, in Lévi-Strauss, the passion of the primitive mind to overcome the contradictions of nature in their synchronic mythologies. [46]

A similar love of one's fate becomes the basis for the pity and poetry which Rousseau claims are the skeletons of all language and which, in the notion of the general will, structure the social contract. Lévi-Strauss observes: "Rousseau saw very clearly that an act of unanimity is the theoretical pre-condition of the existence of a society. . . . The general will is the latent and continuous decision whereby each individual agrees to exist as a member of a group." The perfect embodiments of the general will, those societies without history that we call primitive, are those without entropy and those that function at a temperature of absolute zero. They are the ideal societies to which Nietzsche points in *The Birth of Tragedy*, in which the people and their mythology are one. Heidegger comments upon Nietzsche's antihumanistic perspective and brings together various Nietzschean themes in a structural way:

The predicates that thought has since antiquity attributed to Being Schelling finds in their final, highest, and hence most perfected form in willing. But the will in this willing does not here denote a capacity of the human soul. The word "willing" here signifies the Be-

ing of beings as a whole. It is will. . . . Schopenhauer has the same
thing in mind when he titles his major work *The World* (not Man)
as Will and Representation. And Nietzsche thinks the same thing
when he recognizes the primal Being of beings as the Will to Power.
. . . The highest will to power—that is, the life force in all life—is
to represent transcience as a fixed Becoming within the Eternal Recurrence of the same, and so render it secure and stable. . . .
"Eternal Recurrence of the Same" is the name of the Being of beings.
"Superman" is the name of the human being who corresponds to
this Being.[47]

Is Nietzsche the creator of the structuralist enterprise? Clearly, it is
impossible to give an unequivocal reply. In the long run, he would not
accept a return to a pre-Cartesian rationalistic perspective of man. And
insofar as "we are not getting rid of God because we still believe in
grammar," the death of God is never achieved in structuralism. But, inas-
much as Nietzsche presents an immanentized Christianity and incorporates in himself that which he despises, only to reveal man as dissolved
into the structures that compose him, then Nietzsche is, like Lévi-Strauss,
a "religious" thinker. This Nietzsche is he who, uncompromising, accepts
analytic reason as that quality of man which is most divine and views
"the reality of becoming as the sole reality . . . and [is] unable to bear
this world, even while refusing to deny it." Or this Nietzsche is he who
writes that "a nihilist is a man who decides that the world as it is ought
not to be, and that the world as it ought to be is non-existent. Accordingly existence is meaningless. . . ." He is a nihilist, who, as Ricoeur
concludes of Lévi-Strauss, exposes the non-sense behind sense, a man the
subject of whose books is to have no subject.[48]

Lévi-Strauss as a Sociobiologist

It seems especially clear, at this juncture, that Lévi-Strauss stands in a
tradition that begins to point, today, toward a sociobiological conception of
man. Though he deals only with the social instincts of man and, particularly, primitive man, the obvious allied question must be, is human behavior only one small area of all the thousands of social animal species?
An alternative formulation of this question could be, how primitive is
primitive? That is, can we expect that genetically controlled social behavior begins with man? After all, can we not push Lévi-Strauss's ma-

terialism ("materialisme vulgaire") back, perhaps, to its roots in the DNA structure? If this were the case, then, one would have to agree with Edward Wilson in *Sociobiology: The New Synthesis* (1975) that altruism is simply genetic selfishness. In this view, the genes always operate to increase the chances of survival of those genes that are identical or similar to themselves. The closer the genetic resemblance, the greater likelihood of altruistic behavior, which thus increases the opportunities for some of the genes to survive.

Just as Lévi-Strauss believes that the myths think themselves out in and through individuals, so, too, for sociobiologists, the genes are capable of using individuals for their own self-interests and survival. At the beginning of his *Sociobiology*, Wilson announces his theme:

> The hypothalamus and limbic system of the brain. . . . flood out consciousness with all the emotions . . . that are consulted by ethical philosophers. . . . What, we are then compelled to ask, made the hypothalamus and limbic system? They evolved by natural selection . . . in evolutionary time the individual organism counts for almost nothing. In a Darwinist sense the organism does not live for itself. Its primary function is not even to reproduce other organisms; it reproduces genes, and it serves as their temporary carrier. . . . The organism is only DNA's way of making more DNA. More to the point, the hypothalamus and limbic systems are engineered to perpetuate DNA.[49]

But, what of the uniqueness of language? Surely here, in the capacity of developing symbols with semantic universality, we do not yet encounter any species other than man who has this power in such a developed fashion. The sociobiologist recognizes man's uniqueness in this capacity and that "culture is overriding," but he also postulates that humans may be on a "dual track of evolution." Their "fastest track is cultural evolution," but they have gotten there by "conventional genetic evolution." Furthermore, there are certain limits to direction and distance to which culture can go before "the genetic imperatives will pull it short." [50]

On the other hand, that which distinguishes, in Lévi-Strauss, nature from culture is the presence in the latter of rules and their absence in the former. An example would be the universality, in nature, of temporally limited mating seasons. Somewhere in the evolutionary ladder between the baboons and the higher apes we find that the female becomes receptive during the entire year and even during pregnancy. Rules for mating (kinship systems) must now replace biological functions. The universal or the instinctual is the place of nature; the rule is the place of culture. Culture, for Lévi-Strauss, reminds one of the cunning of Reason in Hegel; it is not merely superimposed upon life, it uses and transforms life to bring about a new order. Culture as the place of rules also seems to express Kant's theme in the *Critique of Practical Reason*, that man is that being who lives not just by law but according to his conception of the law.[51]

Since Lévi-Strauss proposes that all things cultural are languages, the line of demarcation between nature and culture is marked by the presence or absence of articulated speech. He refuses to allow any types of language to the beasts, even the higher apes, and feels that where they have been observed to articulate several monosyllables and disyllables, they have never attached any meaning to them; that is, they never treat these sounds as signs. Yet, at other times, for example in the Preface to the second edition (1966) of *The Elementary Structures of Kinship*, he seems to allow an articulated speech of some sort among some nonhuman species, and he asserts that culture might be reducible to nature: "Ultimately we shall perhaps discover that the interrelationship between nature and culture does not favour culture to the extent of being hierarchically superimposed on nature and irreducible to it." And even as early as 1955, we discover the sociobiological Lévi-Strauss writing, if not of genes, at least of "nerve-cells," on the next to last page of *Tristes Tropiques* (as if such "nerve-cells" alone really "exist"): "Yet I exist. Not, of course, as an individual, since in this respect, I am merely the stake— a stake perpetually at risk—in the struggle between another society, made up of several thousand million nerve cells lodged in the ant-hill of my skull, and my body, which serves as its robot." If Lévi-Strauss is not, at the minimal, ambiguous about the irreducibility of culture to nature, he certainly sounds more and more like the sociobiologist who began the science with his linguistic solutions to anthropological questions.[52]

Notes

Introduction

1. Especially in *Tristes Tropiques.*
2. L–S, *CC*, p. 18; see Jean-Marie Auzias, *Clefs pour le structuralisme*, p. 11; see Yvan Simonis, *Claude Lévi-Strauss ou la 'passion de l'inceste,'* p. 341. Quite frequently, Levi-Strauss refers to his philosophical foundations; see, for example, the last ten pages or so of *LI*, on the *doubts* of Montaigne and Descartes in anthropology (pp. 38–39).
3. Simonis, *Claude Lévi-Strauss*, pp. 87 ff.
4. On the Platonic origin of the problem, cf. Lucien Sebag, *Marxisme et structuralisme*, p. 12. This question appears most frequently today in the discussions involving altruism within the new discipline of sociobiology. Because altruistic behavior lessens the probability of the survival of an individual organism, it has become an enigma in Darwinian evolution theory, stressing, as the latter does, the individual's fight for survival. See Edward D. Wilson, *Sociobiology: The New Synthesis*, p. 4: "Sociobiology is defined as the systematic study of the biological basis of all social behavior."
5. In Lévi-Strauss, it will be a natural, not a conventional, term.
6. *The Dialogues of Plato*, trans. B. Jowett (New York: Random House, 1937), 50: 632.

Chapter 1

1. On Lévi-Strauss's debt to Freud and Marx, see *TT*, pp. 61–63.
   The title *structuralism* is especially important in preventing a confusion with formalism. Peter Caws (quoting from Pouillon's "Essai de definition") emphasizes the distinction between the two: "Structuralism is not formalism. On the contrary, it challenges the distinction between form and matter, and no matter is *a priori* inaccessible to it. As Lévi-Strauss writes, 'form defines itself by opposition to a content which is exterior to it, but structure has no content: it is itself the content, apprehended in a logical

organization as a property of the real' " (Peter Caws, "What Is Structuralism?" *Partisan Review* 35, no. 1 [Winter 1968]: 81).

Elsewhere, Paul Ricoeur has called Lévi-Strauss's position "a Kantianism without a transcendental subject." See Paul Ricoeur, "Structure et hermeneutique," p. 618. In the "Discussion avec Claude Lévi-Strauss" at the end of the issue of *Esprit* containing Ricoeur's article, Lévi-Strauss agrees with Ricoeur's denomination (no. 11 [November 1963], p. 633). His own best designation of structuralism is the one that he himself applies at the end of the discussion: he calls it "a kind of everyday materialism" (ibid., p. 652).

2. Gilles Lapouge, "Freud: Semantics, Not Sex?" p. 45: "From the point of view of the subject, the unconscious is that part of his history which is expressing itself without being understood."

3. L–S, *TT*, p. 62; Tanneguy de Quenetain, "What Are the Building Blocks of Structuralism?" p. 33; Maurice Merleau-Ponty, "From Mauss to Claude Lévi-Strauss," p. 123; *Esprit*, no. 11 (November 1963), p. 652.

4. L–S, *TT*, pp. 55, 60, 61 (English translation, Russell, pp. 51 ff.). The history that has been written by Michel Foucault in *Les mots et les choses* is rightly called by Sartre "a geology: the succession of alternative layers which form our 'earth' " ("Jean-Paul Sartre repond," *L'Arc* 30; 87). Each of these different layers defines the conditions of the possibility of a certain type of thought that triumphed during a certain period.

5. L–S, *TT*, pp. 61–62 (English translation, Russell, p. 57).

6. See Bernard Pingaud, "Comment on devient structuraliste," vol. 26, p. 26.

7. A fundamental distinction, used by all structuralists, is that of *sens* and *signification* (sense and clear meaning). *Sens* is an internal sense (not found in a relation of words to things) and is identical to the function of the word within the language. Language is viewed as a system defined by internal differences, not by relations to external objects. Here it is the combination of the elements within the system that is the bearer of the internal meaning. *Signification* leads out of the system, to the mind of the hearer or the speaker, and is the order explored by a psychologist. See Ambrose McNicholl, O.P., "Structuralism," p. 244.

8. McNicholl, "Structuralism," p. 265. See also Ino Rossi, "Intellectual Antecedents of Lévi-Strauss' Notion of Unconscious," p. 18. Edmund Leach, in his rather positivistic critique of Lévi-Strauss, throws up his hands in despair at his inability to verify the aesthete's self-enclosed system but accepts it insofar as it is an aesthetic enterprise. See Edmund Leach, *Claude Lévi-Strauss*, pp. 122–23. I will consider this critique in greater detail later.

9. L–S, *PS*, pp. 326–27. The reference is to Jean-Paul Sartre, *La Critique de la raison dialectique*, p. 183. Use of the word *aesthete* to characterize the existentialist's opinion of the scientific rationalist is not original with Sartre; it is Kierkegaardian in origin. There are, in Kierkegaard's *Either/Or*, two main manifestations of the aesthetical point of view: the romantic hedonist (exemplified by Mozart's *Don Giovanni*) and the abstract rationalist (exemplified by Goethe's *Faust*). The latter is analogous to Sartre's charac-

terization of Lévi-Strauss. Whereas the hedonist loses his selfhood in the erotic immediacy of his present experience, the rationalist loses his subjectivity in the immediate moment of his speculation, seeking to bypass the responsibility of commitment, and so on. See Sören Kierkegaard, *Either/Or*, trans. David Swenson et al. (New York: Doubleday, 1959), 1:89 ff.

10. L–S, *SEP*, p. viii (English translation, p. xxi).

11. L–S, *TT*, p. 203 (English translation, Russell, p. 178); L–S, *LI*, pp. 6–13.

12. L–S, *SEP*, p. 61; L–S, *IMM*, pp. xxiv ff. (see also E. E. Evans-Pritchard, Introduction to Marcel Mauss, *The Gift: Forms and Functions of Exchange in Archaic Societies*, trans. Ian Cunnison (Glencoe: Free Press, 1954), p. vii); Mauss, *The Gift*, p. 77; L–S, *LI*, pp. 11–12.

13. Emile Durkheim, *De la division du travail social*, p. 46; L–S, *LI*, p. 12; Durkheim, *La division*, pp. 46, 342; On Durkheim and Lévi-Strauss, cf. Ino Rossi, *The Unconscious in Culture*, pp. 13, 83; on the theory of the "total social fact" of Durkheim, see L–S, *LI*, pp. 8–9.

14. Evans-Pritchard, Introduction to Mauss, *The Gift*, p. ix; L–S, *SEP*, p. 71; Mauss, *The Gift*, pp. 11–12.

15. L–S, *LI*, pp. 8–9 (English translation, p. 10). These words portray Lévi-Strauss's usual somewhat ironical tone when speaking of academic philosophy.

16. L–S, *LI*, p. 9 (English translation, p. 11).

17. Mauss, *The Gift*, pp. 37–45; Evans-Pritchard, Introduction to Mauss, *The Gift*, pp. v–vi; Mauss, *The Gift*, pp. 44–45, 68.

18. Howard Gardner, *The Quest for Mind: Piaget, Lévi-Strauss and the Structuralist Movement*, pp. 123–24; L–S, *The Scope of Anthropology*, p. 14.

Chapter 2

1. Merleau-Ponty, "From Mauss to Lévi-Strauss," p. 116·(cf. L–S, *SEP*, p. 98); L–S, *CC.*, pp. 19–20; L–S, *SEP*, pp. 564ff. Anthony Wilden implies that Lévi-Strauss's brand of structuralism is removed from those of Jacques Lacan, the structural psychiatrist (in whom Wilden is particularly interested), and of Jean Piaget, the structural child psychologist (see Wilden, "Structuralism as Epistemology of Closed Systems," in Rossi, *The Unconscious*, pp. 273–90). For Wilden, Piaget is actually a covert phenomenologist, and Lévi-Strauss is a combination of "mechanistic cybernetics" and Kantianism (ibid., pp. 274, 282, 284). I will oppose, presently, Wilden's separation of these three, especially that of Lacan and Lévi-Strauss.

2. L–S, *SEP*, p. 565.

3. De Quenetain, "What Are the Building Blocks of Structuralism?" p. 31; Lapouge, "Freud: Semantics, Not Sex?" pp. 42–44; Danial Lagache, *La psychoanalyse*, p. 54. Lagache feels that the unconscious is the source of language, whereas Lacan contends that language is the source of the unconscious.

4. Lapouge, "Freud: Semantics, Not Sex?" pp. 42–43; De Quenetain, "What Are the Building Blocks of Structuralism?" p. 32. Lévi-Strauss's rejection of Jung's Archetypes as true accounts of mental structures is logically identical to Lacan's repudiation of fixed criteria for the interpretation of dreams. See L–S, *AS*, p. 230.

5. Lapouge, "Freud: Semantics, Not Sex?" pp. 44–45; Lagache, *La psychoanalyse*, p. 34 (on repression, see ibid., p. 43); Sigmund Freud, *The Complete Psychological Works*, Standard Edition, vol. 19, *The Ego and the Id*, pp. 14–15 (unless otherwise indicated, all citations from Freud will be from the Standard Edition).

6. Freud, vol. 21, *Civilisation and Its Discontents*, pp. 76 ff; Lagache, *La psychoanalyse*, p. 20; Freud, *Civilisation and Its Discontents*, p. 76. We are interested in understanding how the pleasure principle dominates the mental apparatus.

7. Freud, *Civilisation and Its Discontents*, pp. 77, 79.

8. Ibid., pp. 76–82.

9. Libido is Freud's name, basically, for the sexual instincts (life instincts): "The name 'libido' can once more be used to denote the manifestations of the power of Eros in order to distinguish them from the energy of the death instinct" *(Civilisation and Its Discontents*, p. 121); See Serge Leclaire, *Psychanalyser, Essais sur l'ordre de l'inconscient et la pratique de la lettre*, pp. 121–45.

10. See Rosalind Coward and John Ellis, *Language and Materialism: Developments in Sociology and the Theory of the Subject*, p. 102; Jacques Lacan, "The Insistence of the Letter in the Unconscious," trans. Jan Miel, *Yale French Studies* 48, p. 143 (my italics).

11. On displacement, see Lagache, *La psychoanalyse*, p. 52.

12. See Anthony Wilden in Jacques Lacan, *The Language of the Self*, p. 110, and the title of Freud's 1938 unfinished essay "Splitting of the Ego in the Defensive Process" and his 1927 essay on "Fetishism," pp. 372–75 and 198–204, respectively, of his *Collected Papers*, vol. 5, ed. James Strachey (New York: Basic Books, 1959). The *fetish* is treated by Freud as a displacement of sexual desire from its ordinary object, the genitalia, to another object that thus substitutes for the first. It is preceded by the splitting of the ego into the area of ordinary reality-functioning and the area of the abnormal (fetishistic) sexual functioning. This divergence is forced upon the fetishist by the fact that reality (civilization) prevents him, for one reason or another, from exercising his sexuality in a nonperverse way. His sexual drives, thus, are turned inward and tend toward the narcissistic in lieu of the anaclytic. See Leclaire, *Psychoanalyser*, pp. 61 ff.

 Lacan cites Freud's explanation of fetishism as "the final seal" on his proposition that the unconscious is structured like a language. In his 1927 article on fetishism and the displacement involved therein, Freud tells of a patient who needed a shine on the nose *(Glanze auf der Nase)* in order to achieve sexual satisfaction. In analysis, this shine *(Glanze)* was traced back to the linguistic displacement, from the forgotten language (English) of the analysand's childhood, of a "glance at the nose," an identification with the child's curiosity for the phallus of his mother. Jacques Lacan, *Ecrits*, p. 170.

13. Freud, *The Psychopathology of Everyday Life*, trans. Alan Tyson (New York: W. W. Norton, 1960), pp. 58–59. On condensation, cf. Lagache, *La 'psychoanalyse*, p. 52.

14. Lévi-Strauss will play the role of psychoanalyst to the collective dreams and collective games of primitive people. This is the heart of his social anthropology.

15. See Lacan-Wilden, *The Language of the Self*, pp. 234–35, 270.

16. Freud, vol. 18, *Beyond the Pleasure Principle*, p. 34; Coward and Ellis, *Language and Materialism*, pp. 3, 96 (citing Lacan in *Ecrits*).

17. Coward and Ellis, *Language and Materialism*, pp. 96–100. On the *points de capiton*, cf. Lacan, *Ecrits*, p. 154.

18. Coward and Ellis, *Language and Materialism*, p. 98; Lacan, *Ecrits*, pp. 172–73; Anika Lemaire, *Jacques Lacan*, pp. 67, 157.

19. Freud, *Beyond the Pleasure Principle*, p. 15. The game is similar to the common children's game of peekaboo.

20. Ibid., p. 15.

21. "There is first the act of speaking and the contexts arise from the awareness within which the individual speaks, but which, at the same time, escapes into shadowy horizons of meaning, present in their absence and absent in their presence, rather than being open to a full and explicit gaze" (Garth Gillan, "Language, Meaning, and Symbolic Presence," *International Philosophical Quarterly* 19, no. 3 [September 1969]: 444). Ultimately, the absence-presence dichotomy will, as we shall see, be the foundation of metaphor. See also Lacan, *Ecrits*, p. 234, on presence and absence in the *Fort-Da* story. See also Lagache, *La psychoanalyse*, p. 21, on the connection of language and the unconscious. The Freudian emphasis on wit, word-slips, language games, and so on, as offering keys to the unconscious, takes on added significance.

22. Again through language, as "an horizon of Otherness." Language is never private, it is learned in a community of speakers (Gillan, "Language," pp. 445 ff.).

23. Jean Deschamps, "Psychoanlyse et structuralisme," pp. 142, 152; Freud, *Beyond the Pleasure Principle*, pp. 16–17, 35. In the work of the American psychologist Jerome Bruner, the stage corresponding to the *Fort-Da* in Freud is the utterance of the holophrase (one word phrase) *all gone*, sometime during the second year of life. *All gone* represents the most primary of all syntactical utterances: "a syntactic structure composed of a closed pivot class, *all gone* and an open class that contains practically every other word in his vocabulary. *All gone* what have you." See Jerome S. Bruner, *Toward a Theory of Instruction*, pp. 104–5. Bruner means that *all gone* (like *Fort-Da*) marks the great leap from nature to culture ("which should be celebrated with an anniversary party each year" [p. 104]) by which the child is enabled to think *metaphorically* (or in *analogies*) or to conceive of something as being both absent and yet present at the same time (as the child in Freud's tale begins

to conceive of his mother, no longer physically present to him yet still somehow not totally absent). This basic syntactic structure enables the child to
construct a vocabulary upon a series of basic "pivot words" about which he
may organize a world (p. 105).

The possibilities of Bruner's being a structuralist *sensu aiente* are minimal
(cf. Jean Piaget, *Le structuralisme* pp. 61–62 [English translation, pp. 72–
73]), but that he is a structuralist *sensu negante* is somewhat more likely.

We shall eventually see that Freud's *Fort-Da* and Bruner's *all gone* correspond exactly in Lévi-Strauss to the notion of mana among primitive peoples.

24. Freud, *Beyond the Pleasure Principle*, p. 15 n. This story is, perhaps, a further
development of Lacan's *stade du miroir* ("mirror stage"), occurring at about
the age of six months, in which the child recognizes his body in the mirror.
See Deschamps, "Psychoanalyse et structuralisme," p. 142, on this Lacanian
stage. The very first signs of the structures of the unconscious appear in
the child's capture of the sense of space.

This mirror stage of absence-presence is the very beginning of the basic
binary opposition to which Lévi-Strauss reduces all other oppositions—that
of nature-culture. See Auzias, *Clefs pour le structuralisme*, pp. 153–54. Lévi-
Strauss will speak of his own work with synchronic structures as work within
the sense of space (rather than temporal structures).

25. See Lacan-Wilden, *The Language of the Self*, pp. 268–69. In some ways,
this interpretation of the Freudian unconscious owes as much to Hegel as it
does to Freud. For, as Wilden writes, "In the Hegelian view, the object
of one's desire is what mediates any relationship to others, since we desire
that object because it is desired by the other" (ibid., p. 163). Especially in the
master-slave dialectic of Hegel's *Phenomenology of Mind* is this view per-
tinent. We shall examine the master-slave dialectic in Lévi-Strauss in a later
section. In Lacan's *stade du miroir*, the child deliberately *alienates* himself
in a split representation, just as in the *Phenomenology*, it is necessary for
consciousness to alienate itself into consciousness of the other, in order to
achieve self-consciousness (ibid., p. 164).

26. Gillan, "Language," p. 434 (I shall explain the relation between the sonorous features of oppositions in greater detail presently); Lacan-Wilden, *The
Language of the Self*, p. 269. See J. Laplanche and S. Leclaire, "L'inconscient: une étude psychanalytique," in *L'inconscient*, VIᵉ Colloque de Bon-
neval, directed by Henri Ey (Paris: Desclee de Brouwer, 1966), pp. 116–17
(I shall return later to this important article).

27. Lacan-Wilden, *The Language of the Self*, p. 163. The best example of this
growth in autonomous status of the object as it is interiorized by the subject is given by Piaget. Bruner cites it as follows: "Piaget's classic demon-
stration of the growth of the idea of the permanent object is still the best:
a one-year-old child presented with a favorite toy, will not cry upon its removal unless he is holding it in his hand. Later, removal will bring tears
if he has begun to move his hand out to reach it. Still later, it suffices to

enrage him that it is removed when his eye has fallen on it. Objects, in short, develop an autonomy that is not dependent upon action. If at first 'a rattle is to shake' and 'a hole is to dig' later they are somehow picturable or conceivable without action" *(Toward a Theory of Instruction,* p. 12).

28. See Piaget, *Le structuralisme,* pp. 54–55; Lacan-Wilden, *The Language of the Self,* pp. 163, 133–34. This mediation is Hegelian in origin as much as Freudian and will reappear in my later section devoted to the master-slave dialetic in Lévi-Strauss.

29. Lacan-Wilden, *The Language of the Self,* p. 163.

30. Lacan-Wilden, *The Language of the Self,* p. 163. See also Gillan, "Language," pp. 432 ff., and Jacques Lacan, "Of Structure as an Investing of an Otherness Prerequisite to Any Subject Whatever," in *The Structuralist Controversy,* ed. Richard Macksey and Eugenio Donato (Baltimore: Johns Hopkins Press, 1972), p. 193. Freud calls intersubjective instincts *anaclytic,* because they literally "prop themselves up" or "lean upon" the self-preservation instincts. For example, the child's first intersubjective instincts arise from his relation to the person who feeds, cares for, and protects this *self,* that is, the mother. The narcissist is the one who has taken as the model not the other but his own self (Sigmund Freud, "On Narcissism: An Introduction," trans. Joan Riviere, in *Collected Papers,* 4: 30–59).

31. Lacan, "Of Structure," p. 164. Deschamps connects this lack that becomes language with its roots in the repressed pleasure principle ("Psychoanalyse et structuralisme," p. 142). Lacan's lack is, I will show, similar to Lévi-Strauss's notion of mana.

32. Lacan, "Of Structure," p. 164. In Lacan's analogy of tropes with *desire,* metonymy is regarded not in the traditional interpretation—as "the part for the whole"—but as "the connection of 'word to word' in the signifying chain, or the combination of signifier to signifier . . . and represents the subject's desire." Metaphor is regarded as "the substitution of 'one word for another' in which the first signifier is occulted and falls to the level of the signified while retaining its metonymic connection with the rest of the chain" (Lacan-Wilden, *The Language of the Self,* pp. 113, 241). We shall presently see that both definitions are related to Jakobson's work on aphasiacs and their "contiguity disorder" and "similarity disorder."

33. During World War II, Lévi-Strauss and Jakobson were colleagues on the staff of the New School for Social Research in New York City.

34. This article was published in Jakobson's *Fundamentals of Language,* pp. 55–82, translated into French as *Essais de linguistique générale,* pp. 43–67. References are given here to both the English original and the French translation. For this quotation, see the English text, pp. 80–81, the French, pp. 65–66.

For a synopsis of this important article by Jakobson, see Roland Barthes, *Elements de sémiologie,* pp. 133–34.

35. Jakobson, *Fundamentals,* pp. 71–72, *Essais,* pp. 57–58.

36. Jakobson, *Fundamentals,* p. 64, Essais, p. 50. The reason for this disability

in understanding *monologue* lies in the structuralist notion that even a *monologue* is an internalized discourse (that is, is metaphorical). On Jakobson's views here, see Bruner, *Toward a Theory of Instruction,* p. 106.

37. Jakobson, *Fundamentals,* pp. 65, 62, 64, *Essais,* pp. 51–52, 50. Camus's central character, Mersault, in *L'étranger* suffers from a type of similarity disorder, as evidenced by the style of language with which Camus endows him. See Roland Barthes, *Le degré zéro de l'écriture,* p. 67. The style aptly suits the alienated Mersault, for he is separated from the collective from which, as we shall see, all metalanguages (codes) derive.

38. Jakobson, *Fundamentals,* pp. 67, 69, 72, 76, *Essais,* pp. 53–54, 56, 58, 61. See Lacan, *Ecrits,* p. 258 wherein substitution produces metaphor, and combination produces metonymy.

39. Deschamps, "Psychoanalyse et structuralisme," p. 145. See Laplanche and Leclaire, "L'inconscient," pp. 106–14, esp. pp. 112, 114.

40. Deschamps, "Psychoanalyse et structuralisme," p. 145; Laplanche and Leclaire, "L'inconscient," pp. 113, 114.

41. McNicholl, "Structuralism," p. 363.

42. Deschamps, "Psychoanalyse et structuralisme," p. 148; McNicholl, "Structuralism," p. 364; Lacan, *Ecrits,* p. 170. One is reminded of the game, based upon metaphor and invented by André Breton as a surrealistic device, called *One in the Other.* The rules of the game are that one of the players secretly decides to identify with a particular object (such as a staircase). The other players then decide that he must pretend to be some other object (such as a bottle of champagne). "He must then describe himself as a bottle of champagne whose characteristics are such that gradually the image of the staircase is superimposed upon and eventually substituted for the image of the champagne bottle." See Roger Caillois, "Riddles and Images," pp. 148–50.
The animating idea of the game is that a poetic image becomes all the more vibrant in proportion to the increase in the distance between the terms it conjoins (ibid., p. 150). In the *Manifeste du surréalisme* (1924), Breton had proclaimed the most powerful image to be the one "presenting the highest degree of arbitrariness" (ibid., p. 148, n. 2). It will be seen that the same animating idea as that of Breton's game vivifies the work of Lévi-Strauss and that the degree of arbitrariness of the symbol also provides some interesting conclusions for the ethnologist.

43. What Lacan calls "des chaines signifiantes" (Laplanche and Leclaire, "L'inconscient," p. 118).

44. Ibid., p. 117. The Platonic theory of participation clearly formulated in the illustration of the divided line in *The Republic* (bk. 6, 510–11; Jowett translation, pp. 771–73) is, properly speaking, the beginning of the scholastics' intrinsic analogy of Being.

45. Laplanche and Leclaire, "L'inconscient," pp. 116–17.

46. Coward and Ellis, *Language and Materialism,* pp. 109–10.

47. Ibid., pp. 112–15. The little girl also suffers, according to Lacan, the castration sense of loss (p. 115).

48. Editor's introduction to Freud, *Civilisation and Its Discontents*, pp. 62, n. 1, 63.
49. See Lacan, *Ecrits*, p. 73.

Chapter 3

1. For an indication of the role of structural psychoanalysis in Lévi-Strauss's work, see: Lévi-Strauss's chapter entitled "The Archaic Illusion" in *SEP*, pp. 98–113 (English translation, pp. 84–97); his article "Le Sorcier et sa magie," reprinted from *Les Temps Modernes* (March 1949) in *AS*, pp. 183–203 (English translation, pp. 161–80); his *IMM*, pp. ix–lii; his "Overture" to *CC*, pp. 9–40 (English translation, pp. 1–32); and finally his article "Le triangle culinaire" in *L'Arc* 26 (1965): 19–29.
2. L–S, *SEP* p. 99. As in Freud's analysis of the *Fort-Da* beginnings of language and culture, Lévi-Strauss's "materialisme vulgaire" does not allow him any departure from his biological base for mental structures. Cf. *IMM*, pp. xi, xv.
3. L–S, *SEP*, p. 99.
4. Ibid., pp. 99–100. Lévi-Strauss is citing throughout from Susan Isaacs, *Social Development in Young Children* (London, 1933).
5. L–S, *SEP*, p. 100. Food alone has an intrinsic value to a person who is starving (ibid.).
6. L–S, *SEP*, pp. 100, 110; cf. Gardner, *The Quest for Mind*, p. 67.
7. L–S, *SEP*, pp. 566, 569 (English translation, pp. 493–94, 496); L–S, *IMM*, pp. xxxxi, xx.
8. L–S, *SEP*, p. 107 (English translation, p. 92).
9. Ibid., p. 109.
10. Glaucon's view of justice is that society and social structures are conventional (that is, artificial). Socrates describes a society in which natural differences exist only in order to be sustained in cultural and social relationships.
11. L–S, *SEP*, pp. 110, 108–9 (English translation, pp. 94, 93).
12. Lacan-Wilden, *The Language of the Self*, pp. 255–57. Phonemes are the actual sounds that are our vowels and consonants. See J.-B. Fages, *Comprehendre le structuralisme*, p. 122, and André Martinet, *Eléments de linguistique générale*, pp. 19–20.
    The morpheme is the grammatical moneme, which is the minimal sign unit composed of phonemes: in the expression "j'ai mal," *j'* (for *je*), *ai*, and *mal* are monemes. Grammatical monemes or morphemes are, therefore, words like *de, pour, avec*, or the Latin genitive, dative, ablative (or even these grammatical endings). For example, in a word like *travaillons*, there are two monemes, *travail* and the morpheme *ons*, which indicate the person and number of the speaker (Martinet, *Eléments de linguistique générale*, pp. 19–21, 117).
13. L–S, *AS*, p. 40. We shall return to these laws presently when we discuss the "system of terminology" and the "system of attitudes" in Lévi-Strauss.

14. L–S, *SEP*, pp. 109, 564 ff. (English translation, pp. 93, 492 ff.); L–S, IMM, p. xxxv; L–S, *AS*, pp. 40–42; Simonis, *Lévi-Strauss*, p. 23.

15. LS, "Le triangle culinaire," p. 19. Lévi-Strauss then proceeds in the article to analyze cooking as a cultural form, as universal as language (in fact, a language itself—a form of communication).

16. Specifically to Jakobson's *Essais de linguistique générale*. See esp. Ruwet's introduction, pp. 12 ff. The opposition *grave/aigu* functions for consonants and vowels, the opposition *compact/diffuse* for the consonant (p. 14).

17. Lucien Sebag, *Marxisme et structuralisme*, p. 105; L–S, "Le triangle culinaire," p. 19.

18. L–S, *SEP*, pp. 109–10; Jakobson, *Fundamentals*, pp. 60–61. Through metaphor, the paradoxical possibility exists of "pronouncing two elements at the same time" (ibid., p. 61).

19. L–S, *IMM*, xxxii.

20. L–S, *SEP*, pp. 105–6, 106–7, 108, 110: A. J. Greimas and F. Rastier, "The Interaction of Semiotic Constraints," p. 93.

21. L–S, *SEP*, pp. 110–111.

22. Ibid., pp. 102; Lagache, *La psychoanalyse*, pp. 117–18.

23. Lagache, *La psychoanalyse*, pp. 30–31. See also Paul Roazen, *Freud and His Followers*, p. 103.

24. See note 12 of Chapter 2, above, on the repressive function of the reality principle upon the pleasure principle.

25. *Synchronic* means in reversible time. See L–S, *AS*, p. 234. I shall return to this term later.

26. L–S, *T*, pp. 145–46 (English translation, pp. 101–2; Jean-Jacques Rousseau, *Essai sur l'origine des langues*, p. 505 (English translation, p. 11); Lagache, *La psychoanalyse*, p. 29.

27. LS, *SEP*, p. 112. I shall examine this splitting in detail in discussing the anthropologist's explanation of village arrangement.

28. L–S, *SEP*, pp. 562–63, 113, 109 (English translation, pp. 93, 113); Auzias, *Clefs pour le structuralisme*, p. 93.

29. L–S, *SEP*, p. 563. Lévi-Strauss is also rejecting here that interpretation of Rousseau's noble savage which would put him also beyond the pale of culture. This interpretation is, as I shall subsequently show, a misinterpretation of Rousseau's notion of an original state of nature.

30. L–S, *SEP*, p. 565. Just as the child engages in a constant repetition of the *Fort-Da* or the infant plays peekaboo endlessly, so primitive societies substitute synchronic structures, such as kinship systems, myths, and such, which turn history into a cyclic process.

31. L–S, *SEP*, p. 568. All the later mythologies studied in Lévi-Strauss's four volumes of *Mythologiques* deal with the relations between man and woman and, therefore, with the basic Oedipal conflict—so that, to this degree, the entire Lévi-Straussian expedition returns to the Freudian grid. See Catherine Backes, "Reflexions sur Lévi-Strauss," p. 15.

32. L–S, *SEP*, pp. 72, 568, 157.

33. Ibid., p. 95. The mathematical functioning of such cross-cousin systems.

would work something like this: the loss of a female is represented as (−), and the gain of one is (+). (Related women are lost; women brought in by marriage are gained.) Given two family lines, A and B, then the marriage of a male from A to a female from B is a (+) for the A line and a (−) for the B line. The collective, working through such mathematically analyzed exchanges, demands that the pluses and the minuses be kept even; if necessary, one generation will correct the asymmetries (or lack of adequate reciprocities) of its predecessor. In the above example, in which family A gained a daughter from B, the son of this union would not marry another female from family B. The structure, of course, is frequently more complicated than this simplified one. See L–S, *SEP*, pp. 151–53.

34. One is, of course, reminded of the Hegelian dialectic: culture is always in "dynamic disequilibrium" before the exchange, which thus brings about equilibrium.

35. L–S, *SEP*, pp. 55–56, 160–61; Auzias, *Clefs pour le structuralisme*, pp. 94–96.

36. L–S, *SEP*, p. 45 (English translation, p. 35); Simonis, *Claude Lévi-Strauss*, pp. 24–25.

37. L–S, *AS*, p. 45; Simonis, *Claude Lévi-Strauss*, p. 25; L–S, *SEP*, p. 552 (English translation, pp. 481–82).

38. Simonis, *Claude Lévi-Strauss*, p. 26, quoting L–S, *AS*, p. 56 (English translation, p. 43); L–S, *AS*, p. 56 (English translation, p. 43); Lévi-Strauss, *The Future of Kinship Studies*, Huxley Memorial Lectures in *Proceeedings of the Royal Anthropological Institute of Great Britain and Ireland* (1965), pp. 13–22, cited in Simonis, *Claude Lévi-Strauss*, p. 183.

39. L–S, "Discussion avec Claude Lévi-Strauss," p. 638.

40. Ferdinand de Saussure, a nineteenth-century French-Swiss linguist, was the founder of structural linguistics and the author of the *Cours de linguistique générale*.
    L–S, *AS*, pp. 342, 326–27; Simonis, *Claude Lévi-Strauss*, pp. 178, 181; Saussure, *Cours de linguistique générale*, pp. 115–24, 86.

41. L–S, *E*, p. 37 (English translation, p. 33).
    Another means employed by primitives of substituting the unchanging for the changing is their mythology. According to Lévi-Strauss, this is evident even from a comparison of the reference points of their mythology and ours. Our myths are rooted in history, theirs in nature. History takes on, for us, mythic dimensions; primitive peoples seek to avoid it entirely. See Lévi-Strauss's remarks in an interview with Paolo Caruso, "Exploring Lévi-Strauss," *Atlas* 2, no. 4 (April 1966): 246.

42. See Simonis, *Claude Lévi-Strauss*, pp. 182 n. 26, in which is explained Lévi-Strauss's reduction of dyadic structures to triadic structures, and p. 183; see also my exegesis, in Chapter 6 below, of the triadic structure of the Bororo village. Culture is that mediatory thirdness which in the mode of Hegel stabilizes an asymmetrical universe.

43. L–S, *AS*, p. 343 (English translation, p. 304); Simonis, *Claude Lévi-Strauss*, p. 182; L–S, *E*, pp. 156, 157. See L–S, *LI*, pp. 25–27 (English translation, pp. 29–31).

44. Auzias, *Clefs pour le structuralisme,* p. 96; L–S, *SEP,* p. 69; L–S, "Le Sorcier et sa Magie," *AS,* pp. 202–3. See L–S, *SEP,* p. 83, and Jakobson, *Fundamentals,* p. 61.

45. L–S, *IMM,* p. xlvii; *L–S,* "Ouverture," *CC,* pp. 20, 18, 19. See Ricoeur, "Structure et hermeneutique," pp. 599–600, and "Symbole et temporalité," p. 9.

46. Fages, *Comprehendre le structuralisme,* p. 124.

47. L–S, "Ouverture," *CC,* pp. 19, 12, 14, 20, 16, 18, *passim.* As in an optical microscope, which cannot reveal matter's ultimate structure to the observer, we can see only progressive enlargements, and each level is relative to another one (ibid., p. 11).

48. See L–S, *TT,* pp. 62–63.

49. This is also a conception of Lacan's. See Lacan, cited in Auzias, *Clefs pour le structuralisme,* p. 152, and L–S, *TT,* p. 60, on neo-Kantian constitution.

50. As the psychoanalyst and the patient work out the symbols of the unconscious by "talking it out."

51. L–S, *CC,* pp. 21–22 (English translation, p. 14). In *Tristes Tropiques,* he speaks of the rare authentic vocations of man as anthropology, mathematics, and *music* (L–S, *TT,* p. 59). All three, of course, are occupations given to coding. Interestingly, he chooses an example of the perfumer, who is also really a coder (or decoder) in the mode of the musician. For example, the thousands of fragrances to be blended are called the "notes," and they are blended on a working table called an "organ."

52. L–S, *CC,* p. 21. In this way, Lévi-Strauss through all four volumes of his *Mythologiques* traces the transformations of basically one myth, the Bororo myth of reference (Backès, "Reflexions sur Lévi-Strauss," p. 13).

53. L–S, *AS,* pp. 241–42. Another favorite image is that the structure of myths is like that of the *nebula:* gaseous, cloudy, and never quite crystallized (L–S, *CC,* p. 10). Another is that of the kaleidoscope, in which there are a limited number of structural arrangements, yet the chances are practically nil that the same configuration will appear twice. In addition, the kaleidoscope image offers an interesting comment on history and structuralism: history is compared to the flick of the finger that brings about the reorganization of the structure (L–S, *LI,* pp. 23–24).

54. L–S, *IMM,* xxxviii. It is a category of thought rather than of the real. See ibid., p. xlvii, and Wilden, "Structuralism," p. 128.

55. L–S, *IMM,* pp. xxxviii, xl, xlv, xliv. Even among ourselves it signifies power, for we, too, have linguistic expressions corresponding to *mana,* such as *ooomph* attributed to a woman, or *what's-it's name,* and so on (ibid., p. xliv). In our society, however, science takes the place of mana among primitives, for, like mana for them, it binds up the universe for us (ibid., p. xliv).

56. L–S, *IMM,* pp. xlv, xliv, xlvi, xlix, 1; L–S, *SEP* (English translation, p. 93). See Barthes, *Eléments,* pp. 151–52.
    A zero-value term in linguistics is one that is neuter or amodal in the sys-

tems of binary oppositions. For example, there are polarities between singular and plural, past and present, subjunctive and imperative. The indicative would be a zero-value term because it would mediate between the terms of this last polarity (Barthes, *Eléments*, p. 67).

57. Barthes, *Eléments*, p. 151. L–S, *CC*, p. 23 (English translation, p. 15).

58. L–S, *CC*, pp. 22–25 (English translation, pp. 14, 15); L–S, *SEP*, p. 73 (English translation, p. 62); L–S, *IMM*, pp. xiv and ff.

59. L–S, *SEP*, p. 113.

60. Lévi-Strauss, in fact, refers to these and similar laboratory illustrations on p. 104 of *SEP*, but he also expresses his reservations regarding the notion of maturation that is involved (see *SEP*, pp. 102 ff.).

61. Fages, *Comprehendre le structuralisme*, p. 124. See also Chomsky's "grammatical transformations" (Noam Chomsky, *Language and Mind*, pp. 25, 63). Grammatical transformations, here, are also the formal mental operations that relate the system of propositions expressing the meaning of the sentence and the sentence as a physical signal (ibid., p. 25).

62. The term *variable* has no mathematical refererent in structuralist thought.

63. Bruner, *Toward a Theory of Instruction*, p. 13.

64. "These discontinuities can be reduced to *invariants*, which is the goal of structural analysis" (L–S, *AS*, p. 325 [English translation, p. 288]).

65. Bruner, *Toward a Theory of Instruction*, p. 9.

66. Ibid., p. 6.

67. L–S, *LI*, p. 27. Consequently, although social anthropology, dealing with the various cultures of man, is a human science, it resigns itself to being considered a social science until the day when it is seen to be a natural science (ibid.). The meaning of this somewhat cryptic aphorism lies in Lévi-Strauss's "everyday materialism." For him, thought is simply "un objet de ce monde" (Michèle Jalley-Crampe, "La notion de structure mentale dans les travaux de Claude Lévi-Strauss," *La Pensée, Structuralisme et Marxisme*, no. 135 [September–October 1967], p. 58). And it is his ultimate hope to reintegrate the laws according to which the collective (unconscious) mind functions with the structural laws governing the natural sciences, by reducing these "conditions of possibility" (of thought) to "physico-chimiques" conditions and, thence, to "réintégrer la culture dans la nature" (ibid., p. 59).

68. L–S, *LI*, p. 27. Recall the coherence theory of truth in Laplanche and Leclaire, noted in Chapter 2 above.

69. Piaget, *Le structuralisme*, p. 55; L–S, *LI*, pp. 24, 23, 27, 26 (English translalation, pp. 27, 30, 26).

70. Literally, the logic of myths.

71. L–S, *AS*, pp. 229–30. What Saussure means here is, briefly, that the link between the signifying sound and the thing signified is arbitrary, so that, for example, although *nuit* has a short and light sound, it yet represents something long, languid, and dark; whereas *jour*, with a long, languid sound, signifies something light and bright. Or, in English, *whale* can stand for a big creature and *microorganism* for a very little one (Bruner, *Toward a Theory of Instruction*, p. 11). Onomatopoetic words are exceptions to this

rule, primarily because they are not signs; that is, they do not "stand for" something else.

The rule of arbitrariness has been expressed in various ways by different linguists. See Roland Barthes, *Eléments*, pp. 122 ff.

72. L–S, *AS*, p. 231. As a consequence, Lévi-Strauss's enterprise with mythology has been called an "à la recherche du temps perdu." This mythic time, which is not the same as diachronic time, will become clearer in the discussion of his distinction between hot and cold societies and dialectical and analytical reason. In the next to last chapter of *PS*, he calls mythic time "le temps retrouve." See Backes, "Reflexions sur Lévi-Strauss," p. 14. For Lévi-Strauss, one of the great losses of technological civilization is this mythic time of the primitives. We seek to replace it with psychoanalysis. See L–S, *AS*, pp. 225–26.

73. L–S, *AS*, pp. 229, 230. Edmund Leach, "Lévi-Strauss in the Garden of Eden," p. 386.

74. L–S, *LI*, p. 26. A further reason for Lévi-Strauss's rejection of Radcliffe-Brown's "structures" is that structure for Radcliffe-Brown is found on the level of empirical observation, not on an unconscious level (ibid., pp. 24–25). Lévi-Strauss differentiates mechanical models from statistical models. The former are those whose elements are on the same scale as the phenomena, whereas the latter are those whose elements are on a different scale (L–S, *AS*, p. 311). Radcliffe-Brown's structures remain on the level of induction and empirical observation, a statistical time (ibid., pp. 315–16). In a similar fashion, ethnography and ethnology are two different levels in the same research (whose final result is the construction of mechanical models) (ibid., p. 314). On the level of mechanical models, deduction takes over (ibid., pp. 316–17).

Lévi-Strauss explicitly acknowledges his debt to psychoanalysis for the inspiration of mechanical models, for it was Freudian psychoanalysis that discovered the means to construct models in a new field, that of the psychological life of the patient considered in its totality (ibid., p. 312).

75. George Ravis, "L'anthropologie et l'histoire," pp. 21–22; L–S, *CC*, pp. 64, 194; L–S, *AS*, pp. 224, 230, passim.

76. L–S, *AS*, pp. 224, 225, passim.

77. Ibid., pp. 232–33. For definitions of phoneme and morpheme, see n. 11 (Chapter 3) above. The sememe is the larger use of words in semantical unities (expressions) (Fages, *Comprehendre le structuralisme*, p. 122).

78. L–S, *AS*, p. 233. On this point see L–S, *CC*, p. 10, and Backes, "Reflexions sur Lévi-Strauss," p. 13. Lévi-Strauss's four-volume *Mythologiques* recounts the variations of the various transformations of one myth, the Bororo myth of reference, chosen arbitrarily by Lévi-Strauss.

79. Sanche de Gramont, "There Are No Superior Societies," in *Molders of Modern Thought*, ed. Ben B. Seligman (Chicago: Quadrangle Books, 1970), p. 207.

80. L–S, *AS*, pp. 235, 233.

81. Ibid., p. 234. In "L'analyse morphologique des contes russes," in the *Inter-*

national Journal of Slavic Linguistics and Poetics, no. 3 (1960), he brings
out their *différential* element by calling them "des paquets d'éléments dif-
férentials."

82. Backes, "Reflexions sur Lévi-Strauss," p. 13. The *code* in its usage by Lévi-
Strauss means the different levels of the structure of culture; that is, there
is in mythology an astronomical code, a culinary code, a matrimonial code,
and so on.

83. "Meta-language: language having for its object an other language" (Fages,
Comprehendre le structuralisme, p. 122).

84. Lévi-Strauss, "L'analyse morphologique," cited in Règis, "Pour une mythologique," p. 620.

85. L–S, *AS,* pp. 234, 235–36, 254, passim.

86. Barthes, *Eléments,* p. 131. For an additional exposition of the same terminology, see Simonis, *Claude Lévi-Strauss,* pp. 162–63.

87. Called "relations" by Hjelmslev, "contiguities" (as we have seen) by Jakobson, "contrasts" by Martinet (Barthes, *Eléments,* p. 132, 131).

88. Barthes, *Eléments,* pp. 132, 133, passim.

89. Emile Benveniste, *Problèmes de linguistique générale* (Paris: Gallimard,
1966), p. 22, cited in Simonis, *Claude Lévi-Strauss,* pp. 163–64; Saussure,
Cours de linguistique générale, p. 171; Barthes, *Eléments,* p. 132.

90. This is Lévi-Strauss's analysis *(AS,* pp. 237 ff.). See also Leach, *Claude Lévi-
Strauss,* pp. 389–90.
    In each of the volumes of *Mythologiques,* there is also a central mediating
    entity (as the Sphinx in the Oedipus story). In *Le cru et le cuit,* it is the
    jaguar; in *Du miel aux cendres,* it is the honey; in *L'Origine des manières
    de table,* it is *the education of women.* See Backes, "Reflexions sur Lévi-
    Strauss," p. 15.

91. L–S, *AS,* pp. 240, 236 ff., 239–40; Leach, "Lévi-Strauss in the Garden of
Eden," p. 338.

92. Règis, "Pour une mythologique," p. 623. The jaguar is the master of fire in
the myths (Backes, "Reflexions sur Lévi-Strauss," p. 15).

93. Règis, "Pour une mythologique," pp. 623–24.

94. Backes, "Reflexions sur Lévi-Strauss," p. 15. On these transformations see
Dan Sperber, "Le Structuralisme en anthropologie," in *Qu'est-ce que le structuralisme?* (Paris: Editions du Seuil, 1968), pp. 223 ff.

95. L–S, *AS,* pp. 254, 255; Bruner, *Toward a Theory of Instruction,* pp. 13, 9,
20; Henri Lefebvre, "Claude Lévi-Strauss et le nouvel eleatisme," *L'homme
et la société, Revue internationale de recherches et de syntheses socio-
logiques,* no. 1 (July–August–September 1966), p. 29. Lefebvre's analysis of
structuralism as a reemergence of Parmenidean Eleaticism will be considered below in my discussion of Lévi-Strauss and Marx.

96. The one area in which Lévi-Strauss is critical of both Durkheim and Mauss
is their uncritical acceptance of the primitives' conscious representations of
the anthropological data, which Lévi-Strauss maintains (as any psychoanalyst would) may be just as remote from the unconscious reality as any other
representation, including that of the anthropologist. See L–S, *AS,* pp. 309–10.

97. Jan Miel, "Jacques Lacan and the Structure of the Unconscious," *Yale French Studies* 36 and 37 (1966): 109.
98. The Freudian cure consists in an acceptance of this Other by the conscious "self"; in the words of Freud: "Wo es war, soll ich werden" ("Where the id was there the ego shall be," better translated by Lacan as "I must come to the place where that was" ["là ou était ça, le je doit être"], *Ecrits*, pp. 128–129, 136, 171). See Yvon Gauthier, "Language et psychoanalyse," p. 638.
99. "Phenomenology I found objectionable in that it postulated a kind of continuity between experience and reality" (L–S, *TT*, p. 62 [English translation, Russell, p. 58]).
100. Lapouge, "Freud: Semantics, Not Sex?" pp. 44, 45; Lacan, *Ecrits*, pp. 135–37, and "The Insistence of the Letter in the Unconscious," p. 143; De Quénetain, "What are the Building Blocks of Structuralism?" p. 33; W. Ver Eecke, "Vers une philosophie de la psychose," *Man and World* 2, no. 2 (May 1969): 299–300 (on Rimbaud's insight).
101. L–S, *TT*, p. 479 (English translation, Russell, p. 414).

Chapter 4

1. See Bronislaw Malinowski, *Magic, Science and Religion,* p. 25; he is citing Lévy-Bruhl's view. However, toward the end of his life, Lévy-Bruhl forsook his earlier position and maintained that the hypothesis of the prelogical state of primitives was one "inadequately founded." The implications of this second position seem to be that in no way at all, "pre"-logical or otherwise, can any cognitive character be assigned to "primitive mentality"; that is, it is all sheer affectivity. See L–S, *LI*, pp. 36–37 (English translation, p. 41). On Lévy-Bruhl and the primitive mind, see Octave Mannoni, "Psychoanalysis and the Decolonization of Mankind," p. 90.
2. L–S, *PS*, p. 332; Edmund Leach, "Brain-Twister," *New York Review of Books* 9, no. 6 (12 October 1967): 6.
3. See E. E. Evans-Pritchard, Foreword to Lucien Lévy-Bruhl, *The Soul of the Primitive*, p. 5, on "participations": "that persons and things in primitive thought form part of one another to the point even of identity." To Lévy-Bruhl, the mind of the primitive is one that injects "participations" into discrete parts of reality; for example, man participates in his totem animal, in his name, and so on. In short, the primitives' mentality is a mystical one. See also Auzias, *Clefs pour le structuralisme,* pp. 162, 74, and Sebag, *Marxisme et structuralisme,* p. 108.
4. De Quenetain, "What Are the Building Blocks of Structuralism?" p. 31.
5. On the analogy between Lévi-Strauss's view of mind and computer data programming, see Edmund R. Leach, "Telestar et les aborigines ou La Pensée sauvage de Claude Lévi-Strauss," *Annales,* no. 6 (November-December 1964), pp. 1100–15.
6. L–S, *T*, pp. 129–30.
7. Hume is considered one of the founders of associational psychology. In his

foreword to the Modern Library edition of *Human Nature and Conduct*
(New York: Random House, 1957), John Dewey wrote a passage that amaz-
ingly, althought it refers to Hume, could literally refer to the central theme
of the work of Lévi-Strauss: "His constructive idea is that a knowledge of
human nature provides a map or chart of all human and social subjects,
and that with this chart in our possession we can find our way intelligently
about through all the complexities of the phenomena of economics, politics, religious beliefs, etc. Indeed he went further, and held that human
nature gives also the key to the sciences of the physical world, since when
all is said and done they are also the products of the workings of the human mind" (p. vi).

8. L–S, *T*, pp. 129–30. It is correct that Lévi- Strauss, like Husserl, is explicat-
ing a logic and not a psychology, but here the analogy ends, for Lévi-Strauss
would never accept phenomenology's rejection of the unconscious. In addition, he would not regard the transcendental reduction of the empirical
transcendent perception to the apodicticity of the immanent perception
(that is, the constitution of essences by the apodictic self) as sufficient to
ground phenomenology "as *a* rigorous science." See Edmund Husserl, *Philosophy as Rigorous Science*, pp. 108–9. For Lévi-Strauss, Husserl's attempt
to reach scientific rigor in philosophy is simply a "sentimentality," an attempt to understand Being "in relation to oneself" and not "Being in relation to itself"—in short, a new way of "finding alibis for metaphysics" and
not true science. And existentialism ends up in "les illusions de la sub-
jectivité" ("the illusions of subjectivity"), called "a sort of metaphysic for
a shopgirl" *(pour midinette)* (*TT*, p. 63).

The roots of Lévi-Strauss's rejection of phenomenology lie in his repudiation of the isolated Cartesian ego.

9. L–S, *T*, pp. 2–3. Frazer is also cited *(The Golden Bough)* as an adherent of
Lévy-Bruhl's position on the primitive (see L–S, *LI*, p. 40). Lévi-Strauss gives
an interesting example of modern-day totemism in the example of the
"Rainbow" Division (the Forty-second Division) of the American Expedi-
tionary Forces in World War I. The anthropologist Linton, who was a
member of the division, recorded the totemic manifestations of the symbol
of the rainbow upon the soldiers (L–S, *T*, p. 10).

10. L–S, *T*, pp. 17 ff., 114–15, 116–17, passim.

11. In *The Two Sources of Morality and Religion*.

12. L–S, *T*, pp. 132–34. On Bergson's role in the French intellectual tradition,
see Gardner, *The Quest for Mind*, pp. 23–24.

13. L–S, *T*, pp. 135, 139 (English translation, p. 94).

14. For a similar functionalistic interpretation of the mind of the native, see
John Dewey, "Interpretation of the Savage Mind," pp. 173–87.

15. L–S, *T*, p. 141. This is what Radcliffe-Brown, who also entered on the path
to a "correct" interpretation of totemism, called the reconciliation of "opposition and integration" (ibid., pp. 142, 140–41).

16. "Participatory," in Lévy-Bruhl's conception of it.

17. L–S, *T*, pp. 140–41 (English translation, p. 98). The quoted passage is from

Henri Bergson's *Les Deux Sources de la morale et de la religion* (Paris: F. Alcan, 1958), p. 221. See L–S, *AS*, pp. 347–49.

18. L–S, *T*, pp. 142, 143. See William James, *Essays in Radical Empiricism* (New York: Longmans, Green and Co., 1912), p. 51.

19. L–S, *T*, pp. 144–46. Sartre postulates that the self is locked in a world of the monadic Cartesian ego, and all other selves act as aggressors, as infringements upon the self's limitless freedom.

20. The coalescence of "totalisation" and "compassion" in Lévi-Strauss functions in the same sense in which Sartre, in *La critique de la raison dialectique*, aligns dialectical reason with totalization. "If dialectical reason exists, it can only be, from the ontological point of view, the synthesis of a multiplicity into a whole, that is, a *totalization* . . ." (R. D. Laing and D. G. Cooper, *Reason and Violence: A Decade of Sartre's Philosophy, 1950–1960* [London: Tavistock Publications, 1964], p. 102).

21. L–S, *T*, p. 145. (English translation, pp. 101–2).

22. Ibid., p. 146.

Chapter 5

1. L–S, *SEP*, pp. 68–69.

2. L–S, *TT*, p. 138.

3. L–S, *TT*, pp. 451, 453 (English translation, pp. 390, 392).

4. On much of what follows, cf. Jacques Derrida, "La violence de la lettre: de Lévi-Strauss à Rousseau," in *De la grammatologie*, pp. 149 ff. (English translation, pp. 101 ff. (hereafter cited as *Grammatologie*).

5. L–S, *TT*, pp. 450, 451 (English translation, pp. 390–91). See also Derrida, *Grammatologie*, p. 169 (English translation, p. 115).

6. John Locke, *The Second Treatise of Civil Government*, p. 62.

7. Jean-Jacques Rousseau, *Discours sur l'origine et les fondements de l'inéqualité parmi les hommes* (New York: Oxford University Press, 1922), pp. 65–66.

8. *The Social Contract*, cited in *Communism, Facism and Democracy*, ed. Carl Cohen (New York: Random House, 1962), pp. 473–74.

9. L–S, *TT*, pp. 421–22; Rousseau, *Du contrat sociale* (Geneva: Les éditions du cheval aile, 1947), p. 173 (English translation: *The Social Contract*, ed. Lester G. Crocker [New York: Washington Square Press, 1971] p. 7) (further citations will be from the translation).

10. Rousseau, *The Social Contract*, p. 22.

11. Ibid., pp. 21–22.

12. L–S, *E*, pp. 29–40, 41 (English translation, p. 37).

13. L–S, *SEP*, p. 61. The *potlatch* among primitives is evidence of this attitude (ibid., p. 62).

14. L–S, *IMM*, pp. xxv, xxxi, xxxii; L–S, *LI*, p. 35; L–S, *SEP*, p. 70.

15. L–S, *SEP*, p. 35.

16. Ibid., p. 4. There are obvious overtones here of the Hegelian "cunning of reason."

17. Ibid., pp. 552, 78, 37 (English translation, p. 32).

18. And this rejection includes that, as we have seen, of the prelogical stage of man in Lévy-Bruhl (L–S, *IMM*, p. xxx).

19. L–S, *SEP*, p. 6 (English translation, p. 5).

20. *The Social Contract*, p. 31; L–S, *PS*, pp. 324–57.

21. See Ernst Cassirer, *The Question of Jean-Jacques Rousseau*, pp. 3–32, pp. 108, 109–10; Peter Gay, Introduction to ibid., pp. 17–18, 27.

22. Cassirer, *The Question of Jean-Jacques Rousseau*, pp. 123–24.

23. Cassirer, a Kantian, looks for *reason* in Rousseau. Lévi-Strauss is under no such constraints.

24. Lévi-Strauss, "Rousseau, The Father of Anthropology," *UNESCO Courier*, March 1963, p. 12. This article is an abridged version of an address given in 1962 to a commemorative gathering in homage to Rousseau at the University of Geneva, and it is usually called "The Geneva Lecture." See Derrida, *Of Grammatology*, p. 114.

25. Lévi-Strauss, "Rousseau," p. 14. One is also reminded of Tolstoy's *Resurrection* and his almost Hindulike but Christian reverence for life.

26. Lévi-Strauss, "Rousseau," pp. 12, 13, 14.

27. Ibid., p. 11.

28. Ibid.

29. Ibid., p. 12.

30. Ibid.

31. L–S, *TT*, pp. 422, 390. On "the universality of human nature," see L–S, *LI*, p. 35.

32. L–S, *T*, p. 142; L–S, *TT*, pp. 451–54.

33. Lévi-Strauss, "Race and History" in *Race and Science* (New York: Columbia University Press, 1961), p. 243. This age Lévi-Strauss calls a "cumulative civilisation."

34. L–S, *TT*, pp. 451–54, 424.

35. L–S, *Race and History*, pp. 233, 235–36. See also L–S, *LI*, p. 39 (English translation, pp. 45–46), and L–S, *TT*, pp. 67–68, 88–89 ff.

36. In the *Leçon inaugurale*, he speaks of this attitude as the "attitude philosophique par excellence"—that "du doute" ("of doubt"). It consists in a radical skepticism—knowing that one knows nothing and exposing what one thought one knew to alien habits, ideas, and so on (ibid., p. 38).

   On another level, the conflict between the *dégagement* of structuralism and the *engagement* of existentialism parallels conflict between the structuralists' analytic logic (the logic of the scientific method, or the logic of skepticism), which breaks down the "object" into its constituent parts, and the Sartrean dialectical logic. See L–S, "Histoire et dialectique," *PS*, pp. 324–57. I shall return to this conflict in a later section.

37. Jean-Paul Sartre, *Literature and Existentialism*, trans. Bernard Frechtman (New York: Citadel Press, 1965), pp. 19–23, 76. The basic opposition between Sartre and Lévi-Strauss on this question is caused, I think, by Sartre's position that man is *en situation* in which he is condemned to be free; that is, he is constantly, by his very nature, changing his position and remak-

ing his world. This is, in essence, Sartre's adaptation to man of the freedom and irrational creativity of Descartes's God. In his later Marxism, Sartre joins a dialectical praxis to the individual ego that constantly reshapes the world. Lévi-Strauss's position is that of the determinist and the scientist: universal laws govern the action of all men, and the action of one culture upon another is not, therefore, creative of its object. Its object already exists and is governed by similar laws. But I shall explore the relations between Sartre and Lévi-Strauss in a later chapter.

38. L–S, "Rousseau," pp. 11, 13.

39. One is reminded of the Kantian dictum that the *a priori* conditions of a possible experience in general are at the same time conditions of the possibility of objects of experience.

40. L–S, *AS*, pp. 309–10; L–S, *TT*, pp. 424, 422–23.

41. L–S, *LI*, pp. 41, 55; L–S, *E*, pp. 37 ff.

42. L–S, *E*, p. 38. Lévi-Strauss does admit, however, that it is unlikely that any society would correspond exactly to either of the two types (L–S, *LI*, p. 42).

43. L–S, *LI*, pp. 43, 44, passim.

44. One is reminded in Lévi-Strauss the moralist, perhaps because of the link through Rousseau, of the Kantian categorical imperative: "So act that the maxim of your will could always hold at the same time as a principle establishing a universal law." See Immanual Kant, *Critique of Practical Reason,* trans. Lewis White Beck (Indianapolis: Bobbs-Merrill Co., 1956), p. 30.

45. L–S, *TT*, p. 454 (English translation, p. 393). Lévi-Strauss specifically refers to the distinction between automata as the area of culture and men as society in eighteenth-century social philosophy, culminating in Saint-Simon. See L–S, *LI*, p. 43.

46. L–S, *OM*, pp. 412–22.

47. De Gramont, "There Are No Superior Societies," pp. 208, 66.

48. Harold Scheffler, "Structuralism in Anthropology," *Yale French Studies* vol. 36–37, p. 82; L–S, *SEP*, p. 10.

49. L–S, *SEP*, pp. 14, 555, 550–51 (English translation, pp. 12, 481); Scheffler, "Structuralism in Anthropology," p. 79. As is well known, exogamy is simply the principle of seeking a wife outside the nuclear family arrangement. "An exogamous group is one inside of which intermarriage is forbidden and which, consequently, requires at least another exogamous group with whom it may exchange its sons and/or daughters for marriage purposes" (Lévi-Strauss, "The Family, p. 282).

50. Scheffler, "Structuralism in Anthropology," p. 80; L–S, *SEP*, pp. 553–54; L–S, *AS*, p. 56; Simonis, *Claude Lévi-Strauss*, p. 26.

51. I rely here especially upon Lévi-Strauss, "The Family," pp. 261–65, 278–79.

52. Lévi-Strauss, "The Family," p. 278. The point is that they are as arbitrary as the sign always is. See Simonis, *Claude Lévi-Strauss*, p. 29.

53. Lévi-Strauss, "The Family," pp. 279, 280, 270, 281, 277; L–S, *SEP*, pp. 16–17, 21 (English translation, p. 18).

54. L–S, *SEP*, pp. 263–64. The principle here is that while the men hunt, till the soil, and so on, the women keep house, nurse the children, and so on.

On the division of labor as structuring a progressively more complicated society, see Karl Marx, *The German Ideology*, trans. and ed. by Erich Fromm in *Marx's Concept of Man*, with a translation from Marx's Economic and Philosophical Manuscripts by T. B. Bottomore (New York: F. Ungar Publishers, 1961), pp. 204–5. Marx traces the division of labor back to an original animal division in the sexual act (ibid., p. 204), tying together, like Lévi-Strauss, *economia* and *erotica*.

55. Lévi-Strauss, "The Family," pp. 277, 278.
56. L–S, *SEP*, pp. 555–56; Lévi-Strauss, "The Family," p. 274.
57. L–S, *SEP*, p. 45 (English translation, p. 49). The essay of Hume to which Lévi-Strauss refers is, cited in the French translation, *Essais moraux et politiques* (Amsterdam, 1764), p. 189.
58. On dualistic organizations, see L–S, *SEP*, pp. 87–88 ff.
59. Luc de Heusch, "Situation et positions," *L'Arc* 26 (1965), p. 9.
60. L–S, *AS*, p. 61 (English translation, p. 49), cited by Simonis, *Claude Lévi-Strauss*, p. 29.
61. Gardner, *The Quest for Mind*, pp. 36–37, 34; L–S, *LI* (English translation, p. 31).
62. The problem with Radcliffe-Brown's exposition is, according to Lévi-Strauss, that he fails to treat the avunculate as one relationship within a system (an error the new linguistics would never make), whereas to understand the system's structure one must group it as a whole (*AS*, pp. 50, 56).
63. L–S, *AS*, pp. 56, 58 ff. (English translation, p. 58); Simonis, *Claude Lévi-Strauss*, pp. 25–26.
64. L–S, *AS*, pp. 58 ff.; Simonis, *Claude Lévi-Strauss*, p. 27.
65. Reuben Osborn, *Marxism and Psychoanalysis* (New York: Delta, 1954), pp. 55–57, 60 (trans. *Marxisme et psychoanalyse* [Paris: Payot, 1965]).
66. Ibid., pp. 58, 60–61. Engels is cited in ibid., pp. 59–60.
67. Ibid., p. 61. Both Engels and Freud were influenced by the view of L. H. Morgan on the group marriage among primitive peoples. On Morgan, see Freud, *Totem and Taboo* (trans. James Strachey [New York: W. W. Norton, 1950], p. 6). For Lévi-Strauss's admiration of Morgan, see *Les structures élémentaires de la parenté*, passim; it is dedicated "à la mémoire de Lewis H. Morgan."
68. See Maurice Godelier, "La pensée de Marx et d'Engels aujourd'hui et les recherches de demain," *La Pensée*, no. 143 (February 1969), pp. 97 ff., 117–20.
69. L–S, *TT*, pp. 330, 356, 331–33 (English translation, p. 310).
70. Ibid., pp. 335, 337, 362–63 (English translation, pp. 314–15).
71. Ibid., pp. 337, 362–63, 37 (English translation, pp. 314–15, 32).

Chapter 6

1. L–S, *TT*, p. 62. See also L–S, *AS*, p. 366, n. 1. The *Eighteenth Brumaire of Louis Bonaparte* is a most important work; in it, Marx elaborates all the basic tenets of historical materialism: the theory of the class struggle and

proletarian revolution, the state, and the dictatorship of the proletariat. In *The Critique of Political Economy,* especially in the posthumously published Preface, he continues the elaboration of these schemes.

Most importantly, the *Eighteenth Brumaire* is an excellent example of how history is achieved as the working out on a collective scale of forces that are unconscious and not willed by the individual. See Engels's letter to J. Bloch, 21 September 1890, in Marx and Engels, *Selected Works* (New York: International Publishers, 1968), p. 693.

2. L–S, *TT*, p. 62 (English translation, p. 58). See also Derrida, *Grammatologie,* pp. 174–75.

3. Lucien Goldmann, *Sciences humaines et philosophie* (Paris: Gonthier, 1966), pp. 89 ff., 94; Frederick Engels, *Speech At the Graveside of Karl Marx,* in Marx and Engels, *Selected Works,* p. 435; Marx and Engels, *Manifesto of the Communist Party,* in *Selected Works,* p. 51; Engels to J. Bloch, 21 September 1890, in Marx and Engels, *Selected Works,* p. 693; L–S, *LI,* p. 25 (English translation, p. 29).

4. Marx, Preface to *The Critique of Political Economy,* pp. 182–83.

5. See Gustav A. Wetter, *Soviet Ideology Today,* trans. Peter Heath (London: Heinemann, 1962), pp. 175–76. See also F. Engels, *Origin of the Family, Private Property and the State,* in Marx and Engels, *Selected Works,* pp. 455–593, especially pp. 473–518. The references throughout *Origin of the Family* are to the influence of Lewis Morgan upon Marx and the materialist conception of history. See pp. 455, 473, 582 ff.

6. L–S, *AS,* pp. 365–66.

7. For example, Radcliffe-Brown, the British anthropologist (L–S, *AS,* p. 340).

8. L–S, *AS,* pp. 305–6, 340, 307, 310. See Maurice Godelier, "Remarques sur les concepts de structure et de contradiction," *Aletheia,* no. 4 (May 1966), pp. 228–29. We have already seen the reason for the precaution of using an unconscious model. The unconscious, the area of the pleasure principle, is always contrary to (not contradictory to) the area of conscious functioning governed by the reality principle; if it were not, there would be no reason for its being repressed by the reality principle. However, since the id does not speak through conscious representations (as in a dream functioning as a rebus), its language can be decoded.

9. Godelier, "Remarques," pp. 229–33. Also, on Marx in Lévi-Strauss, see Godelier, "Systeme, Structure" (English translation: "System, Structure and Contradiction in *Das Kapital*," in *Introduction to Structuralism,* ed. Michael Lane [New York: Basic Books, 1970], pp. 340–59); Deschamps, "Psychoanalyse et structuralisme," p. 150, n. 36, quoting Marx, *Capital,* 3: 96.

10. L–S, *PS,* p. 173.

11. Henri Lefebvre, *Sociologie de Marx,* p. 45, 5–6; Karl Marx and Friedrich Engels, *The German Ideology, Part I,* pp. 6–7. The concept of "species-being" is borrowed by Marx from Feuerbach's *Das Wesen des Christentums.* Feuerbach's own expression is "unmittelbares Wesen des Menschen." See Karl Löwith, *Von Hegel zu Nietzsche,* p. 359.

12. Roger Garaudy, *Karl Marx,* pp. 80–82, and Robert Tucker, *Philosophy*

and Myth in Karl Marx, pp. 138–39; Lefebvre, *Sociologie de Marx*, pp. 5, 53–55.

13. Even before Kojève expounded his Marxist interpretation of Hegel's *Phenomenology* at the Sorbonne in the thirties—lectures attended by, among others, both Sartre *and* Lévi-Strauss—Nicolai Hartmann was terming the formative activity of the slave in Hegel's dialectic the "revolutionizing principle," for in shaping *(bilden)* things, he actually shapes himself. For Hartmann, this becomes "the universal foundation for a philosophy of work." See George L. Kline, "The Existentialist Rediscovery of Hegel and Marx," in *Phenomenology and Existentialism*, ed. E. Lee and M. Mandelbaum (Baltimore: Johns Hopkins Press, 1967), p. 119.

14. See Kline, "The Existentialist Rediscovery," p. 119.

15. Hegel, *Phanomenologie des Geistes*, in *Samtliche Werke*, ed. Hermann Glockner (Stuttgart: F. Frommann, 1951), 2: 157 (English translation: *The Phenomenology of Mind*, trans. J. B. Baillie [London: George Allen and Unwin, 1949], p. 239); Alexandre Kojève, *Introduction à la lecture de Hegel* (Paris: Gallimard, 1947), p. 56 (English translation: *Introduction to the Reading of Hegel*, ed. Allen Bloom, trans. James H. Nichols [New York: Basic Books, 1969], pp. 52–53).

16. L–S, *AS*, p. 365.

17. Paul Radin. *The Winnebago Tribe*, Bureau of American Ethnology Thirty-seventh Annual Report (Washington, D.C., 1923); L–S, *AS*, pp. 149–50.

18. L–S, *AS*, pp. 151 ff. So we have a series of binary oppositions herein established, for example:

central	:	sacred	:	food stored	:	raw	:	bachelors	:	males
peripheral		profane		food eaten		cooked		married couples		females

And, we may add:

raw	:	nature
cooked		culture

19. L–S, *AS*, pp. 159–60. Ultimately, Lévi-Strauss wants the reader to see that the inner ring of the concentric structure plan has the same function as the diametrical line in the village composed of diametric structure.

20. L–S, *AS*, pp. 154–55.

21. Ibid., pp. 156–57.

22. Ibid., pp. 157–60; L–S, *TT*, pp. 254–56.

23. J. Peristiany, "Social Anatomy," *Times Literary Supplement*, 22 February 1957, p. 106; L–S, *TT*, p. 255.

24. L–S, *AS*, pp. 160–61.

25. Ibid., p. 161.

26. Ibid., p. 162.

27. L–S, *TT*, p. 256 (English translation, p. 245).

28. See Lefebvre, *Sociologie de Marx*, p. 6; In the interpretation which follows, see Kojève's commentary in *Introduction à la lecture de Hegel*, pp. 173 ff.

29. Kojève, *Introduction à la lecture de Hegel*, pp. 177–79.

30. L–S, *AS*, pp. 161–62.

31. L–S, *SEP*, pp. 61, 63, 98, 100 (English translation, pp. 84, 86).

32. Ibid., p. 10.
33. Auzias, *Clefs pour le structuralisme,* p. 96; L–S, *AS,* p. 168.
34. L–S, *AS,* p. 176; Simonis, *Claude Lévi-Strauss,* p. 348.

Chapter 7

1. Consciousness is conceived by Lévi-Strauss as the enemy of the human or social sciences, for it allows no way of regarding man (except in the "material" body) as capable of symbolization. He thus argues that, to have a science of man, we must deal with the unconscious. See Jalley-Crampe, "La notion de structure," p. 55.
2. L–S, *IMM,* p. xix.
3. Simonis, *Claude Lévi-Strauss,* p. 342.
4. L–S, *PS,* pp. 326–27; Marx is cited by Ravis, "L'anthropologie et l'histoire," p. 19.
5. And not vice versa, as it is in Sartre's *Critique de la raison dialectique* (L–S, *PS.,* p. 326).
6. L–S, *PS,* pp. 324, 326, 332, 327–28.
7. Ibid., p. 326. Ricoeur also applies this term to Lévi-Strauss in a penetrating criticism *(Structure et hermeneutique,* p. 652).
8. L–S, *PS,* pp. 347, 338; Sartre, "J.-P. Sartre Répond," *L'Arc* 26 (1965), pp. 30, 94; L–S, *IMM,* pp. xiv ff. L–S, *CC,* p. 35. See also Simonis, *Claude Lévi-Strauss,* pp. 57, 81 ff., 104 ff.
9. L–S, *IMM,* pp. xv, xxv, xxx, li, xxxvi ff.; Lévi-Strauss, "The Mathematics of Man," pp. 585–86; L–S, *AS,* pp. 359–60. There is some question of the right of this "qualitative mathematics to claim the name of mathematics. Lévi-Strauss aligns it with set theory, group theory, topology—all branches of modern mathematics ("The Mathematics of Man," p. 586)—calling his own approach "Galilean" (from Galileo), meaning aiming to uncover the laws of variation (read *transformation),* as opposed to the more inductive Aristotelian approach. See L–S, *AS,* p. 332, n. 1.
10. See Chapter 1, p. 2, above.
11. L–S, *CC,* p. 346 (English translation, p. 341); L–S, *PS,* p. 325 (English translation, p. 246).
12. L–S, *IMM,* p. xxxvii; Ravis, "L'anthropologie et l'histoire," p. 24.
13. De Quénetain, "What Are the Building Blocks of Structuralism?" pp. 33–34; Auzias, *Clefs pour le structuralisme,* pp. 140 ff; Mikel Dufrenne, *Pour l'homme,* pp. 45–47.
14. See, for example, Ravis, "L'anthropologie et l'histoire," p. 24: man, though a part of nature, is still the constituting part, through historical praxis, and therefore, for the orthodox Marxist, exists at a different level of nature from the other parts.
15. L–S, *TT,* pp. 477–78 (English translation, p. 413).
16. J.-P. Sartre, *L'Être et le néant* (Paris: Librairie Gallimard, 1949), p. 245: potentiality is put into the world by the *pour-soi,* who, for example, con-

stitutes the half-moon and quarter-moon and full moon, and so on. Without the individual ego, there is no potentiality, no signification; there is just actuality, the thing signified, the moon.

17. J.-P. Sartre, *Existentialism and Humanism,* trans. Philip Mairet (London, Methuen and Co., 1966), pp. 44, 42, 56. See Sartre, *La critique de la raison dialectique,* p. 103, n. 1.

18. Lucien Goldmann, "Structuralisme, Marxisme, Existentialisme," p. 117. See especially Sartre's comments on his Cartesian rationalism in "The Itinerary of a Thought," in *Between Existentialism and Marxism,* p. 37.

19. L–S, *PS,* pp. 329–30 (English translation, p. 249).

20. See, for example, Sartre, *La critique de la raison dialectique,* pp. 103–4, n. 2; L–S, *PS,* p. 330 (English translation, pp. 249–50); L–S, *OM,* p. 422. The "formula" is, of course, from Sartre's celebrated play *No Exit.*

21. J.-P. Sartre, "J.-P. Sartre Répond," *L'Arc* 26 (1965), p. 90. The practico-inert signifies the hard and immobile core that, for Sartre, lies between individual praxis and collective praxis. See Wilfred Desan, *The Marxism of Jean-Paul Sartre,* pp. 119, 135. Sartre, "J.-P. Sartre Répond," *L'Arc* 26 (1965), p. 89.

22. See Catherine Backès-Clément, *Lévi-Strauss* (Paris: Editions Seghers, 1970) pp. 136 ff.

23. L–S, *IMM,* p. xxix. This new humanism of Lévi-Strauss is quite similar to Comte's worship of humanity, existing in Comte's third phase of history, the positivistic one. For an earlier existentialist's critique of this new humanity, one might turn to Dostoyevsky's ironical view of "Life in the Crystal Palace" in part 1 of *Notes from the Underground.*

24. Sartre, "J.-P. Sartre Répond," *L'Arc* 26 (1965), p. 89; L–S, *OM,* pp. 419, 422; L–S, *LI,* p. 47 (English translation, p. 52).

25. L–S, *CC,* p. 21 (English translation, p. 13).

26. L–S, *PS,* p. 334. See Desan, *The Marxism of Jean-Paul Sartre,* pp. 60–61, and Sartre, *La critique de la raison dialectique,* pp. 96–97.

27. Jean Pouillon, "Sartre et Lévi-Strauss," *L'Arc* 26 (1965), p. 59.

28. See note 11 above and L–S, *PS,* p. 325 (English translation, p. 246).

29. L–S, *The Savage Mind* (English translation, p. 250); Sartre, *Between Existentialism and Marxism,* pp. 51–52. Malinowski is quoted in Gardner, *The Quest for Mind,* p. 34. On Malinowski, see also L–S, *LI* (English translation, p. 14).

30. L–S, *The Savage Mind* (English translation, p. 250); Sartre, *Between Existentialism and Marxism,* pp. 38–39, 51.

31. Gardner, *The Quest for Mind,* p. 223; Bernard Pingaud, "Reply to Sartre," in Sartre, *Between Existentialism and Marxism,* p. 223; Sartre, "The Look," *Being and Nothingness,* pp. 340 ff.

32. See Chapter 4 above.

33. René Girard, "Differentiation and Undifferentiation in Lévi-Strauss and Current Critical Theory," pp. 130, 115. Sartre, *Between Existentialism and Marxism,* p. 42. See the almost brutal article "The Man With the Tape-Recorder" in ibid., pp. 199–223.

34. Pouillon, "Sartre et Lévi-Strauss," p. 59; L–S, *CC*, p. 19 (English translation, p. 11); Jalley-Crampe, "La notion de structure," p. 58.

35. Paul Ricoeur, "Symbole et temporalité," pp. 24, 10; L–S, *CC*, p. 19. But see also Raphael Pividal, "Peut-on acclimater 'La Pensée Sauvage'?" pp. 561–62: Pividal claims that the great difference between Kant and Lévi-Strauss is that, whereas the former constructs a logic of the *a priori*, the latter shows that this must be a logic of the *a posteriori*.

36. L–S, *CC*, p. 19 (English translation, p. 11).

37. See Raphael Pividal, "Signification et position de l'oeuvre de Lévi-Strauss," pp. 1095–98.

38. Ibid., p. 1097; Maxime Rodinson, "Racisme et civilisation," pp. 120–40, 132; Roger Caillois, "Illusions a rebours," *Nouvelle Revue Française*, December 1954, pp. 1010–24, January 1955, pp. 58–70.

39. See, for example, Henri Lefebvre, *Le langage et la société*, and "Claude Lévi-Strauss et le nouvel eleatisme," p. 27 and passim. See also Sartre, "J.-P. Sartre Répond," *L'Arc* 26 (1965), pp. 89–90.

40. L–S, *AS*, pp. 369, 370. This is all worked out in an article by Maurice Godelier, "La Pensée de Marx et d'Engels aujourd'hui et les recherches de demain," *La Pensée*, no. 143 (February 1969), pp. 117–18.

41. L–S, *AS*, pp. 369, 368.

42. Ricoeur, "Symbole et temporalité," p. 9.

43. Lefebvre, quoted in De Gramont, "There Are No Superior Societies," p. 222; Frederick Copleston, S.J., *A History of Philosophy*, vol. 1, pt. 1 (New York: Doubleday and Co., 1962), pp. 66–67; W. T. Stace, *A Critical History of Greek Philosophy* (London, 1920), pp. 49–52, cited in ibid., p. 68.

44. McNicholl, "Structuralism," p. 365; Louis Althusser, "Freud and Lacan," pp. 200, 201–3, 198.

45. Mark Poster, *Existential Marxism in Postwar France*, pp. 342, 349; McNicholl, "Structuralism," p. 366.

46. Poster, *Existential Marxism*, p. 351; Miriam Glucksmann, *Structuralist Analysis in Contemporary Social Thought: A Comparison of the Theories of Claude Lévi-Strauss and Louis Althusser* (London: Routledge and Kegan Paul, 1974), pp. 147–48.

47. McNicholl, "Structuralism," p. 366; Poster, *Existential Marxism*, p. 352.

48. Glucksmann, *Structuralist Analysis*, p. 109; Louis Althusser and Etienne Balibar, *Lire le Capital*; Poster, *Existential Marxism*, pp. 352–58; McNicholl, "Structuralism," p. 369.

49. See Glucksmann, *Structuralist Analysis*, pp. 167–73; Poster, *Existential Marxism*, p. 340, n. 81, in which is contained an excellent listing of articles and statements by leading French intellectuals about Althusser's position, and n. 87, p. 345; George Lichtheim, *George Lukács*, pp. 63–73; and Martin Jay, *The Dialectical Imagination*, pp. 88–100, 74–75.

50. Ricoeur, "Symbole et temporalite," pp. 19 ff. Sartre, "J.-P. Sartre Répond," *L'Arc* 26 (1965), pp. 89–90, alludes to the same sort of critique, but not in any great detail.

51. Lévi-Strauss likes to compare structures with games, especially chess. See, for example, "Preface de la deuxième édition" (February 1966), *SEP*, pp. xxix, 63–64; there he remarks, as noted previously, that in primitive societies exchange exists primarily on behalf of group solidarity and alliance security, as is evident from the fact that there is no more real transfer of goods than in a game of chess in which the players do not give each other the pieces they move forward, but merely move to provoke a counter-move.

52. Andre Handricourt and Georges Granai, "Linguistique et sociologie"; Pividal, "Signification," p. 1095; L–S, *AS*, pp. 92–110; Ricoeur, "Structure et hermeneutique," pp. 352–53.

53. Paul Ricoeur, "The Task of Hermeneutics," pp. 141, 149.

54. De Gramont, "There Are No Superior Societies," p. 207; Ricoeur, "Hermeneutics," p. 147.

55. For the distinction, see Jonathan Culler, *Structuralist Poetics* (Ithaca, 1975), pp. 6 ff.

56. Ricoeur, "Structure, Word, Event," *Philosophy Today* 12 (Summer 1968): 115, 123; Jonathan Culler, *Structuralist Poetics*, p. 9; Rollo May, *Existential Psychology*, p. 16.

57. John Lyons, *Noam Chomsky*, pp. 36, 37–38; Ricoeur, "Structure, Word, Event, p. 124. See Noam Chomsky, *Cartesian Linguistics* (New York, 1966).

58. Culler, *Structuralist Poetics*, pp. 26–29. See also Robert Detweiler, *Story, Sign, and Self*, pp. 177–87, on "Ricoeur and Structuralism."

59. John Searle, "Chomsky's Revolution in Linguistics," *New York Review of Books* 18, no. 12 (29 June 1972): 16–24.

60. *Annales*, no. 6 (November-December 1964), pp. 110–16.

61. Ibid., p. 112. The distinction is between analog computers and digital computers.

62. See Pividal, "Signification," p. 1096, and G. Gurvitch, "Le concept de structure sociale," *Cahiers internationaux de sociologie* 19 (1955); Gurvitch is answered by Lévi-Strauss in chapter 16 of *AS*.

63. See Sartre, *Critique de la raison dialectique*, p. 18, note 1 on this earlier conflict.

64. Pividal, "Signification," p. 1096; The editors of *La Nouvelle Critique*, "Réflexions sur Claude Lévi-Strauss" 205, no. 4 (May 1969): 12; L–S, *AS*, pp. 360–66.

65. Culler, *Structuralist Poetics*, pp. 16, 92–93, 225–26, 92; Leach, *Claude Lévi-Strauss*, p. 92. L–S, *CC*, pp. 18, 25–26 (English translation, pp. 10, 17–18); L–S, *AS*, pp. 229–31.

66. May, *Existential Psychology*, pp. 17–18. On the case of Ellen West, see *Existence*, ed. Rollo May, Ernest Angel, Henri Ellenberger (New York: Simon and Schuster, 1958), pp. 237–364.

67. Viktor Frankl, *The Doctor and the Soul*, p. 31, and *Man's Search for Meaning*, p. 166.

68. Allan Janick and Stephen Toulmin, *Wittgenstein's Vienna*, pp. 75–77; Thomas Szasz, *Karl Kraus and the Soul-Doctors*, pp. 27–30.

69. Philip Pettit, *The Concept of Structuralism*, pp. 88, 89.

70. Anthony Quinton, "Freud and Philosophy," pp. 78–79. See also Karl Popper, *The Logic of Scientific Discovery*.

71. See Leach's puzzlement regarding the meaning of Lévi-Strauss's *esprit humain* in Edmund Leach, *Genesis as Myth* (London: Jonathan Cape, 1969), pp. 25–27; also see Edmund Leach, "The Legitimacy of Solomon: Some Structural Aspects of Old Testament History, in Michael Lane, *Introduction to Structuralism* (New York: Basic Books, 1970), p. 248.

72. L–S, *IMM*, p. xix; Leach, *Claude Lévi-Strauss*, pp. 85–86; Pettit, *The Concept of Structuralism*, p. 90. See also L–S, *TT*, p. 64 (English translation, p. 59).

73. Yvan Simonis, "Two Ways of Approaching Concrete Reality," pp. 384, 380, 385.

74. Quinton, "Freud and Philosophy," p. 80.

75. Ibid., pp. 80–81, 82.

76. Seymour Fisher and Roger P. Greenberg, *The Scientific Credibility of Freud's Theories and Therapy*.

77. Leach, *Claude Lévi-Strauss*, pp. 127, 122–23.

Chapter 8

1. In the second part of the *Discourse on Method,* Descartes writes, "Among those who previously sought truth in the sciences only the mathematicians have been able to find any demonstrations, i.e. any reasons which are certain and evident" (Descartes, *Oeuvres de Descartes,* 6: 19 (hereafter cited as *AT*).

2. S. V. Keeling, *Descartes*, pp. 23–24n; Descartes, *Oeuvres et lettres*, p. 595 (*Principes* 53) (hereafter cited as *AB); AT*, 2: 268; *AT*, 8: 79; *AT*, 6: 19–21; Jean-Claude Piguet, "Les conflits de l'analyse et de la dialectique," p. 547.

3. *AB*, p. 587 (*Principes* 37): "the principle perfection of man is to have a free will, and that is what makes him worthy of praise or of blame."

4. *AB*, pp. 278 (*méditatione seconde*), 582 (*Principes* 24), 583; Etienne Gilson, *The Spirit of Medieval Philosophy*, pp. 95 ff.

5. Jean-Paul Sartre, "Cartesian Freedom," p. 183.

6. The phrase is similar to Lacan's statement, previously cited here, "The order of the symbolic can no longer be understood as constituted by man, but as constituting him" (cited in Auzias, *Clefs pour le structuralisme,* p. 152).

7. Ricoeur, "Structure et hermeneutique," p. 620; Sartre, "J.-P. Sartre Répond, *L'Arc* 26 (1965) p. 88; Auzias, *Clefs pour le structuralisme*, p. 108. On Lévi-Strauss and Cartesianism, see Derrida, *Grammatologie*, p. 172.

8. Auzias, *Clefs pour le structuralisme,* p. 101. As Lévi-Strauss himself avers, structuralism abhors all dualism: the structure is the intimate union of sensible and intellectual. See Bernard Pingaud, "Comment on devient structuraliste," p. 2.

9. Auzias, *Clefs pour le structuralisme*, p. 99. The influence, again, is originally from Rousseau. As Derrida points out, Rousseau substituted symbols for the conscious ideas of Descartes *(Grammatologie*, p. 147).

10. Auzias, *Clefs pour le structuralisme*, p. 91. Note, as Derrida points out, that in Descartes there is the possibility of a private language only. In Rousseau, as in Lévi-Strauss, there can be no public language (Grammatologie, p. 147).

11. L–S, *CC*, p. 35; De Quénetain, "What Are the Building Blocks of Structuralism?" p. 34.

12. In this way, it is correct to speak of Lévi-Strauss's primitive as Piguet does, as "un sauvage cartésianise" ("Les conflits," p. 566).

13. L–S, *CC*, p. 18 (English translation, p. 10); *AB*, pp. 279–33 *(méditatione seconde)*; Dufrenne, *Pour l'homme*, p. 82 (this book is an admirable attempt by a phenomenologist and professor at Nanterre to defend existential humanism from structuralism's inroads); L–S, *AS*, p. 360 (English translation, p. 326). Thus, as noted above, Lévi-Strauss compares structural analysis to musical composition and hopes for the day when logical properties will be revealed as attributes of things just as directly (and, we might add, in as ordered a fashion) as are savors and perfumes (L–S, *CC*, p. 22).

14. Leach, *Claude Lévi-Strauss*, pp. 123–26; L–S, *CC*, pp. 24, 25, 26, 23 (English translation, pp. 16, 17 [cited in Leach, *Claude Lévi-Strauss* p. 126], 18, 15.

15. See Friedrich Nietzsche, *The Birth of Tragedy*, pp. 949–1088. Also see Sarah Kofman, "Metaphol, Symbol, Metamorphosis," pp. 201–14.

16. Gilson, *Medieval Philosophy*, p. 99. See Pingaud's citation of Lévi-Strauss's youthful meditation on the daffodil, which presents this "sacramental" character and the diacritical function of signs: "he gives himself over, one Sunday, to contemplation of a daffodil. . . . to see it, one must, at the same time see it in relation to the other plants, and oppose it to them" ("Comment on devient structuraliste," p. 3). Simonis calls Lévi-Strauss's structuralism a logic of aestheticism (*Claude Lévi-Strauss*, pp. 316 ff.). We can begin to see why, in this passage from Pingaud.

17. Auzias, *Clefs pour le structuralisme*, p. 91. This sacramental interrelatedness (which Lévi-Strauss in *Tristes Tropiques* aligns to Buddhism (pp. 471 ff.) reverses our usual conception of moral pollution. Our Judeo-Christian "world, the flesh, and the devil" has traditionally been viewed by Western man as the source of moral infection of the *subject* (by the object). The primitives, however, have always known (as their logic shows us) what we, with our problems of environmental pollution, are just discovering: that the world is pure and the subject is impure, that man is the source of moral infection and the universe must be protected from him (on "l'impureté du sujet," see L–S, *OM*, pp. 418 ff.).

18. See Barthes and the neuter writing of the structuralist authors of fiction: A. Robbe-Grillet, M. Leiris, and others (Barthes, *Le degré zero*, p. 67).

19. L–S, *IMM*, pp. xlix, l and its note, xlvi, xlvii; Barthes, *Le degré zero*, pp. 152, 132.

20. On semantic and cryptic forms, see pp. 45–46 of Adolph Portmann, *New Paths in Biology*. "Unaddressed" are those "phenomena whose sole purpose

it is to express the phenomenal essence of an animal or plant." On the pearly butterfly, see pp. 77–82. On "display" and the mollusk's shells, see Marjorie Grene, "Portmann's Thought," *Commentary*, August 1965, p. 34.

21. Alfred Hitchcock, quoted in François Truffaut, *Hitchcock*, pp. 99–100, 98.

22. Ibid., pp. 103, 11 (quoting Eric Rohmer and Claude Chabrol, *Hitchcock* [Paris: Editions Universitaires, 1957]).

23. Dufrenne, *Pour l'homme*, p. 86. The thesis of Dufrenne's book is that Heidegger is the harbinger of structuralism. Dufrenne's interpretation accords with my own in showing structuralism as a revival of essentialism.

24. Simonis, *Claude Lévi-Strauss*, p. 308; Auzias, *Clefs pour le Structuralisme*, p. 101; L–S, *CC*, p. 22 (English translation p. 14).

25. Gilson, *Medieval Philosophy*, pp. 134, 377–78.

26. L–S, *IMM*, pp. xlvii-xlix; Lévi-Strauss, "Discussion avec Claude Lévi-Strauss," *Esprit* (November 1963), p. 646. See Derrida's article on this difference between language and knowledge: "La structure, le signe, et le jeu," in his *L'écriture et la différence*, pp. 423 ff.

27. Thus, as in Rousseau, for Lévi-Strauss all language was first figurative. See Rousseau, *Essai sur l'origine des langues*, pp. 505–6.

Rousseau gives an interesting example of the way that man's first speech begins with figurative language. A savage man, when meeting others, will initially be frightened. *He sees these others as different from himself.* He calls them giants (the first figurative language, expressing the discontinuity of the self and the other). Then, after many experiences, he recognizes that these "giants" are neither bigger nor stronger than himself. Therefore, he invents another name common to both other men and himself and he calls them and himself "man," relegating "giant" for the fictitious object of his early illusion (ibid., p. 506).

28. The zero-value is, as Simonis points out, really *man* himself, in the sense of the scientific humanity of Comte or the absolute humanity of Rousseau, meaning nothing more than the rules of the unconscious (*Claude Lévi-Strauss*, pp. 308, 97–98).

29. Gilson, *Medieval Philosophy*, pp. 97–98.

30. L–S, *PS*, p. 348 (English translation, p. 263). There are, of course, quite a few areas where the parallel I have drawn between medieval scholasticism and modern structuralism becomes somewhat tenuous. For example, the notion of the freedom of the will was a very important one in scholasticism, whereas it is nonexistent in structuralism. In addition, and most importantly, Lévi-Strauss introduces ideas of an impersonalized *human spirit* (Dufrenne, *Pour l'homme*, pp. 86 ff.) and of a decentralized structure (Derrida, *L'écriture*, pp. 413 ff.), both of which may be alien to the spirit of medieval thought. These discrepancies are understandable if we remember that Lévi-Strauss is closer to Comte than to Aquinas.

31. On this point, there is, obviously, a certain semblance between Lévi-Strauss and Hegel. Kostas Axelos, in the "Discussion avec Claude Lévi-Strauss," refers to this analogy by calling Hegel "the father of structuralism" and by comparing Hegel's "Grande Logique" to "Lévi-Strauss's "pensée sauvage

globale" (pp. 645–46). Axelos distinguishes between two types of genealogical thought: that in which events follow one after the other, generation by generation, and that of the phenomenology of the mind, in which a total and initial structure develops nontemporally and nonspatially (ibid.). In Hegel, the gradual conquest of nature by the Idea, which conquest leads to the coming of the Spirit, is quite similar to the conquest of nature by culture in Lévi-Strauss, which leads to the realization of a total salvation in the idealized humanity.

32. Or like the innocent (natural) savage in Rousseau, who, as I have shown, never exists apart from society (in *both* Rousseau and Lévi-Strauss).

33. L–S, *SEP*, pp. 569–70; Simonis, *Claude Lévi-Strauss*, pp. 306, 307–26; L–S, *CC*, p. 25.

34. Terence Hawks, *Structuralism and Semiotics*, p. 149. On Derrida, see ibid., pp. 145–50, and Detweiler, *Story, Sign, and Self*, pp. 187–91.

35. Roman Jakobson and Morris Halle, "Phonology and Phonetics", p. 8 (p. 108 of the *Essais*); L–S, *AS*, p. 108.

36. L–S, *AS*, p. 107 (English translation, p. 92).

37. Jacques Derrida, "Structure, Sign, and Play in the Discourse of the Human Sciences," pp. 247–72.

38. Ibid., pp. 254–55, 257–58.

39. Ibid., pp. 256, 261–62, 260, 262–64.

40. Alfred Freedman, Harold Kaplan, and Benjamin Saddock, *Modern Synopsis of Psychiatry II*, p. 1228.

41. John Murray Cuddihy, *The Ordeal of Civility*, pp. 162, 158–59.

42. Ibid., pp. 162, 160, 151–52.

43. Stanley Diamond, "The Myth of Structuralism," pp. 320–25.

44. Poster, *Existential Marxism*, p. 223. Ricoeur, "Hermeneutics," p. 153. Sartre is cited in Diamond, "The Myth of Structuralism," p. 325.

45. Nietzsche, "The Gay Science," in *The Portable Nietzsche*, selected and trans. by Walter Kaufmann (New York: Viking Press, 1965), p. 102.

46. See Gilles Deleuze, "Active and Réactive," pp. 100–103; Nietzsche, *Thus Spake Zarathustra*, in *The Portable Nietzsche*, pp. 340–43.

47. L–S, *E* (English translation, pp. 37, 38). Martin Heidegger, "Who Is Nietzsche's Zarathustra?" pp. 71–77.

48. Nietzsche, quoted in Culler, *Structuralist Poetics*, p. 96, and in Karl Jaspers, *Nietzsche*, p. 244; L–S, *CC*, p. 12 (English translation, p. 4).

49. Wilson, *Sociobiology*, p. 3.

50. Edward O. Wilson, "Sociobiology: Nature and Nurture Come Out Swinging," p. E 18.

51. L–S, *SEP*, pp. 10, 4 (English translation, p. 4); Simonis, *Claude Lévi-Strauss*, pp. 36, 37; Alex Comfort, *The Nature of Human Nature*, p. 24.

52. L–S, *SEP*, pp. xvi, 6–7, Preface to the Second Edition (English translation, p. xxx). L–S, *TT*, p. 478 (English translation, Weightman, p. 414).

Selected Bibliography

Althusser, Louis. "Freud and Lacan." In *Lenin and Philosophy and Other Essays*. New York: Monthly Review Press, 1971.

Althusser, Louis, and Balibar, Etienne. *Lire le Capital, I, II.* Paris: François Maspero, 1968. In English, *Reading Capital.* Translated by Ben Brewster. New York: Pantheon Books, 1970.

Auzias, Jean-Marie. *Clefs pour le structuralisme.* Paris: Seghers, 1967.

Backès-Clément, Catherine. "Reflexions sur Lévi-Strauss: Presentations des 'mythologiques.'" *La Nouvelle Critique*, no. 24 (May 1969).

Barthes, Roland. *Eléments de sémiologie.* Paris: Editions Gonthier, 1964. In English, *Elements of Semiology.* Translated by Annette Lavers and Colin Smith. Boston: Beacon Press, 1970.

———. *Le degré zéro de l'écriture.* Paris: Editions Gonthier, 1964. In English, *Writing Degree Zero.* Translated by Annette Lavers and Colin Smith. Boston: Beacon Press, 1970.

Binswanger, Ludwig. "The Case of Ellen West." Translated by Werner M. Mendell and Joseph Lyons. In *Existence,* edited by Rollo May, Ernest Angel, and Henri Ellenberger, pp. 237–364. New York: Simon and Schuster, 1958.

Bruner, Jerome. *Toward a Theory of Instruction.* New York: W. W. Norton, 1966.

Caillois, Roger. "Illusions a rebours." *Nouvelle Revue Française*, December 1954, January 1955.

———. "Riddles and Images." *Yale French Studies*, no. 41 (September 1968).

Cassirer, Ernst. *The Question of Jean-Jacques Rousseau.* Translated and edited by Peter Gay. Bloomington: Indiana University Press, 1954.

Charbonnier, G. *Conversations with Claude Lévi-Strauss.* Translated by John and Doreen Weightman. London: Jonathan Cape, 1969.

Chomsky, Noam. *Language and Mind.* New York: Harcourt, Brace and World, 1968.

Comfort, Alex. *The Nature of Human Nature.* New York: Avon Books, 1966.

Coward, Rosalind, and Ellis, John. *Language and Materialism: Developments in Sociology and the Theory of the Subject*. London: Routledge and Kegan Paul, 1977.

Cuddihy, John Murray. *The Ordeal of Civility: Freud, Marx, Lévi-Strauss and the Jewish Struggle with Modernity*. New York: Basic Books, 1974.

Culler, Jonathan. *Structuralist Poetics*. Ithaca: Cornell University Press, 1975.

De Gramont, Sanche. "There Are No Superior Societies." Reprinted in *Molders of Modern Thought*, edited by Ben B. Seligman. Chicago: Quadrangle Books, 1970.

Deleuze, Gilles. "Active and Reactive." In *The New Nietzsche*, edited and introduced by David B. Allison. New York: Delta Books, 1977.

De Quénetain, Tanneguy. "What Are the Building Blocks of Structuralism?" *Réalités*, no. 207 (February 1968).

Derrida, Jacques. *De la grammatologie*. Paris: Minuit, 1967. In English, *Of Grammatology*. Translated by Gayatri Spivak. Baltimore: Johns Hopkins University Press, 1974.

——. *L'écriture et la différence*. Paris: Editions du Seuil, 1967.

——. "Structure, Sign, and Play in the Discourse of the Human Sciences." In *The Structuralist Controversy*, edited by Richard Macksey and Eugenio Donato. Baltimore: Johns Hopkins University Press, 1970.

Desan, Wilfred. *The Marxism of Jean-Paul Sartre*. Garden City, N.Y.: Doubleday, 1965.

——. *The Tragic Finale: An Essay on the Philosophy of Jean-Paul Sartre*. Cambridge, Mass.: Harvard University Press, 1954.

Descartes, René. *Oeuvres de Descartes*. Edited by Charles Adam and Paul Tannery. 12 vols. Paris: Leopold Cerf, 1897–1910. Cited in the notes as *AT*.

——. *Oeuvres et lettres*. Edited by André Bridoux. Paris: Gallimard, 1953. Cited in the notes as *AB*.

Deschamps, Jean. "Psychoanalyse et structuralisme." *La Pensée*, no. 135 (September-October 1967).

Detweiler, Robert. *Story, Sign, and Self*. Philadelphia: Fortress Press, 1978.

Dewey, John. "Interpretation of the Savage Mind." In *Philosophy and Civilisation*. New York: Capricorn Books, 1931.

Diamond, Stanley. "The Myth of Structuralism." In *The Unconscious in Culture*, edited by Ino Rossi. New York: E. P. Dutton, 1974.

Dufrenne, M. *Pour l'homme*. Paris: Editions du Seuil, 1968.

Durkheim, Emile. *De la division du travail social*. Paris: Presses universitaires de France, 1960.

Fages, J.-B. *Comprehendre le structuralisme*. Toulouse: Privat, 1968.

Fisher, Seymour, and Greenberg, Roger P. *The Scientific Credibility of Freud's Theories and Therapy*. New York: Basic Books, 1977.

Foucault, Michel. *Les mots et les choses*. Paris: Gallimard, 1966. In English: *The Order of Things*. New York: Pantheon Books, 1970.

Frankl, Viktor. *The Doctor and the Soul*. New York: Bantam Books, 1967.

——. *Man's Search for Meaning*. New York: Washington Square Press, 1963.

Freedman, Alfred, Kaplan, Harold, and Saddock, Benjamin. *Modern Synopsis of Psychiatry II.* Baltimore: Williams and Wilkins, 1976.

Freud, Sigmund. *The Complete Psychological Works.* Standard Edition. Translated by James Strachey, Anna Freud, Alix Strachey, and Alan Tyson. London: Hogarth Press, 1961.

———. *The Psychopathology of Everyday Life.* Translated by Alan Tyson. New York: W. W. Norton, 1960.

Garaudy, Roger. *Karl Marx.* Paris: Seghers, 1964.

Gardner, Howard. *The Quest for Mind: Piaget, Lévi-Strauss and the Structuralist Movement.* New York: Random House, 1974.

Gauthier, Yvon. "Language et psychoanalyse." *Dialogue: Revue Canadienne de Philosophie* 7, no. 4 (1969).

Gilson, Etienne. *The Spirit of Medieval Philosophy.* Translated by A. H. C. Downes. New York: Charles Scribner's Sons, 1940.

Girard, René. "Differentiation and Undifferentiation in Lévi-Strauss and Current Critical Theory." In *New Directions for Criticism,* edited by Murray Krieger and L. S. Dembo. Madison: University of Wisconsin Press, 1976.

Godelier, Maurice. "System, Structure and Contradiction in *Das Kapital.*" In *Introduction to Structuralism,* edited by Michael Lane. New York: Basic Books, 1970.

Goldmann, Lucien. "Structuralisme, Marxisme, Existentialisme." *L'Homme et le Société,* no. 2 (October-November-December 1966).

Greimas, A. J. and Rastier, F. "The Interaction of Semiotic Constraints." *Yale French Studies,* no. 41 (1968).

Handricourt, André, and Granai, Georges. "Linguistique et sociologie." *Cahiers Internationaux de Sociologie,* July-December 1955.

Hawks, Terence. *Structuralism and Semiotics.* Berkeley: University of California Press, 1977.

Heidegger, Martin. "Who Is Nietzsche's Zarathustra?" In *The New Nietzsche,* translated and introduced by David B. Allison. New York: Delta Books, 1977.

Husserl, Edmund. *Philosophy as a Rigorous Science.* Translated by Quentin Lauer. New York: Harper and Row, 1965.

Jakobson, Roman. *Essais de linguistique générale.* Translated by Nicolas Ruwet and A. Adler. Paris: Les Editions de Minuit, 1965.

Jakobson, Roman, and Halle, Morris. "Phonology and Phonetics." In *Fundamentals of Language.* The Hague: Mouton and Co., 1956.

Janik, Allan, and Toulmin, Stephen. *Wittgenstein's Vienna.* New York: Simon and Schuster, 1973.

Jaspers, Karl. *Nietzsche.* Chicago: Henry Regnery, 1965.

Jay, Martin. *The Dialectical Imagination: A History of the Frankfurt School and the Institute of Social Research, 1923–1950.* Boston: Little, Brown, 1973.

Keeling, S. V. *Descartes.* London: Benn, 1934.

Kofman, Sarah. "Metaphor, Symbol, Metamorphosis." In *The New Nietzsche,* translated and introduced by David B. Allison. New York: Delta Books, 1977.

Lacan, Jacques. *Ecrits*. Translated by Alan Sheridan. New York: W. W. Norton, 1977.

———. *The Language of the Self: The Function of Language in Psychoanalysis*. Translated with notes and commentary by Anthony Wilden. Baltimore: Johns Hopkins University Press, 1968.

Lagache, Daniel. *La psychoanalyse*. Paris: Presses universitaries de France, 1955.

Lapouge, Gilles. "Freud: Semantics, Not Sex?" *Réalités*, no. 202 (September 1967).

Leach, Edmund. *Claude Lévi-Strauss*. New York: Viking Press, 1970.

———. "Lévi-Strauss in the Garden of Eden." *Transactions of the New York Academy of Sciences* 23 (1961).

Leclaire, Serge. *Psychoanalyser: Essais sur l'order de l'inconscient et la pratique de la lettre*. Paris: Editions du Seuil, 1968.

Lefebvre, Henri. *Le langage et la société*. Paris: Gallimard, 1966.

———. *Sociologie de Marx*. Paris: PUF, 1968.

Lemaire, Anika. *Jacques Lacan*. Translated by David Macey. London: Routledge and Kegan Paul, 1977.

Lévi-Strauss, Claude. "The Family." In *Man, Culture, and Society*, edited by Harry L. Shapiro. New York: Oxford University Press, 1960.

———. "The Mathematics of Man." *International Social Science Bulletin* 6, no. 4 (1955).

Lévy-Bruhl, Lucien. *The Soul of the Primitive*. Translated by Lilian A. Clare. New York: Praeger, 1966.

Lichtheim, George. *George Lukács*. New York: Viking Press, 1970.

Locke, John. *The Second Treatise of Civil Government*. Edited by J. W. Gough. Oxford: Clarendon University Press, 1946.

Löwith, Karl. *Von Hegel zu Nietzsche*. Stuttgart: W. Kohlhammer Verlag, 1941.

Lyons, John. *Noam Chomsky*. New York: Viking Press, 1970.

McNicholl, Ambrose, O. P. "Structuralism." *Irish Theological Quarterly* 35, no. 3 (July 1968), 35, no. 4 (October 1968).

Malinowski, Bronislaw. *Magic, Science and Religion*. Garden City, N.Y.: Doubleday Anchor, 1954.

Mannoni, Octave. "Psychoanalysis and the Decolonization of Mankind." In *Freud, The Man, His World, His Influence*, edited by Jonathan Miller. Boston: Little, Brown, 1972.

Martinet, André. *Eléments de linguistique générale*. Paris: Armand Colin, 1960.

Marx, Karl, and Engels, Friedrich. *The German Ideology, Part I*. New York: International Publishers, 1947.

Mauss, Marcel. *The Gift: Forms and Functions of Exchange in Archaic Societies*. Translated by Ian Cunnison, Glencoe, Ill.: Free Press, 1954.

May, Rollo. *Existential Psychology*. New York: Random House, 1969.

Merleau-Ponty, Maurice. "From Mauss to Claude Lévi-Strauss." In *Signs*, translated by Richard C. McCleary. Evanston: Northwestern University Press, 1964.

Nietzsche, Friedrich. *The Birth of Tragedy*. Translated by Clifton P. Fadiman. In *The Philosophy of Nietzsche*. New York: Modern Library, 1954.

Pettit, Philip. *The Concept of Structuralism*. Berkeley: University of California Press, 1977.

Piaget, Jean. *Le structuralisme*. Paris: Presses universitaires de France, 1968.

———. *Structuralism*. Translated and edited by Chinanah Maschler. New York: Basic Books, 1970.

Piguet, Jean-Claude. "Les conflits de l'analyse et de la dialectique." *Annales,* no. 3 (May-June 1965).

Pingaud, Bernard. "Comment on devient structuraliste." *L.Arc* 26 (1965).

Pividal, Raphael. "Peut-on acclimater 'La Pensée Sauvage'?" *Annales,* no. 3 (May-June 1965).

———. "Signification et position de l'oeuvre de Lévi-Strauss." *Annales,* no. 6 (November-December 1964).

Popper, Karl. *The Logic of Scientific Discovery*. London: Hutchinson, 1959.

Portmann, Adolph. *New Paths in Biology*. Translated by Arnold J. Pomerans. New York: Harper and Row, 1964.

Poster, Mark. *Existential Marxism in Postwar France*. Princeton: Princeton University Press, 1975.

Quinton, Anthony. "Freud and Philosophy." In *Freud: The Man, His Work, His Influence*, edited by Jonathan Miller. Boston: Little, Brown, 1972.

Ravis, Georges. "L'anthropologie et l'histoire." *La Nouvelle Critique*, June 1969.

Ricoeur, Paul. "Structure et hermeneutique." *Esprit*, no. 11 (November 1963).

———. "Symbole et temporalité." *Archivio di Filosofia*, nos. 1–2 (1963).

———. "The Task of Hermeneutics." In *Heidegger and Modern Philosophy*, edited by Michael Murray. New Haven: Yale University Press, 1978.

Roazen, Paul. *Freud and His Followers*. New York: New American Library, 1974.

Rodinson, Maxime. "Racisime et civilisation." *La Nouvelle Critique*, no. 66 (June 1955).

Rossi, Ino. "Intellectual Antecedents of Lévi-Strauss' Notion of Unconscious." In *The Unconscious in Culture*, edited by Ino Rossi. New York: E. P. Dutton, 1974.

Rousseau, Jean-Jacques. *Essai sur l'origine des langues*. Paris: Bibliothèque du Graphe, 1967. In English, *Essay on the Origin of Languages*. Translated by John Moran and Alexander Gode. New York: Unger, 1966.

———. *The Social Contract*. Edited by L. G. Crocker. New York: Washington Square Press, 1971.

Sartre, Jean-Paul. *Being and Nothingness*. Translated by Hazel Barnes. New York: Washington Square Press, 1975.

———. *Between Existentialism and Marxism*. Translated by John Mathews. New York: William Morrow and Co., 1974.

———. "Cartesian Freedom." *Literary and Philosophical Essays*. Translated by Annette Michelson. New York: Collier Books, 1962.

——. *La critique de la raison dialectique.* Paris: Editions Gallimard, 1960.

——. *L'Être et le néant.* Paris: Librairie Gallimard, 1949.

Saussure, Ferdinand de. *Cours de linguistique générale.* Paris: Payot, 1969.

Sebag, Lucien. *Marxisme et structuralisme.* Paris: Payot, 1964.

Simonis, Yvan. *Claude Lévi-Strauss ou la 'passion de l'inceste.'* Paris: Aubier Montaigne, 1968.

——. "Two Ways of Approaching Concrete Reality: 'Group Dynamics' and Lévi-Strauss' Structuralism." In *The Unconscious in Culture,* edited by Ino Rossi. New York: E. P. Dutton, 1974.

Szasz, Thomas. *Karl Kraus and the Soul-Doctors.* Baton Rouge: Louisiana State University Press, 1976.

Truffaut, François. *Hitchcock.* New York: Simon and Schuster, 1967.

Tucker, Robert. *Philosophy and Myth in Karl Marx.* Cambridge: The University Press, 1961.

Wilson, Edward O. "Sociobiology: Nature and Nurture Come Out Swinging." *New York Times,* 26 February 1978.

——. *Sociobiology: The New Synthesis.* Cambridge, Mass.: Harvard University Press, Belknap Press, 1975.

Index

Aestheticism, 4, 120
Althusser and his structural Marxism, 107 ff.
Analogical relationships, 18–19; in Lévi-Strauss, 39–49, 66
Analytic reason, 64; founded by Rousseau, 67; in structuralism, 97
Antihumanism: and dissolution of man, 97, 100; and Lévi-Strauss, 66
Aristotle and Lévi-Strauss, 123
Atom of kinship, 75
Auzias, Jean-Marie, 123

Bachelard and the epistemological break, 107
Bergson: as source of Sartrean freedom, 104; and totemism, 54–55
Binarism, importance of and limitations of, 114–15
Binswanger and Ellen West, 116
Bricolage in Lévi-Strauss and in Marx, 109
Bruner, Jerome, and experiments relating to analogical reasoning, 40 ff.

Cassirer: as interpreter of Rousseau, 64–65; contrasted with Lévi-Strauss's interpretation, 65
Chomsky and structuralism, 112–14
Commitment: in existentialism, 69; as opposed by Lévi-Strauss, 69–70
Compassion: as pity in Rousseau, 66; as primary passion in Rousseau, 56
Condensation-displacement, 10–12

Culture-nature, 98–99
Cumulative societies defined, 68–69

Death of man in structuralism, 99, 123
Decentered structure in Derrida and Lévi-Strauss, 131 ff.
Dédoublement: in Freud, 28–30; in Marxism, 86; as mirror-image in Bororo village structure, 90; as mirror-stage, 19; as progressive-regressive analytic method in both Sartre and Lévi-Strauss, 102
Derrida, Jacques, 130 ff.
Descartes, 12; and the Nambikwara chiefs, 81; repudiation of, in structuralism, 50–51, 72–73; reversal of, in Lévi-Strauss, 121 ff.
Diachronic: in the collective, 83; in kinship systems, 78
Dialectical materialism: and Bororo village structure, 86–92; development as a science of, 107 ff.
Dialectical reason as subordinate to analytic reason, 97 ff.
Dilthey and hermeneutics and life, 111 ff.
Durkheim and ethnology, 4–5

Eidetic intuition of essences, 111–12
Essentialism and Lévi-Strauss, 123 ff.
Everyday materialism of Lévi-Strauss, and mind as a thing among things, 115
Exchanges, 4–6; loss of, 94–95